D0991611

ALSO BY FRANK TANNENBAUM

•

SLAVE AND CITIZEN:
The Negro in the Americas

THIS IS A *Borzoi Book*

PUBLISHED BY *Alfred A. Knopf* IN NEW YORK

MEXICO:
The Struggle for Peace and Bread

MEXICO

The Struggle for Peace and Bread

B Y

FRANK TANNENBAUM

ALFRED A. KNOPF: NEW YORK: 1950

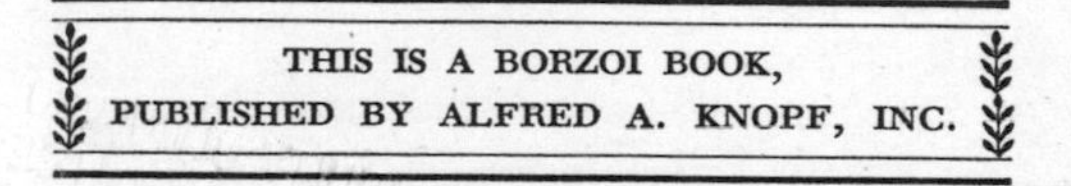

FIRST EDITION

TO THE MEMORY OF

Moisés Sáenz and Miguel Othon de Mendizabal

WHO DEVOTED THEIR LIVES TO

THE MEXICAN PEOPLE

Introduction

THIS BOOK was begun as a study of the issues at stake between Mexico and the United States since 1910; but the matters in dispute between the two governments cannot be understood apart from the Mexican social milieu. It therefore seemed necessary to describe the Mexican complex of economic and social tensions that gave the diplomatic dispute its peculiar flavor and significance. So that the disputes between the two countries, summarized in the last chapter, may be seen against the proper setting, this is a book about Mexico. The Revolution of 1910 merely added to the complexity of the Mexican scene and made it even more difficult for Americans to understand Mexico's inner stress and strain.

Looked at objectively, the discussion as it developed between the two countries was really beside the point and never came to grips with the issues. Under the circumstances, it could not do so. The Mexicans were concerned with preserving their freedom to work out the changes implicit in their Revolution, the United States with the defense of American rights adversely affected by the Mexican social upheaval.

The American argument persisted in restating the traditional position of the rights of foreigners contractually acquired under previous law. The Mexicans denied the very basis of the contract, not only for Americans, but even for Mexicans. In their view, the American thesis had no validity, being based upon a series of assumptions that they denied. This was especially true after the Constitution of 1917 came to rule Mexican political thinking. The Mexicans could not repudiate the program the Constitution sanctioned, and the United States could not accept it. Had the Americans really meant to assert the arguments they were elaborating in diplomatic notes, their only recourse would have been military intervention.

Two world wars, as well as two broad political changes in the United States—the New Freedom and the New Deal—intervened in the discussion, and American foreign policy, proclaiming the doctrine of the self-determination of nations and upholding the policy of equal sovereignty within the community of American nations, found intervention impossible. The result was that Mexican governments had their way, and the United States receded in fact, even if not in theory.

In the end it became clear that the issues were broader than those involved between American private interests in Mexico and the Mexican governments. The Revolution really represented something that a large part of the American people believed in: the vindication of popular rights and the assertion of self-determination. We finally acceded to Mexico's program because in some way it really was also part of a developing American program in international affairs.

The two world wars served to strengthen the American belief that the rights of smaller nations must be defended, even if in the process the interests of American nationals are adversely affected. If we lost the diplomatic argument, we won the greater one, that of moral leadership in defense of the right of the little nation to a dignified place in the community of nations. Had we pursued our difference with Mexico to its logical conclusion of intervention, we would have wrecked the Pan-American system and would have had no moral grounds for our role during the Second World War. In fact, our experience with Mexico and the statement of international doctrines it evoked have served to fortify the influence of the United States in the contemporary world. In a strange and unexpected way the original statement that Mexico was free to work out its own policies, even if it injured the interests of United States nationals, and that the territorial integrity and political independence of Mexico were inviolate has, like bread cast upon the waters, returned a thousandfold. It has increased the moral and political role of the American people and given our government a place of trust and leadership in the world which it could not have achieved by a mere show of force. American foreign policy has been hammered out on the Mexican anvil.

Acknowledgments

THERE REALLY IS NO WAY by which I can acknowledge my indebtedness to those from whom I gathered the substance of this book. It is a product of many years of interest in and contact with Mexico. I first went to Mexico in 1921, and over the years have been privileged to enjoy the friendship and kindness of many people. I owe a greater debt than I can repay to those friends who—like Ramón Beteta, Daniel Cosío Villegas, Jesús Silva Herzog, Manuel Gamio, and Gonzalo Robles, among many others—tolerated my inquisitiveness and my very American self-assurance. Perhaps, too, this is the place to acknowledge the kindness of the late Josephus Daniels and of Mr. Sumner Welles. The friendship of General Lázaro Cárdenas stands apart and by itself.

Two Mexican friends, Silvio Zavala and Victor L. Urquide, helped me by reading sections of the manuscript. The former read Chapter iii, the latter Chapters xi, xii, and xiii. The manuscript was read and commented upon by Robert Warren and Winfield Riefler. Two of my colleagues, John H. Wuorinen and Dwight C. Miner, read the final chapter. Mrs. Bertha Singer and Mrs. Rhoda Metraux both read the manuscript in its earlier stages, and my secretary, Mrs. Dorothea Boardman, suffered through all its changes.

I want especially to acknowledge the editorial going-over that the manuscript received from Mr. Herbert Weinstock. Finally, if it is permissible for an author to say a kind word about his publisher, I should like to express my appreciation to Mr. Alfred A. Knopf for his interest in this volume.

FRANK TANNENBAUM

Columbia University
August 25, 1949

Contents

MEXICO:
The Struggle for Peace and Bread

The people must learn that they can be governed without terror.

—LÁZARO CÁRDENAS

CHAPTER 1

The Configuration of the Land

MEXICO is an isolated country. Geographic obstacles have impeded communication and fostered a local, inward view and an aloofness from the outside that has proved not merely physical, but political and spiritual as well. Mexico is unlike any other country in the world, and almost every Mexican community enjoys its own quality of uniqueness. The physical geography could not have been better designed to isolate Mexico from the world and Mexicans from one another.

The central part of the country rises steeply out of the sea to perpetually snowcapped peaks like Orizaba (18,700 feet), Popocatépetl (17,887 feet), and Ixtaccíhuatl (17,343 feet), while numerous other mountains of lesser height contort the earth. It is within sight of these mountains that most of the Mexican people have found their homes, built their largest cities, and developed the greater part of their economy. The V-shaped plateau stretching to the American border, formed by the two mountain ranges that fan out from the center, contains the greater part of the country's population.

This plateau, which contains something like one third of the area of Mexico, gradually widens as it rolls on its way toward the American border, and its declining elevation may be indicated by the location of some of the cities on it. At the head of the plain are Toluca at 8,600 feet above sea level, and Mexico City at 7,500. Guadalajara, farther north, stands at 5,000 and El Paso, on the border, at 3,600. Many of the basins within this vast plain contain shallow ponds and swamps that have no outlet to the sea because they were blocked by volcanic activity. Volcanic cones dot central Mexico, and in some places there are extensive remains of ash, cinder, and lava.

The peaks towering over central Mexico are the hub of the Sierra Madre Occidental, the western range, and the Sierra Madre Oriental, the eastern range, which make the walls of the plateau. These ranges have imposed a barrier reaching to both the Pacific and the Gulf of Mexico. It is, for instance, only thirty-six miles as the crow flies from Mexico City to Cuernavaca, but to get there one has to climb to nearly 10,000 feet after leaving the city, and then make the precipitous drop down 5,500 feet into the sunny valley containing the capital of the state of Morelos. To the south of the great peaks the land descends steeply to the narrow Isthmus of Tehuantepec. which is only 700 feet above sea level. In this rapid fall the valleys grow narrower, the ravines deeper, the changes in climate sharper along the mountain slopes, and the cities fewer in number. The pockets that permit towns and villages to survive are often riven and torn, and man holds onto a steep mountainside for a habitat because no other is available.

The land rises again from Tehuantepec to form the state of Chiapas, which has a plateau comparable in altitude to that of the northern plain. The low coastal states of Tabasco and Campeche and the limestone peninsula of Yucatán lie east of Chiapas. This low-lying southeastern region, like the northwestern territory of Lower California, has been cut off from central Mexico by the lack of roads.

The two great mountain ranges meeting in the center of the country dominate Mexico's physical structure, condition the distribution of its temperatures and rainfall, influence the flora and fauna, and make a country of sharp climatic contrasts.

Vera Cruz in the east and Acapulco in the west, for instance, are hot, moist, tropical, and crowded with vegetation. They lie in the *tierra caliente* (hot land). But when one climbs up the mountains the hot land gives way to the *tierra templada* (temperate land). The coconut, banana, orange, and mango are left behind, and one enters another world. At 6,000 feet oaks begin to dominate the scene. Firs and pines make their appearance at 10,000 feet and increase with the altitude until they almost completely replace every other tree. The upper tree limit is somewhere between 12,500 and 13,500 feet, and the permanent snow line lies between 14,600 and 15,000. Temperature, vegetation, and human habitat are determined by altitude, and the distance from perpetual snow to the seeming paradise of eternal warmth is very short. In central Mexico it is possible to leave the tropics lying at sea level in the morning, reach a cold and semi-freezing temperature in the shade at high noon, and be back again in the tropics on the other side of the slope by night. As one goes from sea level toward the mountaintops and then down again, there is a visible modification in the texture of the land every few hundred feet, even its color seeming to change with the changing altitude.

A crop map of Mexico is a crazy quilt. The banana is grown in almost every part of the country, and it can be seen in a northern state like Tamaulipas, in a southern one like Chiapas, and in central states like Oaxaca and Michoacán. What is true of the banana is true of corn, wheat, and fruits, tropical or temperate. The determining influence is altitude, not latitude.

The diversity of physical feature leaves general description misleading and makes Mexico an unknown country even to Mexicans. States like Chihuahua and Durango, known for their deserts, have large forest reserves if one climbs high enough, while a warm small state like Morelos has, rising high above it, the cold wind-swept slopes of volcanic Ajusco, where little can be grown. Mexico is a country of climatic pockets, with their own humidity, heat, moisture, rain, and soil. The locality transcends the larger political unit and imposes a cultural, economic, and political localism. The people often differ from region to region in appearance, language, economy, and social mores. Diversity, separateness, and isolation are the rule.

Local particularism has been a constant feature in Mexican history. Unification on a national scale has been difficult because geographical diversity is the rule and because isolation has fostered a continuing separatism. Except among middle-class intellectuals the very idea of the nation has, until recently, been on the defensive.

The difficulties created by physical structure are aggravated by the uneven distribution of rainfall. As one goes from Lower California and northwestern Sonora to Tehuantepec, Chiapas, and Tabasco, one travels from a waterless sandy desert to a water-soaked, soggy, saturated earth that makes life and labor as difficult there as in the desert. Lower California and northwestern Sonora have, on the average, less than ten inches of rain per year, while most of northern Mexico, stretching from the American border down to latitude 20° N. and covering a good third of the entire country, has an average of less than twenty inches of rain per year, insufficient for agriculture and barely enough for pasture. If it were not for the mining camps with their neighboring cities and their bits of tillable land, this northern area would be an almost abandoned country. Anyone crossing Zacatecas, Durango, Chihuahua, or Coahuila on horseback will find the carcasses of cattle dead of thirst, and except in a few regions the very use of the land, even for pasture, depends in part upon the windmill that taps underground water. Agriculture in this large part of Mexico rests upon recently developed systems of irrigation.

The north is parched and water-hungry; the central part of

the country has barely sufficient moisture for plant life; the south is saturated with water. On the eastern coast the rains increase to the south, varying from forty inches per year in Tamaulipas to over a hundred in Tabasco. In central Mexico the rains are seasonal, coming chiefly between June and September. During these months it rains almost every day; heavy clouds darken the skies in most of central and southern Mexico and pour out their waters in torrents reminiscent of the Biblical flood. The rainy season is followed by more than six months of clear skies and dry, moistureless days, when the sun yellows the grass and parches the earth, while the wind blowing from the mountains fills the air with great swirls of dust.

The distribution of rainfall in Mexico may be dramatically summarized by noting that one half of the country has insufficient moisture throughout the year, another third has inadequate moisture in the winter, and only about thirteen per cent has enough rain through the year. Those parts of Mexico which have sufficient rain are tropical and poorly inhabited. On the central plain only the small basin running from Mexico City to Aguascalientes has sufficient (though irregular) rainfall during the summer to make possible agriculture without irrigation.

Temperature, governed by altitude, has given Mexico marked variation in local climates. On the upper plateau, Mexico City, which lies south of 20° N., has an average temperature of 60.1° F., with the warmest month at 65.1° and the coldest at only 54.3°. It is no wonder that Mexico City seems to Americans a city of eternal spring. And there are many localities in Mexico with a climate milder and more equable than that of Mexico City.

The hottest parts of Mexico lie in the desert regions near the Gulf of California or in the river valleys along both the Caribbean and the Pacific coasts. But the proverbial heat of the tropical coasts and the idyllic temperature of the plateau are broken, every now and then, by cold winds sweeping down from the north. Many an American in Mexico City has been surprised by a sudden blackening of the sky, an almost freezing cold, and the falling of a heavy hail at high noon of what had started as a sunny day in July.

The absence of sufficient moisture is the chief barrier to Mexican economic well-being. Water is unobtainable where it is most needed. The rains are sparse and undependable. Where rivers exist they lose themselves in the desert, go underground, or spill off high mountain ranges into the sea in torrential streams. The air in the winter is dry, the earth parched, and the atmosphere filled with blowing dust. Even the valleys, green during the rainy seasons, are surrounded by barren mountains that tell their story of land eternally thirsty. The isolated hut on the desert or hugging some steep cliff merely evidences a bit of moisture where man could locate. All about him the land rises, layer upon layer of desiccated mountains cut by innumerable gullies and uncounted ridges, each higher than the other until hidden in perpetual snow.

Man in Mexico, for all his works, is but a puny creature hidden in some inaccessible gully, scratching at the earth with his wooden stick or iron hoe. The mountain mass overshadows all his efforts, and he finds a place against its side as a refuge from cold or wind and goes to some natural spring or running brook to quench his thirst. He coddles the earth to yield him his food. Looked at from a distance, the scene is breath-taking in its majesty: the combination of bronzed mountains, snow-covered peaks towering against the sky, and green earth in the valley, all cut away against some deep mountain cleft and bathed in midday light or set aglow by a setting sun, is beyond description. As a human habitat, however, this scenery merely provides a splendid setting for a difficult world and a hard life. Scenically the country warms the heart of the wanderer from afar, but for the native folk Mexico is a hard, if not a niggardly country within which to nurture the human body, and it is only with the greatest difficulty that even a sparse living may be won from its smiling but recalcitrant earth. Mexico is a beautiful place in which to live and a hard place in which to make a living.

CHAPTER 2

The People

MEXICO, which is about one fourth the size of the United States, has approximately twenty million people and a density of 25.9 per square mile.

The Mexican population has grown very slowly. We have two separate estimates for 1521, of seven and nine million respectively. The years following the Conquest saw great devastation among the natives. War, forced migration, labor in the mines, and epidemics of native and, especially, European origin worked great havoc among the people. Smallpox, brought to Mexico by a Negro from Cuba in 1519, proved a great scourge; typhoid became known after 1531, and typhus in 1545. Entire communities were wiped out, and people died like trees attacked by an unknown blight. Two hundred and seventy years later, Mexico had only four and a half million;

even in 1872, nearly three and a half centuries after the Conquest, the population approximated the number the Spaniards had encountered.

Instead of being evenly distributed, the population is dense on the central plateau and declines sharply toward the coasts and borders. The Federal District, in the center, has a population density of over three thousand per square mile, and Quintana Roo, in the southeast, of only one. These are extremes, but the contrast is persistent. Tlaxcala has a density of 144.1, whereas Sonora has 5.2, Guanajuato 88.7, and Campeche 4.6 per square mile. The Mexican people prefer to live at high altitudes: seventy per cent of them are located at over 3,000 feet above sea level and 29 per cent at over 6,000. The combination of altitude, temperature, and rainfall has made the central part of Mexico the natural habitat for the Mexican people. The five states whose capitals have a mean altitude of 7,713 feet, with an average temperature of 58.7° F., contain approximately twenty-five per cent of the population in only 4.2 per cent of the area of the country. In contrast, the eight states whose capitals have a mean altitude of 2,234 feet embrace over half of the Republic, but have a mere thirteen per cent of the population.

Mexico is preponderantly a country of little villages. Instead of living stretched along the countryside in separate farmsteads, the people are grouped together in thousands of little hamlets, villages, and towns. In 1940 there were 105,185 communities in Mexico, of which 75,876, or 72 per cent, were hamlets of one hundred people or less. Even more striking is the fact that 98,967 inhabited places in Mexico, or 94 per cent of all, have under 500 people each. Mexico City, with 1,700,000 inhabitants, is larger than the other twelve cities of over 50,000 combined; the second largest city, Guadalajara, has 229,235, and the third, Monterrey, has 186,092. There is only one other city, Puebla, with more than 100,000.

Structurally the distribution of the population of Mexico is unbalanced. Most communities possess none, or almost none, of the modern tools and no effective means of communication.

The twenty-one cities with a population of 25,000 or over are the centers of local political power and prestige. With few exceptions, they are the only parts of Mexico that in a technical sense belong to the contemporary world. Only a few other towns have newspapers, theaters, paved streets, modern sanitation, secondary schools, and colleges, or lay claim to participation in the political and the cultural life of the country. Far above them Mexico City stands like an absorbing octopus, a great and beautiful city in its own right, but, because of its disproportionate place in the hierarchy of Mexican communities, overshadowing and dominating all else. Mexico City claims all, rules all, and does its best to absorb all—in politics, in income, in culture.

The overwhelming power and influence of Mexico City are particularly noticeable because the vast majority of the people are country folk and know nothing of city life. Of the thirty-two political units only one—the Federal District, where Mexico City is located—is preponderantly urban. For the country as a whole, 64.9 per cent of the population lives in rural districts. If we look at this matter from another angle, the fact is even more impressive: 99.2 per cent of all inhabited places in Mexico in 1940 had a population of less than 2,500. Only 0.7 per cent were urban. All discussion of Mexico must begin with this.

The Mexican cultural complex is riven internally between the European and Indian elements. The European has, on the whole, predominated in the cities, and the Indian has, on the whole, prevailed in the country. It is true, of course, that even in Mexico City there are strong Indian cultural influences as soon as one gets away from the narrow European circle and goes among the mass of the city's population—the *mestizos* (of mixed blood). It is equally true that even in the remotest places in Mexico one finds some European influence—for instance, candles and cattle among the Huicholes.

These separate cultures vary greatly in their relative importance in different parts of Mexico. The northern part of Mexico is *mestizo* and therefore more European; the southern part is largely native and therefore more Indian in both race and culture. The Mexican government has given up the attempt to count the number of Indians in Mexico as a race apart, on the grounds that *indio* is an inaccurate and undefinable term, and has begun instead to enumerate the people who speak Indian tongues. For 1940, we are told that there were 1,237,018 individuals over five years of age who spoke only one of the thirty-three Indian languages tabulated in the census. There are also 1,253,891 persons who speak both Spanish and an Indian tongue. This adds up to 2,490,909: 14.8 per cent of the population five years of age or over speak Indian languages. At best this is only an approximate figure. I am morally certain that no one counted the Chamula Indians one by one, or the Huicholes, or the Lacandones, or the Mixes, or even the Otomís, who are in the very center of the country. Linguistically the thirty-three languages, even in the same region, may prove as different from each other as Hebrew, Chinese, and Finnish.

To these two and a half million Indians it is necessary to add at least an equal number of the rural population who, if not Indian, live at an Indian cultural level. There are, thus, perhaps five million people whose food habits, tool equipment, family and social organization, basic attitudes, and notions about the world are Indian rather than European. These people constitute in fact a series of isolated folk cultures within the nation.

The folk cultures are sometimes very small, as witness the remnant of the Yaquis. I shall always remember a visit to this small but remarkable little "nation," so quiet in speech, so dignified and reserved in its formal relations with outsiders and officials, so formal about its own rights, so willing to defend them to the death, that even the Mexicans who are most eager to make a big nation out of the little ones must pay tribute to this little group of human beings that for four hundred and fifty years has resisted every attempt either to conquer or to exterminate it and, in the process, has given racial color and character to the state of Sonora. The possession of a little Yaqui blood by any Mexican is a matter of pride.

I remember that on a visit a president of Mexico offered to build the Yaquis a school. They said: "If you wish to build us a school down here near the railroad tracks, we reserve the right to burn it at any time, so please build it out of wood, for a school will attract the settlers of other 'nations' [meaning *mestizos*], and they will soon begin claiming our lands and we will be forced to drive them out. But if you will build a school for us up there in the mountains, it will be safe, for no strangers will disturb us there." They beat their little drum that called the nine villages from the mountains together for the occasion —for the drum can be heard far and wide, and they use it to communicate among themselves. As it was explained to me by one who had fought against them in a battle in his earlier days as an army officer: "Their drum always beats forward, forward, forward, and you can never get away from the sound that it makes, and you know that they are always with you."

There was an evident feeling of dignity and self-confidence and a sense of good government and discipline among them. They were then at peace. They had been given their lands, and under President Lázaro Cárdenas an attempt was being made to bring them into the nation. As one man said to me, "We have much to learn from them. They are on a higher moral plane than we are."

The issue raised by this remark is a very real one. The difficulty of assimilation and incorporation in this and other instances lies in the fact that the *mestizo* has often so little to give, morally and spiritually speaking, that he makes but a poor case for "incorporation." As we left the Yaqui region, one friend remarked reflectively: "*Somos estranjeros aquí*"—"We are foreigners here." That is the key to the situation: there are many areas, small and large, where the official language, manner, and way are foreign. That is true of such places as Yucatán, where the Maya is one of the larger folk cultures. Its 400,000 people have shown remarkable powers of self-preservation in custom, tradition, habitat, and even language. It is true of the Trique Indians in Oaxaca, who are about 40,000 in number; it is true of little groups like the Coras, in Nayarit, and of many others, small and large.

The problem is not solved by mere linguistic incorporation, even when that finally occurs, for there remains a residue of tradition and belief which is local, specific, and peculiar, and which still leaves unfilled the gap between the national culture and the local way of life. The majority of the Indians, and of the *mestizos* closely related to them culturally, are chiefly located in central and southern Mexico. Northern Mexico, the Mexico closer to the United States, is not typical of the rest of the country. It was inhabited by migratory tribes before the Conquest and has remained sparsely settled ever since. Where the language has passed away, the cultural elements of the Indian still survive. The point to remember is that while many of the Indian groups and languages have disappeared since the Conquest, there are numerous groups that still retain non-European culture traits. Among these are the Mayas, the Otomís, the Aztecs, the Chontals, the Mixes, the Zapotecs, the Tarascans, and the Triques. It will be a long time before these characteristics completely disappear.

While the Indians have everywhere taken on some of the European traits, European culture in Mexico has in turn been profoundly influenced by the Indian. It has been said, for instance, that two thirds of Mexican place names are of Indian origin and that a true dictionary of the national language—not, mind you, the Spanish language—would show one half of the words to be of Indian origin. Even the Supreme Court has found difficulty with purely Spanish terms because of the many Indian words and concepts that have crept into legal terminology.

This mingling of the cultures has its counterpart on the physical level. From the days of the Conquest the Mexican has been the child of an Indian mother and a European father. There were never as many Europeans as Indians in Mexico, never as many *criollos* [1] as Indians, and, until very recently, never as many *mestizos* as Indians. The Indian strain has predominated in the Mexican population. In 1793 the Indian population was given as 52 per cent of the total, and in 1810 as 60 per cent, whereas the European and native white elements were given as 15.2 and 18 per cent, respectively, for the same dates. Alexander von Humboldt estimated that the populous state of Oaxaca had six whites out of every hundred inhabitants, Puebla nine.

The unexpected and permanent European contribution to Mexico was the unplanned appearance of the *mestizo.* He arrived upon the scene soon after the Conquest and has become the most important element in the Mexican population. He became both the unconscious carrier of European culture to Indians and the natural link between the racial and linguistic groups in Mexico. It was he who supplied the armies that fought the wars of Independence, and from him has come the greater part of the men active in public life since then.

The *mestizo* is generally the only Mexican who has a sense of the nation. The Indian has remained parochial, the *criollo* has hungered for Europe; the *mestizo,* close to his Indian mother and yet aware of the larger world, has consciously and unconsciously striven for the making of a nation out of the heterogeneous elements in his country. The process has been slow, the task difficult and continuing, but the future belongs to the *mestizo.* To him will go the credit of having created a common people out of the many diverse groups on Mexican soil.

The European has always been on the defensive, and if we are to accept the theories of Mexican anthropologists, the Indian and the *mestizo* have shown greater physical resiliency. They better fitted the Mexican environment. The white man has been a bird of passage, either as a European or as a *criollo.* The *mestizo* has arisen from the strife between European and Indian to rule the present scene.

[1] A *criollo* is one both of whose parents were Spaniards.

During the colonial period the *mestizo* was lost in one of the many *castas* (sixteen of them were counted and recognized) and denied access to the opportunities of the time, except in menial trades. There were many individual exceptions, true enough, but these *were* exceptions. The wars of Independence offered the *mestizo* his first real opportunity to make his presence felt, and he took full advantage of the occasion to become a military leader, a soldier, and a politician.

The participation of the *mestizo* has become progressively more important, and even the Revolution of 1910, which was nominally made by and for the Indian, was really a revolution officered, guided, and developed by the *mestizo*. The Indian motif was strong, but the directing hand has been the *mestizo's*.

Tradition has endowed the *mestizo* with two traits: personal ambition and lack of scruples. It is only by stating the case as crassly as this that one can even attempt to find a rationalization of the complete chaos of the Mexican Independence period. The lack of scruples expressed itself in violence, and violence in conspiracy, and conspiracy in revolution, which in turn led to further violence. In the Constitutional Convention of June 16, 1856, one of the deputies, amid the applause of his fellows, said: "Among us . . . the spirit of restlessness and ambition has such standing . . . that conspiracy has become a profession, and the abuse of the most precious rights a title to glory and applause. Peace has few followers and prudence fewer still."

Psychologically the Mexican milieu is underlaid with an ingrained morbidity that derives from the traumatic character of Mexican experience. All of life, personal, social, political, and even cultural, is burdened by the expectancy of sudden injury, violence, and death. The very physical environment seems to fit in with this description of the universe. The sudden earthquake, the unexpected, newly born volcano, the rapid change of weather that in an hour turns a balmy warmth to shivering cold accompanied by a flood of water pouring down from the sky, or that brings the hard wind-driven hail that flattens the crops, are common experiences. Equally certain is the sudden disease—even if only smallpox or typhoid—that takes the little children away and leaves the schoolhouse empty. Above all, there is the possible appearance of armed men who rob and kill and destroy. There is a kind of expectancy of death—sudden and meaningless—that makes fatalism and indifference to life a common feature of all groups and of all classes. On more than one occasion, when one asks for an old friend, the reply is: "*Ya lo mataron*"—"He has been killed." Or one hears a man say, as a matter of course: "*Me iban a matar*"—"They were going to kill me." I myself have seen a man roll up his sleeve to show bullet wounds on his left arm and explain: "They ambushed me, but I fell on the ground and pulled out my pistol with my right hand and killed three of them, and the rest ran away."

It is not that society is violent, brutal, and ungracious. Quite the opposite. The society is quiet, generous, friendly, and overflowing with vitality, but it is lived in the very day, at the very moment, because no one can tell what will happen tomorrow. One hears from everyone: "In Mexico anything can happen." Life really has no sense of permanence. All existence is on the verge of disaster. This peculiar fatalism results in irresponsibility, in a sense of futility, in a feeling that tomorrow, "*mañana,*" will be time enough, if there is a tomorrow. It tempers every act, every belief, every arrangement, every promise. The presence of death is so imminent that its actual coming by violence is accepted as a matter of course and leaves behind it much less feeling of horror than in other civilized societies.

To some extent this is a psychology of battle. Survival is a matter of luck and miracle, a product of accident or hidden charm. It is due to the protective influence of the favorite saint. He who survives is lucky, brave, or specially favored.

Mexican history has been peculiarly tragic, violent, and remorseless. At various times the Mexican people have seen the sudden apparition of an enigmatic evil that destroyed whatever made life worth living. The Conquest killed the Indian leaders, destroyed their temples, burned their records, and almost destroyed the identity of the people with their own past. It would almost seem as if the attempt was to strip the Mexicans of their psychological continuity as a people. The Spaniard denied the Indians their gods, their art, their writing, their temples, their law, their morality, and their ethics.

The Indians never recovered from this blow, and the tragedy was as much in its seeming purposelessness as in its destructive character. The "why" had no answer. Very much the same can be said of the other violent experiences of the Mexican people. The long and destructive wars of Independence, with their avowed purposes of freedom and justice, provided a cover not merely for terror and bloodshed, but for the denial of the essential human values inculcated during hundreds of years of colonial teaching. The fifty years of continuing strife that followed the wars of Independence merely confirmed the Mexican people in their feeling that life was a temporary survival on the brink of death.

The breaking away of Texas and the war with the United States were both like a sudden cutting of the body in two, which had the psychological effect of a dismembered body left alive. The body lived on, the injury healed, but the morbidity remained as a permanent characteristic of the psychology of the people. In the struggle with the Church the thing in evidence was the years of cruel and rapacious civil war. On the part of the leaders the battle might be for high ideals. For the mass of the people it was like the hurricane, purposeless, directionless, impersonal, and utterly destructive. The Díaz regime rested upon orderly and systematic terror, if such a phrase makes sense. Life was lived upon sufferance. The Revolution of 1910 merely re-created the older form of violence that for ten years at least reproduced all the moral turpitude and horror of many an older Mexican experience.

The Mexican—not the *criollo* or the educated person who has in some measure overcompensated—lives in a world where faith in one's fellows has been stretched to the breaking-point. He lives in a world where skepticism and cynicism are a healthy sign, a means of survival. The Mexican intellectual either does not know this or denies it because he has immersed himself in European and American concepts and ideas. He gives simple explanations of Mexican ills: economic exploitation, political corruption, lack of education, and the like. But the deeper basis of all the ills is the tragedy of Mexican history. It has affected the attitude of the mass of Mexicans toward one another and toward the world outside. It has given them the assumption that the worst is to be expected from any new contact. It is not fear. It is the deep lesson of experience. They know that tragedy and death lurk around every corner. It is no accident that the villagers in the hills speed the departing traveler by saying: "May you go with Cod, and may nothing new happen to you." IIe who would understand Mexican politics and policy must understand this.

A Short View of a Long Subject

TWO THEMES run through all of Mexican history—regionalism and cataclysm. It is only recently that a semblance of unity has been achieved. Long before the white man reached its shores, the area was divided into "empires," "principalities," "kingdoms," "states," tribes, races, and languages, each in its own locale, each at war with the rest, or kept in subjection and paying tribute. The one thing it did not have was unity. It was not a country, a nation, or an empire. It had no common loyalty, rule, or governance. It was a welter of particular cultures, no one strong enough to dominate all of the others. Violence and war ruled the political scene.

The history of ancient Mexico is a puzzle, unrevealed even to the most assiduous student. What we know of its hidden story is half conjecture, half surmise. For in spite of much research and the archæological ruins uncovered, the great questions still remain unanswered. Who were the Indians of Mexico? Where did they come from? How did they manage to be so divided that we do not know how many races, languages, or cultures there were at the time of the Conquest? How was it possible that in one area so sharp a divergence of culture and language as the Aztec and the Otomí should be found crowded almost one on top of the other? How, too, does one account for the variation in stature, in color, and in physical type of a people to whom we give a common name and for whom we claim a common origin?

If we ask the simple question: "Who were they?" the honest answer is that we do not know. We are not even sure how long the Maya, for example, stayed in the recognized Maya area or how long it took for them to develop that particular form of hieroglyphic writing of which we can now decipher at least the dates. What we ask about the Maya can be asked about every other group. We seem to have a somewhat more specific record of the Toltecs and Aztecs. But what about the Otomís? There are still nearly one hundred thousand of them in the central plateau. They cannot be related linguistically, even by the most optimistic students, to any other language groups in Mexico. Not only is there no agreement as to the number of Indian groups at the time of the Conquest, but even today scholars differ as to the number of races and languages still in existence.

If the peoples of Mexico had a common origin, what was the process of differentiation; and if they have no common origin, which seems incredible to the modern student, how did they get where they were and where they have survived? How many layers of civilization lie buried one on top of another in the valley of Mexico? Every now and then an archæologist uncovers a hitherto unknown culture beneath a lava bed and gives it a name—"the archaic culture," for instance—and when he asks the geologist to tell him how long ago that particular lava poured down into the valley, he may get an answer ranging from ten to thirty thousand years. Why was the process of acculturation so slow, so incomplete, that when the white man reached the Mexican shores in 1517–19 he encountered, in spite of the extensive Aztec Empire and widespread Nahua language, a multiple universe so difficult to deal with that one good friar wrote to the King that only the devil could have sown so many languages in such close proximity for the ungodly purpose of making it impossible to teach neophytes the true faith?

Mexican scholars say that prehistoric man in Mexico may be assumed to have existed ten thousand years ago. They also assert the existence of an archaic culture that spread over the greater part of the country between five and ten thousand years ago. The origin of the earliest archæological ruins some of them put back twenty-five hundred years. But their datings may be wide of the mark, and a group of archæologists in Mexico in the fall of 1946 decided that it was necessary to put some dates back a thousand years because the periods had become too crowded to be credible. Recent discoveries in the state of Vera Cruz seem to push the horizon still farther back.[1]

To this background of archaic culture there was added some time long ago the culture of the Huastecas, extending from the eastern cordillera to the Gulf of Mexico. But where they came from is not known. After them came the Maya. Each author, or almost each, has his own story to tell. Mexican scholars prefer to assume that the Maya originated somewhere in the basin between the Grijalva and Panuco rivers; others would have them come from the Mississippi Valley or from Cuba. Nor is there agreement upon the time of their origin or arrival: a thousand years B.C., six hundred, one hundred, are all dates suggested by reputable scholars.

The Maya spread over Tabasco, Chiapas, Guatemala, and Honduras, and built such magnificent temples as Copán, Qui-

[1] "The evidence so far, then, suggests that man . . . lived at La Jolla [California] something like 40,000 years ago." (George F. Carter: *Transactions of the New York Academy of Science*, May 1949, page 256.) The question of when men first occupied the New World remains unanswered.

riguá, Palenque, and later in Yucatán, Chichén-Itzá, Mayapán, and Uxmal. The Maya were great architects, lived in populous cities, had a highly developed culture. They were notable astronomers and divided the year into eighteen months of twenty days each, adding five days at the end of the year, thus making a year of 365 days, and counted a cycle of forty years. It has been said that their cumulative errors in computing time would not in a thousand years have equaled one day.

In later periods came the Toltecs, but as with both the Maya and the Huastecas there is a difference of opinion as to their origin. Some Mexican scholars doubt that they came from the north and prefer to believe that they originated in the Huasteca, that is, northern Vera Cruz and parts of Puebla, Hidalgo, and San Luis Potosí. The Toltecs apparently built the archæologically famous cities of Tula, Teotihuacán, and Cholula. Seemingly pacific, deeply religious, and skilled in the arts, they spread over a great part of central Mexico. They were, we are told, tall, robust, and hard-working.

The Zapotecs seem to have come from the north to settle in the valley of Oaxaca. To them belong the famous ruins of Mitla and of Monte Alban, with its fifteen square miles covered with monuments, edifices, and graves. Out of one of these graves have come some of the most interesting artistic remains found in America. The Zapotecs had a year of 365 days and a system of writing that contained both ideographic and phonetic elements. They worked in jade, knew how to cut even the hardest stones, and did beautiful work in weaving and with feathers.

The Mixtecs, who seem to have come from the headwaters of the Panuco, settled in the northeastern part of Oaxaca. They too had a calendar of 365 days. They were perhaps the best workers in metals; and among their skills they included the art of soldering gold and silver. The most precious jewels discovered to this day come down from them. They worked in jade, bone, and obsidian.

About the origins of the Tarascans we know nothing, and yet these people spread over what is now the state of Michoacán and parts of Jalisco, Guanajuato, Nayarit, Colima, and Guerrero. They were an agricultural and fishing people, working communally, and possessed, like others in Mexico, varied skills in making pottery, working with gold and feathers, and weaving. They divided the year into four parts and measured time by lunar months. They had a detailed religious calendar and filled the year with ceremonies. Their language was absolutely different from that of any of the others. They believed, as other Indians did, in immortality and in a paradise. Their dynasty as an organized "kingdom" dates back to the twelfth century and was extinguished by the Spaniards in the 1530's, when Tangaxoan II was tortured to death by Nuño de Guzmán in an effort to extort gold from the Indian ruler.

The Aztecs presumably came from the north and settled in the valley of Mexico. These warlike people ultimately extended their influence over a great part of the central and southern part of the country, reaching in places what is now Central America. Their arrival and settlement on an island in one of the lakes of the valley of Mexico can be dated 1325. They exacted tribute from lesser tribes and forced the conquered communities, which numbered 372 at the time of the Spanish Conquest, to supply them with all sorts of agricultural and industrial products. They were great merchants and soldiers and wandered far and wide. They were a people of refined tastes in clothes and food, possessing a great variety of dishes and fruits; and their upper classes cultivated the luxury of music and entertainment during meals. Their government was an elective but absolute monarchy; and for political reasons they formed an alliance with Texcoco and Tlacopán. It was a species of agricultural democracy, with an oligarchic leadership based upon clans, with the land held in common.

The land was for them the source of life, and he who failed to use it lost his civil rights. Like the Greeks and the Romans, they had many gods, the chief of whom was Huitzilopochtli, who represented the sun and to whom human sacrifices were common. They were an exceedingly religious and mystical people, with a numerous priesthood, who watched over the individual from the cradle to the grave.

Like other Indians in Mexico, the Aztecs had a calendar of 365 days, divided into eighteen months of twenty days each, with five additional days at the end of the year; and they also had a religious calendar of thirteen months. Their cycle was of a hundred and four years, divided into two "centuries" of fifty-two years each. At the end of each fifty-two years they destroyed their personal possessions, put out the fires, covered their heads with ashes, and waited in anguish for the rising sun, fearing that the end of the world was upon them. Their temples were raised on pyramids, and their better houses were built of stone. They have left extensive remains of pottery and their weaving was of great distinction. They worked in obsidian and with feathers, were skilled in sculpture and in painting, and carried on an active commerce. They bartered, and used cocoa for money.

These widely diffused Indian cultures in Mexico were but high points in Indian achievement. In addition to them there was a great horde of other cultures, ranging from the most primitive in northern Mexico to others that approximated those mentioned. Miguel Othon de Mendizabal, a Mexican scholar who devoted a lifetime to the study of Mexican Indian populations before the coming of the white man, classifies the settled native populations into nine separate groups, with 127 subdivisions.

In the north and northeast, embracing the greater parts of what are now the states of Hidalgo, Guanajuato, Zacatecas, San Luis Potosí, Chihuahua, Durango, Coahuila, and Nuevo León, and the area between the Panuco and Bravo rivers on the Gulf of Mexico, were the non-agricultural hordes, living by hunting, fishing, and the collection of wild fruits. Most of these were in small groups whose languages have disappeared or have remained unclassified. They drank fermented drinks made from cactus fruit and agaves and indulged in the smoking of peyote.

To the west, in the valleys and *barrancas* of the Sierra Madre Occidental and on the coastal plains that border the Gulf of California, were the first of the territorial groups classified under twenty-seven different headings and devoted to intensive agriculture, fishing, and hunting. Some of them, like the Yaquis and the Mayos, worked the lands along the rivers; still others, like the Tarahumaras, were great hunters of deer. They raised maize, kidney beans, squash, and cotton and used wild tobacco.

To the south, beginning with the Mocorito River in Sinaloa, we find the first organized "small states," of which the modern scholar identifies twenty-one. These states had been formed by conquest, and represented a military and religious hegemony of one "tribe" or village over many others. These conquered, incorporated, or subdued groups within each "state" were themselves often different in race and language. We find among them the beginnings of social hierarchy, governing classes, and organized commerce. We begin to see a more formal division of labor, established religious institutions, a priestly class, and the construction of temples. Many of the groups in these "states" have since disappeared, but among these small "states" are such present-day groups as the Mixes and Zoques.

When the Spaniards reached Mexico, there were also in existence expanding "kingdoms" and "empires" actively encroaching upon their neighbors. Among these were the kingdom of "Colima," of recent growth, which boasted fourteen provinces, and the "kingdom" of Michoacán. But these were overshadowed by the Aztec confederation. While Mexican served as a sort of lingua franca, at least twenty-four other languages were spoken in the Aztec Empire.

In the midst of this prolixity of "states," "empires," "lordships," and "republics," the Aztec confederacy, with the city of Tenochtitlán (Mexico) at its center, was the chief political unit, holding in subjection numerous people whom it treated as conquered and inferior beings. Such was the hatred for this central and all-absorbing caste among the villagers for hundreds of miles around, forced to carry to it annually hundreds of thousands of pieces of individual tribute in cloth, cotton, fruits, food, and precious metals, that the Spaniards found among them natural allies against the Aztecs.

Mexico before the Conquest was not a state or nation, a people, or a culture. This precolonial particularism remained a persistent influence all through the three hundred years of the colonial period, continued after the Independence, and has only been diminishing since 1860 and more particularly since 1910.

If regionalism has been one of the two leading motifs of Mexican history, cataclysm has been the other; for the conquest of Mexico (1519–21) was a cataclysm. It was sudden, unexpected, and catastrophic. The Spanish Conquest destroyed the Aztec confederacy and demolished Tenochtitlán, its capital. The first four hundred soldiers, with Hernán Cortés at their head, climbed from Vera Cruz over the narrow mountain passes. After two months of bitter fighting with the Indians, much blandishment, and reckless courage all combined, they found themselves in the pass, at about 12,000 feet, between Ixtaccíhuatl and Popocatépetl, overlooking the city of Tenochtitlán on a little island in the great lake of Texcoco. As they looked down upon its great towers, its canals, and the causeways connecting it with the mainland, a sense of the power, prestige, and beauty of this city surrounded by waters came upon them, and they said aloud to each other in astonishment: "Not even Venice is richer or more beautiful."

Down below, the precious jewel lay ready for the plucking, but the effort to take it would, as they were to discover to their embarrassment, prove difficult and costly. The whole enterprise, from the landing on the coast to the final destruction of the city, is a tale out of the *Arabian Nights*. It cost the Spaniards nearly a thousand lives. Received reluctantly by Moctezuma, the "Emperor," who came to meet them in a bejeweled canopy carried on the shoulders of his nobles, they finally found themselves prisoners of the Aztecs, risen in rebellion because of unprovoked outrages against their pride. It was only the fortitude and hardiness of the Spaniards that enabled them to save a remnant of their numbers on the memorable *Noche Triste,* when they fought their way out of the city and back to the mainland, wounded, exhausted, and defeated, seeing their fellows taken prisoner and sacrificed to the Indian gods high up in the temple placed on the dominating pyramid in the center of the city. They could see the white bodies of their countrymen drawn over the sacrificial stone, and the exulting Indians around them, all revealed in the shadows of the fire.

The first real encounter with the Aztecs had been a bitter and humiliating defeat, but Cortés and his fellows licked their wounds and fortified their spirits. The Tlaxcala Indians took them in, nursed and nourished them, disregarding the advice of one of their own chieftains that this was the hour to make an end of the eternal war with the Aztecs and with them to destroy the newcomers while there was still time. The advice of the old and the prudent prevailed. With the support of their Indian allies, the people of Tlaxcala and others, the Spaniards gradually disrupted the Aztec Empire by attacking its outposts, devastating its allies, destroying its prestige; and when all was ready, backed by many thousands of Indians and strengthened by new arrivals attracted by the tales emanating from Mexico, Cortés and his men returned to the fight.

The Aztecs resisted to the bitter end. They were surrounded on water and by land—for the Spaniards had built thirteen ships and launched them on the lake. Their food had given out, their water supply had been cut, their dead and dying lay in the streets, but they would not yield. After forty days of unending siege and war Cortés offered them a truce, saying that he did not wish to destroy the city. But the Aztecs refused, and the siege continued fifty-three days longer. Unable to use their horses, the Spaniards ordered their Indian allies to pull down the houses one by one and to fill up the canals, thus gradually demolishing the entire city. This destruction was ultimately accomplished, while the Aztecs chided their Indian enemies in the service of the Spaniards by saying to them: "Go on, destroy the city. If we win, you will have to rebuild it for us; if the white men win, you will have to rebuild it for them." Cortés adds: "And it pleased God that this last should turn out to be true."

The Aztec heroism awoke the admiration and even the compassion of the Spaniards, but was to no avail. Tenochtitlán, the great symbol of Indian power in North America, was obliterated, and with it the very ethos of the Indians. Their spirit was broken.

The adventure of expanding the Spanish hold continued for a long time in isolated and distant places. Cortés sent his followers far and wide, to the Pacific Ocean, to Guatemala in the south, to Michoacán in the north. These in turn were followed by others, who wandered in search of the "seven cities." They listened to strange stories told to them by a Negro who had a tale made up of a thousand miracles. The Conquest expanded the horizon of the Spaniards and opened their minds to a new world more fabulous than their strangest dreams.

The Indian political power lay in the dust, not to revive again, and with it all of their values, arts, and sciences. The Conquest, as if by design, had destroyed all the leaders of Mexico, all its wise men, all its priests, all of those who carried in them the accumulated wisdom of a strange and heroic people. Spiritually the cataclysm was complete, as if the head had been severed, but the body, by some miracle, was permitted to wriggle on in the dust. When the military conquest was over, the religious conquest began. And it was the religious conversion that ensured the ultimate success of the Spanish enterprise. It was the gradual substitution of new values by the Church that made the new dispensation acceptable.

The Indian was now to survive as a stranger in a stranger's house, with little of his material wealth remaining to him. But his tragedy was also deeply spiritual; the gods he had symbolized in stone statues were rolled down the temple steps and shattered, the buildings he had adorned were pulled down, and his written hieroglyphic records were burned. With their wise and their learned dead and their arts destroyed, the Indians were left to vegetate in a universe robbed, for them, of an ethical basis.

Spain next set itself to the task of converting the natives into good Europeans on the Spanish model. The Indians were to be endowed with all the immunities, like unto "our subjects in Spain." But the ideal was compromised in the process because the Crown's officials proved weak and corruptible, the Spanish colonists rebellious, and the Indians, immersed in their ancient superstitions, apathetic to European blandishments. The eight or nine million human beings of varying cultures at different stages of development, scattered over a large and difficult terrain, could not be easily molded; and the good intentions of the King were frittered away in the conflicting interests of the Crown, the Church, and the Spanish colonist.

The Crown wanted the natives free, governed by Spanish law, converted to the true faith, paid for their labor in honest coin, and protected against abuse. It attempted to defend the Indians in their lands, and even to preserve those good Indian traditions which were not incompatible with the true faith or with loyalty to the King. The aim was high, the task Herculean, and the effort largely ineffective. Perhaps no more generous attempt was ever made by a conquering power to cast the mantle of protective justice over a defeated people. Solicitude for the welfare of the Indian was expressed in a thousand laws and ordinances. But the distance that separated the King from his native American subjects was great physically, even greater spiritually. The long reach of the Spanish kings faltered, and a penchant for minute regulation, for prescribing every detail, so clogged the administrative machinery as to make it nearly impotent. The law reflected an aspiration toward the ideal. The practice proved fallible when not corrupt, inadequate when not self-defeating. The attempt to do everything perfectly made it almost impossible to do anything well. And the persistent jealousy, if not fear, on the part of the Crown that its agents in America, from viceroy to corregidor, would escape its surveillance led it to keep changing its officials every few years and undermining their effective authority. It enabled the conquistadores and their descendants to nibble away at the administrative rules by obdurate noncompliance.

The ideal aims of the Crown met obstinate resistance on the part of the Spanish conquerors. They, too, had an interest to defend and an aim to achieve. They had risked their lives and expended their fortunes in the Conquest. The country and the Indians, they felt, were rightfully theirs. They were not disloyal to the Crown, but they too had an ideal to maintain: to convert Mexico into a feudal paradise, a paradise where the land would be carved up into great estates and cultivated by submissive Indians as serfs. It seemed to them just and politic that they should be allowed to enjoy the fruits of their labors in recompense for the faithful service they had rendered to the King. Each conquistador was to become something of a feudal lord all by himself, rendering a nominal obedience to the King in Spain.

That the aim was not entirely an empty dream can be seen from the grant to Cortés of a title of nobility and an estate with many towns and villages and at least 23,000 Indians. If the newly conquered country was not to be abandoned by its conquerors, then the needs of the Spaniards for Indian labor had to be satisfied, for there was, in fact, no other labor available. It was the Indian who had to work in the mines, till the fields, construct the houses, raise the churches, clean the streets, and do the things that must be done if a community is to survive. The great battles between the Crown and the conquistadores were fought out on this issue.

Opposed to both was the Church, especially the great religious orders. The religious orders acquired a preponderant influence over the Indians by acting as their natural defenders. In a subtle sort of way the religious orders had the loyalty and the confidence of the Indians because they were, in fact, closer to them than the other Spaniards. They were the only ones on the scene who had the real interests of the Indian at heart and, in some measure, saw the world in non-individualistic fashion as did the Indians themselves. The communal practices of the orders and the religious mysticism of the Fathers fitted in well with the Indians' great devotion and lack of personal ambition. By training and belief the religious orders were the natural defenders of the Indians against the conquistador and even against the Crown, for they too opposed its centralizing influence. This was generally true in spite of the fact that the orders became rich in material goods and politically powerful.

The cross-purposes of the Crown, the colonists, and the religious orders prevented, in the long run, any one of them from establishing its own particular ideal; but the effort would probably have failed in any case. The gap between the European and the native was, culturally speaking, too great and their inner bent too divergent.

The fundamental difficulty lay in the incompatibility of an individualist culture and a communal culture. The Indian could never accept the ethical implications of the Spaniard's extreme individualism. The Indian was communal, impersonal, submissive, mystical, and self-denying. He wanted little for himself and aimed merely to live out his round of days in an unperturbed universe, following an ancient pattern and living by old rules. He was parochial in his vision and, after the Conquest, remained broken in spirit and oblivious of outside stimulus. He mainly wished to be left alone. The Spaniard, on the other hand, was arrogant, self-assertive, and ambitious. He had a sense of direction. He wanted to get on in the world, acquire land, silver, houses, servants, and honors. He could assume individual responsibility and was a man in his own right. The individual incentives of the European made no appeal to the Indian. The white man found that he could not bribe the Indian to labor for him by the payment of a wage, and so resorted to one or another form of compulsory service.

This recalcitrance of the Indian to European incentives was symbolic of a subtler incompatibility, and the two races were doomed to suffer each other in contempt and fear, in assertive arrogance and passive but stubborn self-withdrawal. The mingling of the races and their culture took the form of attrition, a long process of wearing each other down that has now lasted for four and a half centuries and whose end is not yet in sight. In this process the Indians had the advantage of numbers, pertinacity, and physical adaptability to the climate, the soil, and the altitude. They persisted in their ways, their languages, their manners, food, customs, superstitions, and way of being. The Spaniard could escape the Indian impact only by taking refuge in the large city. Only there could he live like a Spaniard. Even there, however, the overwhelming weight of numbers, customs, and ancient habit was on the side of the Indian. In time the Indian accepted some of the things the white man had to offer, but chiefly in the cities. It was mainly through the *mestizo* that Spanish culture found an increasing role in Mexico. But the process required centuries.

In the meantime the pressing problem of getting the work of the colony done had to be solved. It was solved in the beginning by forced labor and slavery, and as late as 1550 there were still some thousands of slaves; but it was solved primarily through the *encomienda*, whereby a given number of Indians were entrusted to a conquistador in payment for the service he had rendered to the Crown. In return the *encomendero* was supposed to assume the responsibility of converting the Indian to the true faith and to pay the priest. The bitter agitation against personal subjection, however, carried on by Bartolomé de las Casas and others, was so persistent that the Crown attempted, through the "New Laws" in 1542, to abolish the *encomienda*. The threat of a rebellion forced a modification of these laws. The Indian paid a head tax to the *encomendero* and was paid in turn for his labor, but the Indian did not wish to work and did not want the money, and to some degree personal service continued in spite of the laws. Another method of recruiting labor was worked out in the *repartimiento*, by which each Indian community was forced to supply a given number of laborers each week to the public service, defined to include most needs for labor. They were paid at the end of the week, but even this system was subject to great abuse and only in the seventeenth century was it so regulated as to reduce its worst evils. The only free labor that developed was in the mines, in the towns about the mines, and, to some extent, in the cities, where the *mestizos* congregated and became craftsmen and laborers.

In the *obrajes* (cloth factories) the Indians were nominally free men working off a debt or prisoners working out a penalty imposed by a court. These laborers were locked in their workshops from sunup to sundown. They were not permitted to see their families more than once a week, their food was thrown in to them, and they were whipped if they failed to complete their task. In agricultural labor upon the plantations debt peonage became an almost universal rule before the end of the colonial period and was not finally abolished until after the Revolution of 1910.

From the point of view of the future Mexican nation, the deliberate endowment of the Indian communities, by the Crown, with the right of self-government and of the election of their own officials was of great importance. Given the complexity of the Mexican racial and linguistic structure, this was probably inevitable in some measure, but it was not inconsistent with the Spanish tradition of town government. In effect, the elected local Indian caciques and *gobernadores* were themselves often as poor as mice. They received no salary and their only emolument consisted in being freed from paying the "tribute." They also enjoyed the right to the service of a few Indians.

During the colonial period Mexico came to be divided into two types of social organization, villages and plantation communities, a division that in a measure still persists. Where the land was rich and fruitful, the villages tended to disappear. On the other hand, in the mountains of states like Oaxaca or Puebla, the villages persisted in great number, and, with the villages, the language, the custom, and the tradition. That Mexico came through three hundred years of Spanish influence with the older Indian pattern so largely intact is in no small measure owing to the policy of self-government "in accord with ancient custom" prevalent in these Indian villages during the colonial period.

For the future of Mexico the Spanish emphasis upon mining was of great importance. It set in motion a reorganization of the economy and a redistribution of the population. It involved the exploration of the arid north, the carrying of large groups of Indians to a new habitat, and their enlistment to labor in the mines. It created in the desert a series of new urban centers that had to be fed from newly developed agricultural areas, and it also produced an important transportation industry for the supplying of such mining towns as Guanajuato, Zacatecas, and Chihuahua. This placed an additional burden upon the Indian population, for it required numerous human and animal carriers to supply these distant communities. The development of these and other cities meant that the declining rural population was forced to feed an increasing number of urban communities. What the Spaniards had brought in European foods, animals, and tools was not, in the first century, sufficient to make up for the new demands placed upon the natives.

This new bias in the economy was further complicated by the introduction of private property. To the Indian, land was and has largely remained a communal possession; to the Spaniard, land belonged to the individual. It was upon this difference in attitude toward land that a large part of the history of Mexico was made to turn. The conflict came to be embodied in two distinct institutions, the village versus the plantation.

But the greatest influence of the Spaniards on Mexico is to be found in the unplanned growth of a new race, the *mestizo*. With the *mestizo* as an unconscious instrument, the Spanish language won increasing use in the country, until it has become the medium of most of the population. The Spaniards, too, gave Mexico a common religion. We thus have three great unifying elements, derived from the Conquest, upon which the future of Mexican nationalism was to be built: a common race, the *mestizo;* a common language, Spanish; and a common faith, Catholicism. With these came other features of European culture: tools, animals, fruits, and grains important to all the people, but always more important to the European and the *mestizo* than to the Indians.

With the mixture of races in Mexico added to by the bringing in of Negroes in sufficient numbers to leave their mark upon the population in certain parts of the country, we have the basis of the social structure that characterized Mexico throughout the colonial period and in some degree continues to this day. The Spaniard—that is, the born European—was at the top in politics, in the Church, and in prestige. The *criollo*, his American-born child, stood at a lower level. He inherited most of the wealth, but was denied any important role in political administration. The *mestizo* and the dozen different *castas* that resulted from the mixtures of European, Indian, and Negro in their various degrees and kinds were still lower.

In spite of the deep division in Mexican society, the country had lived so long in peace and loyalty to King and Church that the Spanish Crown seemed part of the very order of nature and the Spanish Empire the center of the earth. The isolation of the country was so profound that the American and French Revolutions and the liberal philosophies they embodied barely touched the mass of the Mexicans. To the few intellectuals and priests who in the privacy of their studies read the forbidden books it all must have seemed like a strange and incredible apparition. In spite of the great convulsion in Europe, the first years of the nineteenth century succeeded one another in Mexico without any visible omens of the tragedy that lay just ahead. The news in 1808 of the abdication of Ferdinand VII and his imprisonment by Napoleon was like a catastrophe that numbed the spirit and lamed the body. The people put on mourning and moved about in a confused and irresolute way, not knowing where to turn or what to do. When they recovered their senses, they gathered in crowds and vowed to remain loyal to their unfortunate monarch and swore never to accept any other. That was clear in their minds. What was not clear was what to do in the interim period. Who was now the ruler of Mexico? From whom did authority derive? The King was in prison. Did Mexico owe allegiance to the popular juntas, which had, on their own account, assumed authority to govern

Spain in the name of the King? Or were the people of Mexico, like the people of Spain, equal within the Crown and competent to do what the Spaniards were doing: organize their own government and rule the country against the time of the return of their King?

The Mexicans, following the Spanish example, reverted to the ancient tradition of popular sovereignty. It was on this political issue that the first blood since the Conquest was to be shed between the Mexicans and the Spaniards. The Spaniards, who had so long ruled the country, were fearful that the theory of popular sovereignty might lead to self-government, and certainly would lead to an undermining of the political dominance they had enjoyed for the preceding three centuries. To the *criollos* it seemed logical and natural to claim the same rights that were being exercised by their Spanish brothers in Spain. They were no lesser subjects of the King than those living across the sea. The Spaniards, not trusting the Viceroy, José de Iturrigaray, organized a conspiracy under the leadership of a rich Spanish plantation-owner named Gabriel de Yermo, and one night invaded the palace and replaced the Viceroy by an old man closer to their hearts. They won the first skirmish, but in the end it was to prove a very expensive one. It was they who had broken the principle of the legal succession of power and had shown that the government could be overthrown in the middle of the night by a few armed men. The Mexicans were to learn that lesson and practice it for many years to come.

Napoleon's occupation of Spain released forces that could not be controlled by a few conspirators in Mexico City. The inner social rift was suddenly illumined and widened, and the classes fell apart to fight an utterly destructive war.

A fatherly priest, Miguel Hidalgo, over fifty years of age, whose head was filled with ideas gathered from the French philosophers he had read in secret, came to be the leader of the first great social convulsion in Mexico since the Conquest. His career and tragic end are compressed into a few months that span the period from September 16, 1810, when in the early dawn he rang the church bells to summon his little flock in the small town of Dolores in the state of Guanajuato, to July 31, 1811, when he was killed by a firing squad in Chihuahua. His head was cut off, placed in a cage, and hung on the blood-soaked walls of the Alhóndiga in Guanajuato, to stay there until 1821 as the visible symbol of the tragedy that was tearing Mexico apart. He has since become one of the fathers of his country. The day of the *grito de Dolores,* when he first raised the image of Our Lady of Guadalupe as the banner of his rebellion, with the cry: "Long live Ferdinand VII, and death to the *gachupines!*" (Spaniards), has become a national holiday. But Hidalgo did not achieve Mexican independence. The few Indians he raised by the ringing of the parish bells soon swelled to a mob of 80,000 armed with knives, sticks, and stones, which pillaged, sacked, and butchered as it paraded through central Mexico. Most towns and cities surrendered out of fear or were overwhelmed by numbers. When, as in the city of Guanajuato, the armed mob met with resistance, it mercilessly killed all of those who fell into its hands. The cry of "Long live Ferdinand VII, and death to the *gachupines!*" was amended along the march. Hidalgo freed the slaves, abolished the tribute, and had himself declared the Captain General of America. He was treated as a serene highness and received under a canopy, as were the viceroys.

This was really a rebellion of the masses against their masters, the first serious uprising against the Spanish Conquest in three centuries, and a reassertion of the native against the foreigner. The leaders were swept along until the first serious setback at the Battle of Las Cruces, just above Mexico City. The rebels won, but Hidalgo would not or could not take advantage of his victory. Mexico City lay open just below and could have been taken, and, if taken, sacked and pillaged. The terrified Viceroy, in despair, brought to Mexico City the Virgin of Los Remedios, a "rival" to the Virgin of Guadalupe, and prayed to her for deliverance. The retreat from Las Cruces was the beginning of the end. Hidalgo's army never won a battle again; and the final chapter proved to be the betrayal of

Hidalgo by one of his own followers, his degradation and excommunication by the Inquisition, and his death in sorrow and repentance.

Hidalgo was not the only priest killed at that time. Before he was executed, the Spaniards shot six other priests who had followed him in his crusade. The parish priest was the natural leader of the masses in his early campaign for independence. It was another priest, José María Morelos, a half-caste with Negro blood in his veins, a poor man who worked as a laborer on a plantation and as a mule-driver until the age of twenty-five, who became the next leader of the Revolution. He had sought for holy orders in his poverty and, as a student, had known Hidalgo. Under Morelos the Revolution took on, in idea at least, the form of a clearly marked social movement. He was a simple, unpretentious, soft-spoken, and stubborn man. And the army he organized, disciplined, and commanded for five years tested the Spanish power in Mexico to the straining-point and very nearly defeated it.

In this instance we get a glimpse of the basic issues that in one form or another were to underlie Mexican political history for a century to come. Morelos's program is the clearest fore-shadowing of the Mexican Revolution of 1910. He wanted, as the Constitution issued at Chilpancingo in 1813 makes clear, to make Mexico independent, deriving its sovereignty from the people; to break up the large estates; to divide the wealth of the rich between the poor and the government; to abolish slavery, caste distinctions, judicial torture, government monopolies, the sales tax, the tribute; and he hoped to organize a government of law. Finally, he devised a federal constitution based upon universal suffrage. But the day of federal government had not yet come. In spite of his stubborn competence and great military leadership, he too was finally defeated, betrayed, and executed. With his death, on December 22, 1815, the mass movement for Mexican independence came to an end.

The uprising had been too vast to die a quiet death. Other leaders of lesser stature fought on in the hills. Many of them were captured and killed; others, such as Vicente Guerrero and Guadalupe Victoria, hid out in the impassable mountains and survived all vicissitudes. The war had been bloody and merciless on both sides. The killing of prisoners was the rule except for the striking instance of Guadalupe Victoria. The marauding armies sacked towns and burned plantations. The visible wealth accumulated during three centuries of peaceful life and labor was destroyed. Worst of all, the habit of peace was now dead and the rule of violence had been enshrined. Little men with a few armed followers discovered a key to power, prestige, and wealth, and the self-improvised leader had learned to stand against the King, the government, and the nation. The quiet that followed the execution of Morelos was a troubled peace, and the central government was not for many generations to have that unquestioned authority which had characterized Mexican politics for nearly three centuries.

The independence movement had been defeated chiefly by the relentless energy of Felix María Calleja, the best general of the Spaniards and later Viceroy of Mexico. One of his officers was Agustín Iturbide, a *criollo* of middle-class origin who had proved mercilessly cruel to the rebels, reckless in personal courage, and not too scrupulous in the handling of public funds. A man of little instruction and much ambition, he was to succeed in giving Mexico the independence the simple men of faith had failed to achieve, but it was to be under a different guise and to serve different ends. Instead of being, as it was under Hidalgo and Morelos, a movement not only against Spain but also against the dominion of those who had inherited power through the Conquest, the rebellion was to be a means by which the Spaniards in Mexico saved their property, the Church its powers, and the *criollos* their dream of equality in the affairs of the State.

A new turn of events in Spain in 1820 once again so reshuffled the cards that the conservative Mexican upper class, who for twelve years had fought against independence, now turned in favor of it, not because they had changed their principles, but because they wished to preserve them. Ferdinand

VII, who had returned to Spain after the defeat of Napoleon, had been forced to reintroduce the liberal Constitution of 1812 once again, and in Mexico the Spanish colony and hierarchy, who preferred the ancient rule, were willing to disrupt the Spanish Empire rather than assent to the liberal principles of the Constitution of 1812. They conspired to arm Agustín Iturbide with power to carry out their purpose. With the pretext of suppressing the smoldering rebellion under Guerrero in the south, they persuaded the Viceroy to give Iturbide an army. No sooner was he free of Mexico City than he in turn induced the rebels he had been armed to destroy to join him, and with him to achieve that independence for which the Mexican people had so long aspired.

The new uprising, under the Plan of Iguala—that is, with Mexico a monarchy under Ferdinand VII or another prince of Spanish lineage, with the maintenance of the rights of the Church, and with equality between Spaniards and Americans—swept the country. Iturbide rode into Mexico City in triumph on September 27, 1821. The end of the Spanish control of Mexico had come just three centuries after the Conquest. The refusal of Ferdinand VII to accept the peace treaty made in Mexico gave Iturbide the opportunity to occupy the seat of the older viceroys and later to assume for himself the crown he had helped take from the Spanish kings. He set up a regency of five and called for the election of a congress, which met in February 1822.

The art of congressional government was not to be learned overnight, however, and with political squabbles, high oratory, an empty treasury, and an army of 80,000 that had to be paid, the prospect of peaceful democratic government was not bright. The ambitions of the rude soldier who had so suddenly risen to power were still to be satisfied. On March 18, 1822, within a month after the meeting of the Congress, Pío Marcha, a sergeant in the army, raised the cry of "Long live Agustín I!" The tumult rose, crowds gathered, the streets were soon jammed by mobs shouting: "Long live Agustín I!" and Iturbide, pretending unwillingness, agreed to accept the crown. The next day a delirious mob imposed its will upon the Congress.

Thus, by the simple device of a city tumult, a new dynasty was to be saddled upon the country. This new, unlettered monarchy, dressed in royal trappings, learning the courtly arts from a French modiste, adorned itself with borrowed jewels and homemade tinsel. Iturbide had himself crowned in the cathedral of Mexico City on July 25, 1822. After the coronation he showered titles of nobility upon his followers and adherents. It was a famous show that delighted the *léperos* and the innocent children of the city streets, but it lacked substance. With a recalcitrant Congress, no money, rising prices, and a discontented army, the throne proved an uneasy seat. Not even the forced dissolution of Congress helped matters. On February 19, 1823, less than eight months after he had been solemnly crowned, Iturbide abdicated the throne when he was threatened by a rebellion in Vera Cruz led by a young officer named Antonio López de Santa Anna. He was exiled from the country and given a pension to remain abroad. But the end of his career was not yet. He returned to Mexico on July 15, 1824, landed in Tamaulipas, and was shot five days later by local authorities. Thus came to an end the career of the man who had first opposed and later, by treason to his superiors, accomplished the Independence, snatched a crown from a howling mob, and driven the first elected Congress from its seats by the bayonet. Iturbide had taught ambitious Mexican soldiers and politicians all the lessons they needed for the future ruin of their country, and they set about accomplishing that ruin with great assiduity and self-importance.

An explanation of the chaos may be sought by ascribing it to the sudden release of energy and ambition in the social classes previously confined by the traditional obedience to Spanish rule. The *criollo,* who in general terms was also a conservative, came into his own with the Independence, the *mestizo,* who was a "radical," with the civil strife and the reform movement of the sixties. The conservative party favored a centralized government that would give Mexico City control over the country. The liberals, who wanted a federal government based upon the local provincial caciques, were generally middle-class provincials eager to despoil the Church. The conservatives, trained in the Spanish tradition, were monarchical, supported Iturbide, and played a role in bringing in Maximilian. The Federalists, trained in the law and under the influence of French ideas, were republican, anticlerical, and in favor of free competition. They opposed the corporate ownership of the Church and of the communal Indian village lands as well. The conservatives favored the special privileges of the clergy and the army as against other citizens. The Federalists were opposed to special privileges and in favor of the doctrine that all men are equal before the law. The Indians played little or no active role throughout this period and were not a party to the argument except in individual instances, like that of Juárez, who became the leader of the Federalists.

Three men, Antonio López de Santa Anna (1794–1876), Benito Juárez (1806–72), and Porfirio Díaz (1830–1915), symbolize the bitter, tragic years of Mexican history between the Independence and the Revolution of 1910. Santa Anna is the evil genius of Mexican destiny. No other character in that turbulent and chaotic period embodied in his own person so much evil and charm. No description of Santa Anna in ordinary terms makes sense. His hold over the people of Mexico partakes of the unreal. His gifts were those of a ventriloquist or a magician, and his power over the Mexicans had something of the pathological in it. He began his career by betraying Iturbide and developed betrayal into a fine political art. But nothing he did seemed sufficiently degrading to drive him permanently from public office. He was shallow, bombastic, unprincipled, florid, and a showman. He dressed in gaudy uniforms; decorated himself with shining badges, stars and ribbons; gave himself innumerable titles, such as "savior" and "father of the country." He was sentimental, cruel, voluptuous, and unprincipled, but decorative and enchanting. He built monuments to himself at public expense; and when his leg, shot off by a French cannon ball, was brought to be buried in Mexico, the city turned out to do homage to something that seemed to have become a sacred relic, while Santa Anna, in gilded braid, watched the scene from his presidential chair as if it were a matter of the gravest national concern. The leg, in another turn of the wheel, was dug up from its grave by a mob and dragged through the streets.

This man, the chief architect of the dismemberment of Mexico through the loss of Texas and the defeat of the Mexican army during the war with the United States, continued even after these two national disasters to be called back to public office to continue the role of demagogue and tyrant. The defeat of Mexico by the United States and the taking from Mexico of more than half her national territory as a result of the Treaty of Guadalupe Hidalgo left the country demoralized and internally torn, so that it seemed as if every state, every district almost, would separate from the rest and set up a government of its own. The inner strife was more compelling than the external tragedy. The defeat by a foreign army was over and accepted. The struggle of who was to rule what was left of Mexico, and on what basis, remained unanswered and, in a measure, unanswerable. Neither side had the power to crush completely or to persuade the other; and the art of political compromise was unknown and perhaps, under the conditions, unacceptable.

The old struggle between the conservatives and the liberals continued as before. The conservatives aspired to non-democratic government and, as a last desperate effort, were willing to gamble with a foreign monarchy. When, in 1853, Lucas Alamán, the outstanding leader of the conservatives, turned the government over to Santa Anna for the ninth and last time, it was with a definite antidemocratic program. The program included the destruction of the states, the division of the country into departments, and the organization of a dictatorial government resting upon the influence of "the hierarchy, the landowners, and all of the serious-minded people." Santa Anna, the incredible Santa Anna, who called himself "Most Serene Highness" and declared himself "perpetual Victor," was the hope and the instrument of this new effort of the conservatives to control the country. The effort failed, and the Revolution of Ayutla (1854) finally drove Santa Anna from the political scene. He tried at least once more "to save the nation" during the French invasion, by offering his services first to Maximilian, who would not have them, and then to Juárez, who also did not feel the need for Santa Anna's "heroic arm" and "unquenchable patriotism." Santa Anna found himself unwanted at last. Twenty years later he returned to Mexico and wandered along its streets an old, forlorn, and pitiful creature. His magic was gone.

The Revolution of Ayutla (1854), under the leadership of Juán Álvarez, an old regional cacique who dominated a large part of southern Mexico, precipitated the next great cycle in Mexican history. This was the reassertion of the Federalists and their natural allies, the young liberal lawyers and intellectuals. Theirs was to be the next turn. They wrote their program into the Constitution of 1857 and laid the basis for the bitter three years' war (1858–61). The liberals won; but the conservatives were not yet beaten. They had been defeated, but a better day perhaps awaited them under a monarchy set up with foreign help. Maximilian of Austria and his beautiful and devoted Carlotta were to be the new victims of the gods of Mexico; and a new war—a war against French armies that was to last from 1862 to 1867—was once again to drench the fields of Mexico in blood and lead Mexicans to murder one another over issues that seemed to have no solution.

The story need not be repeated here. Maximilian was shot one early dawn in 1867 by order of Benito Juárez, who turned a deaf ear to all pleading for mercy. It was all so simple. The end of the American Civil War and the policy of William H. Seward, the American Secretary of State, who had consistently maintained the attitude that it was contrary to the interest of the United States for any foreign monarchy to subvert any republican form of government in the Western Hemisphere or to acquire any territory on this side of the Atlantic, played no small part in the final victory of the Mexican liberals. They won, or at least seemed to have won, the long battle that had begun with the Independence.

The figure of Juárez is the dominant one all through the period that runs between 1856 and 1872. Juárez was a full-blooded Indian. He was taciturn, righteous, a believer in the law, unyielding, stubborn, and, on a matter of principle, without mercy. He would try to destroy the Church and the army with their special privileges and make Mexico into a democratic and federal republic. The Constitution, above all things, had to be upheld, the nation preserved against foreign invasion and saved from internal treason. He came close to achieving his ends, but destiny willed otherwise. One thing seems clear: it is not until the end of the Juárez period that we can properly begin to speak of a Mexican nation. Until then it was little more than a conglomeration of regions loosely bound together and at war with one another.

It was left for Díaz to consolidate the Mexican nation. The centralized tyranny against which the Revolution of 1910 was to be fought was a creation of the years 1876–1910. The achievement was a remarkable one, but the cost proved high. Internal peace was secured by the ruthless destruction of all local and regional leadership. By the end of his regime there was only one source of power in Mexico. Banditry was exterminated or else the bandits were dressed in uniforms and given authority to capture and kill those who would not yield. Political opponents were given the choice of accepting government favors and surrendering their political independence, or of facing the prospect of a sudden end.

The issues of centralism versus federalism were compromised by leaving the Constitution intact and governing as if it did not exist. The conservatives had their centralized government, the Federalists their Constitution. The governors were repeatedly "elected" as lifelong lackeys of the President. The local municipalities were supplanted by *jefes políticos* responsive to the will of Díaz. The legislature was filled with friends kept in office, and the press was completely muffled. The Church issue was sidetracked by leaving the law intact but only partially enforced, and the Church, as long as it did not prove politically troublesome, could enjoy a large measure of freedom. The conflict between the wealthy landowners and the rising middle-class lawyers and liberals was compromised by the progressive developments derived from the encouragement of extensive foreign investments in railroad-building, public improvements, telegraphs, telephones, sanitation, and mining.

The intellectuals and lawyers who had quarreled with the aristocracy over who should govern Mexico found employment with the foreign companies as lawyers and concession-hunters. They found a hundred ways of keeping busy and growing prosperous. Díaz's control extended to the courts. The courts understood that the foreigner was to be protected because he was making Mexico into a progressive nation. Positivism came to be the ruling philosophy, and ideals of order and progress were the dominant notes in the Díaz regime. During this period a great part of the land found its way into foreign hands, and, with it, all the mining and manufacturing, a substantial part of the commerce, and the new oil industry as well. For the first time in its history Mexico had peace internally and standing as a nation abroad. Its credit was good, its budget was balanced, and the danger of internal rebellion and dismemberment had seemingly passed away.

The achievement, as time was to prove, rested upon poor foundations. In spite of the many years of strife, the inner structure of Mexico had remained strangely static. The rebellions had been fought out between the upper and middle classes, between the centralists and the Federalists. The mass of the population, the Indians and the poor peasants, remained outside the quarrel and served in it only as cattle driven to slaughter. The plantations had increased in size and number, and many of them belonged to foreigners. The rising cost of living was not balanced by an increased wage, and the declining yield of an eroding soil was met by higher tariffs upon agricultural produce. The new industries, for all their importance, touched only a fraction of the population. These changes were justified by a theory of progress that declared the Indian retrogressive and that required his elimination to make room for the European and American immigrants who were to take his place.

As the regime consolidated, it became more and more oppressive; and with the years Díaz came more and more under foreign influence and was less and less in contact with the needs of the people. When the regime seemed strongest, when its work seemed most admirable to the foreigner, and when people inside and outside of Mexico talked of it as something eternal, it proved shallow and weak, ready to be knocked down by the first strong wind that blew against it. The year 1910, when the centennial of the Independence was celebrated with so much pomp and applause for the old dictator, was also the year that saw the beginning of the end.

CHAPTER 4

The Revolution: 1910–46

The Revolution that began on November 20, 1910 against the dictatorship of the octogenarian Díaz is the point of departure for contemporary Mexico. The Revolution, headed by Francisco I. Madero, himself the scion of a great landowning family of northern Mexico, was unadorned by any philosophy of politics, meager in its social program, and opportunistic in its immediate objectives. The Madero Revolution was motivated by narrowly defined political aims; chief among these were the placing of young men in office and the electoral defeat of Díaz. Díaz, who had governed Mexico since 1876, had grown old, and his associates in the Cabinet, the governors of the states, and his political henchmen in and out of public office had grown old along with him. Among the members of his Cabinet, the Secretary of War and the Secretary of Justice were over eighty; the heads of the Departments of Communications, of the Interior, and of Public Works were seventy; and the others around sixty. Among the governors of the states two were past eighty, six were over seventy, and seventeen over sixty years of age. Like the dictator himself, the governors had continued in office year in and year out. The Terrazas family had ruled the state of Chihuahua since 1860, Tlaxcala had been governed by one man for twenty-six years, Aguascalientes for twenty-four years, Tabasco for twenty-two years. Puebla had regularly re-elected the same Governor for eighteen years, and Vera Cruz had done the same for nineteen years. So the story ran for most of the states.

The men around Madero were imbued with modern ideas. Madero himself had been educated abroad and had lived in Europe and in the United States. The movement was political rather than social or economic. It was military because there was no other way of uprooting the dictatorship; it was military in the special sense of a Mexican revolution, reminiscent of the middle of the nineteenth century. The armies were composed of small bands of barefooted men, poorly armed, living off the country, led by self-appointed leaders, and fighting petty engagements, described as major battles only because their opponents proved incompetent to meet their onslaught.

The uprisings in many parts of the country were spontaneous, un-co-ordinated, and owing allegiance to their own immediate leaders. Madero merely symbolized the rebellion. The effective leadership came from the common people, from men like Pascual Orozco and Pancho Villa, who gathered small groups of personal followers that swelled with every skirmish because every peon found the adventure exciting and the promise that lay beyond the horizon—especially if one had a gun in one's hand and a brave leader to follow—irresistible.

The uprising, to its own great surprise, proved successful in toppling the Díaz government and in electing Madero to the presidency. The victory of Madero proved easy—too easy. The great flood of popularity with which he was literally carried to the presidential chair was ominous. As never before in the history of Mexico, the common folk—the poor, the illiterate, the voiceless, the people who had never been heard from—appeared upon the scene in thousands of little villages, in interior towns, and in the capital cities. In Mexico City itself crowds greater than had been seen before hailed the "apostle" and cheered him along his way when he took office on November 6, 1911. Observers of that day in Mexico were puzzled and perturbed. Such an outpouring of sudden enthusiasm at a mere change of government was unreal; for the leader of the movement was, after all, a mild little man, kind and well-intentioned, but not a zealous bearer of a lighted torch. It was not his purpose to set a new world aglow or to tear the old order apart. His mission, as he saw it, was a limited one: to re-establish the older system of political succession by regular election.

To say re-establish is to misstate the historical fact. It was to establish, for Mexico had never had free and regular elections. Of the seventy-two Mexican governments during the nineteenth century only twelve had had a seemingly legal origin. The slogan of the Madero Revolution: "Effective suffrage and no re-election," was not new. Even Díaz had proclaimed it in his day, when as a young man he achieved the presidency by revolution against the then existing government. What was new was the stirring of the masses, who insisted on making Madero a symbol of something he did not represent. They would make him an "apostle" against his will. Madero was to symbolize a deeper urge than a mere change of political powers. The urge, however, was undefined, perhaps unconscious.

What time was to reveal, and that quickly, was an upsurge of the rural folk and a breaking down of the system of habit, law, and tradition that had for so long defined the social structure in Mexico. What was at hand was a social revolution. It had no intellectual leadership and no great name. No new philosopher, prophet, or poet was on hand to stir the folk. Their restlessness responded to something less formalized, but perhaps more real. They were hungry for land. They had been hungry for land for a long time and had striven for it in isolated instances, each village by itself. Now, for reasons not clear, but perhaps explainable, the movement had taken on a general character. In the early days it was still largely inarticulate. The arguments were still mainly about political matters. The intellectuals and the politicians were still mainly concerned over the issues of good government, honesty in politics, justice before the courts. But the underlying movement of the rural folk gradually swamped all else and subordinated all other issues to this basic one of land for the people. It was symbolic that Emiliano Zapata, in the state of Morelos, would not lay down his arms after Madero came to office. He insisted that land must be given to the villages. But he was almost alone among the supporters of Madero in seeing clearly the issues at stake. For the rest the objectives of the Revolution remained implicit and could not be voiced by inarticulate men.

The Mexican Revolution can perhaps best be characterized as an emerging nationalism. It was directed toward identifying the people of Mexico with the Mexican nation and toward giving unity to a people who had from time immemorial been divided by language, race, culture, and class. In that sense it aimed at giving coherence to what had always been a conglomerate, even a contradictory, pattern. The ruling theory in Mexico, since the conquest by the Spaniards in 1519, had always been that the Indian was incompetent, a child at best, or, as the later doctrine would have it, an inferior being condemned by nature to be the eternal pariah as against the "civilized," "cultured," and better-endowed elements in the population. The Indian was the servant of the upper classes, for he was, so the argument ran, fit for nothing else. The natural rulers of Mexico were the military, the hierarchy, the politicians, the landowners, the business men, and the well-bred. Between them and the poor Indian or *mestizo* there was a gap that could not be bridged because the lower classes, it was believed, were naturally lower.

Mexico was not really a nation. It was a land of locally bred colonists, who for all purposes felt themselves living in a foreign country and sought their inspiration outside the bounds of their native country, especially in France. Their painting, literature, art, and architecture in the second half of the nineteenth century had the exotic quality of things imported from the outside. The large landowners, the educated, the philosophers, all belonged intellectually to a non-Mexican universe, and even some of the first leaders of the Mexican Revolution of 1910 were of the same lineage. The movement, once initiated, soon took a different turn. The Mexicans, so to speak, discovered themselves and turned their eyes toward their own people.

The gap between the upper class and the poor, between the aristocrat and the *pelado*, between the city and the country, was of a seemingly absolute quality. In spite of the fact that in theory the Indian and the white man were equal before the law and in spite of the fact that an occasional Indian, like Juárez, could, by the accident of revolution and political upheaval, climb to the presidency, it remained true that for all other purposes the gap between the "Spanish" and the "white" *criollos* on one hand and the underlying population on the other remained unbridgeable.

In spite of a hundred years of independence and of endless rebellions, in spite of civil wars, foreign invasions, and changes in the Constitution, the basic economic, social, and political pattern had altered little. The wars had been among the rulers of the nation, or, better perhaps, among the ruling institutions. The quarrels had taken place between the monarchists and the republicans; between the Church and the State; between the federalists and the centralists; within the middle class, lawyers on one side and priests on the other. But these groups, taken together, were numerically small and were all imbued with an underlying contempt for the Indian and the peon. They all believed that Mexico was to be ruled by its "natural" rulers.

The significance of the Revolution of 1910 lies in the fact that it repudiated this doctrine. The mass of the people, who until then had been neither consulted nor considered in the battles fought over who would rule them, asserted their claim to participate in the government itself.

If the Revolution is to be defined as an emerging nationalism, it is in the sense that the common people who now asserted their rights had, so to speak, been considered by their "natural" rulers as alien, as something apart and of a lesser order; and the people, when they found a voice, instinctively defined their rulers as alien. It was thus that the lines were drawn as the battle developed, and it was expressed by the phrase that Mexico had become the mother of the foreigner and the stepmother of the Mexican.

The students of the University of Mexico, who abandoned their classes by the hundreds in 1915 and joined the Revolution, were turning their backs upon foreign influence and seeking for new values in the soil of Mexico itself, among the barefooted, bronzed, poor Indians and *mestizos* whose companions they became. The movement was nativistic and, because it was that, it also became antiforeign. The foreign influence was everywhere: in the Church, in mining, in industry, in landholding, in education, in art, architecture, and fashions. The movement turned to the past, idealized the Indian tradition, and fought the Conquest all over again. The foreigner became defined as the conqueror—the Spanish conqueror and his more recent allies in European or American dress. To re-create a "true," a native Mexican nation became a kind of dream. Nostalgia for the past ruled the scene.

The Revolution begun by Madero had unconsciously moved from the question of political succession to a nativistic nationalism that altered the character of the upheaval. Instead of being a political uprising, it became a mass uprising that repudiated the very basis upon which the older order rested. A new theory of government came to rule the day. The people were the government, and they had been denied moral status under the older order. Mexico turned from the educated, well-born, and rich to find salvation at the hand of men come from the soil. The leaders of the Revolution were poor men nourished on the land.

It was the peasant who forced his personality and finally his program upon Mexico. The leaders were such men as Emiliano

Zapata, a peasant born in a little village in the state of Morelos, who saw the lands of his people taken away and was pressed into the army against his will. Pancho Villa, in the north, was an illiterate bandit, quick on the draw and indifferent to the meaning of life. He became an imaginative and reckless leader, adored and feared by his followers, and at one time had forty thousand armed men under his command. Álvaro Obregón was a peasant rancher in Sonora. He was "practical," sagacious, and skilled in blandishments, and he developed into the greatest military and the shrewdest political leader of Mexico. Plutarco Elías Calles, a poor schoolteacher, who wore his first pair of shoes at sixteen, defended Mexican nationalism against an angry and hostile world and dominated Mexican politics for almost a generation. Lázaro Cárdenas was a poor boy with three years' schooling, who at the age of twelve had to support a widowed mother and a number of brothers and sisters. He joined the Revolution at sixteen and came to be the most beloved and disinterested figure in modern Mexico. These men, and hundreds like them of lesser importance, are symbolic of the upheaval. The folk had come out of the depths to carve a new and better world for themselves and in doing so destroyed the visible forms of an older society.

Madero had promised land for the people in a half-hearted sort of way. He had also proposed the nationalization of the railroads, the restoration of the Constitution of 1857, the reestablishment of the local town governments, and the abolition of the *jefes políticos*. But he proved incompetent as an executive. He surrounded himself with men of his own type, placed his brothers in the Cabinet and in high office, had little contact with the people, and did not understand the urgency of the demand for land distribution. Worse, he confided in the older military, the former henchmen of Díaz, and, like a child in innocence and dignity, prayed for a political peace in Mexico without recognizing that the peace he wished for would wait upon a new balance of the social forces he had unwittingly helped to upset. The passions roused by Madero proved beyond his competence to guide, and he was engulfed by the anger he had kindled. The day called for political sagacity, for the traditional qualities of the *caudillo*, and for the intuitive wisdom of a great leader of the people, and Madero possessed none of these. His time in office was to prove short and troubled. He was barely seated in the presidential chair in November 1911 when he had to meet a serious rebellion by Pascual Orozco in Chihuahua in the early months of 1912; and, that suppressed, a new one in October in Vera Cruz led by Felix Díaz, a nephew of the old dictator. This, too, was defeated, and, in his kindness, Madero spared the lives of its leaders. Felix Díaz was imprisoned in Mexico City, where he and Bernardo Reyes could conveniently plot from their prison cell with the older military elements who resented their loss of prestige and influence. On February 9, 1913 an uprising broke out in Mexico City led by the men whose lives Madero had spared.

It was typical of the Mexican milieu that the regular army officers who led this rebellion against Madero should convert Mexico City into a battleground and for ten days bombard the palace over the heads of the populace. It was also typical that Madero, encased in the National Palace, should turn for support to the least scrupulous among his soldiers, Victoriano Huerta, and entrust to this inebriate not only his life but the fortunes of the movement that had carried him to office. Huerta soon betrayed his trust and, inside the American Embassy, signed a compact with the enemies of Madero. The American Ambassador, Henry Lane Wilson, introduced him as the future provisional President of the Republic to the hastily gathered diplomatic corps. All of this took place before Madero had resigned the presidency. Madero was seized on February 18, his resignation was extracted from him on the 19th, and he and his Vice-President, José María Pino Suárez, were assassinated on the 22nd by men responsible to Huerta while being carried to the national penitentiary. The shadow of the prospective tragedy ran before the event, and the wife of Madero and members of the diplomatic corps begged Henry Lane Wilson to save the life of the man to whom he was an accredited Ambassador, and even the Texas legislature telegraphed to President Taft asking our intervention on behalf of Madero.

Huerta not only was recognized by the leading European powers, but was also accepted by most of the governors of the states, for they, like the Mexican army, belonged in spirit to the Díaz regime. Only Venustiano Carranza, Governor of Coahuila, José María Maytorena, Governor of Sonora, Zapata in Morelos, Saturnino Cedillo in San Luis Potosí, and a few scattered and insignificant forces here and there refused to accede to what was acclaimed as the end of the Revolution, now sealed by the death of its most conspicuous representative.

Madero's cold-blooded murder merely symbolized the eternal tragedy of Mexico. Life, even the life of the head of the State, was a mere incident to be swept aside by political passion. The murder of Madero presaged the nature of the struggle to come.

A state of mind came to prevail that tolerated such characters as "Major" Fierro, Pancho Villa's "personal killer," who murdered untold prisoners in cold blood with his own hands. Political murder was not murder, and a kind of self-assertiveness and self-reliance took hold of the people because there could be no reliance on anyone else. As one surveys the years of turbulence of that period, the wonder is that out of the Revolutionary chaos a sense of direction ever emerged. Equally remarkable is the fact that men were found who could make passions coalesce into government, even if not into law; for the government and the law were two different things, and remained so for a long time.

The upheaval was greater than its leaders, broader than its expressed objectives. It sought for ways of social peace by means of traditional violence. Huerta merely continued an older tradition; and others, on every side of the battle and for many years, did likewise. The Revolution worked its way with these instruments and in spite of them.

The murder of Madero split Mexico wide open. It became evident that even the limited political purposes of the Madero Revolution would involve the country in bitterness and war.

Huerta, in the saddle, attempted to quiet opposition and to impose his will by murder of such men as Senator Belisario Domínguez, who protested the usurpation. The fact that he did not succeed was owing to many things, among them the refusal of the Wilson administration to recognize a government come to power by the murder of the legally elected President. From Mexico City, Madero's adherents escaped and made their way toward the north to join Carranza. On March 26, 1913 Carranza formally issued the Plan de Guadalupe, assuming the title of First Chief of the constitutional army. He promised to defeat the usurper and re-establish constitutional government. Groups of men under their own leaders appeared everywhere, all intent upon avenging the death of Madero. These bands carried their women with them, armed themselves as they could, and grew with each battle. Individual leaders, bringing their own men, joined together under some better-known chieftain, formed armies that, starting in the north and northwest, defeated and drove the Mexican regular armies southward, and by July 1914 forced Huerta to abandon Mexico City. Most conspicuous for their success as military chieftains were Pancho Villa and Álvaro Obregón, one from Chihuahua, the other from Sonora. But the defeat of Huerta merely marked the beginning of new and greater strife.

The Revolution had so far produced no formalized programs, and when Huerta was defeated the military forces were divided between those of Villa and Carranza. Carranza as chief of the constitutional forces proved stubborn and intractable, Pancho Villa petulant, capricious, and undependable. An attempt to compromise the difference between these two in the Convention of Aguascalientes in October 1914 failed. Villa's armies marched on Mexico City, which they occupied jointly with Zapata, while Carranza was forced to flee to Vera Cruz. Obregón, Carranza's leading general, finally drove Villa north again and, in the Battle of Celaya, in March 1915, defeated this old-time bandit and very great cavalry leader. The military crisis precipitated by Villa forced Carranza to seek popular support among those to whom the Revolution had become a social movement. It was thus that what had begun as a political revolution came to be a social revolution. The decree laws issued by Carranza, and among them the first agrarian law—that of January 6, 1915—were in time to be amplified in the Constitution of 1917. But in the meantime they brought Carranza the support he needed.

With this program in hand, and with Obregón, who had become in his own way the spokesman of the "radicals" of the Revolution, Carranza received the support of the labor unions, the agrarians, and all those bent upon reducing foreign influence. A considerable group of intellectuals, with Luis Cabrera at their head, labored in Carranza's offices in those days and attempted to formulate a body of laws that would express the social content of the Revolution. With Villa defeated, it became necessary to give a legal basis to Carranza's power; and a convention to reform the Constitution of 1857, rather than an election, was decided upon.

The convention that met in Querétaro in December 1916 represented the successful military faction headed by Carranza. It was composed mainly of soldiers fresh from the field of battle, the intellectuals who surrounded Carranza, and a few labor leaders. The air was tense, and factional bitterness dominated the scene; untamed military groups still ravaged the country, while fear of the United States, which hung over the convention, was revealed in its debates. It was called together to reform the older Constitution of 1857, but instead produced a document that was to become the source of a profound social and economic revolution. This Constitution embodies two contradictory conceptions of the role of the State and of the relation of the individual to the government. It reiterates all of the concepts of democratic government contained in the Constitution of 1857. Freedom of association, worship, and speech, representative government, universal suffrage, periodic elections, the separation of the powers, the independence of state and municipal governments, the rights of trial by jury, and the right to property—all are retained. In fact, the political ideals of the American and French Revolutions find their restatement in the Constitution of 1917.

There was something in addition about which a few members of the convention were concerned, for it was clear that these principles now reaffirmed had not protected Mexico from either political chaos or tyranny. If the Revolution was not once again to prove a vain and useless effort, something was needed that would re-establish a balance in Mexican society. The independence from Spain in the early part of the nineteenth century had so weakened the State that it could not contend against the other entrenched institutions within the Mexican body politic. These institutions were defined by the members of the Constitutional Convention as the Church, the large plantation, and foreign interests. It was therefore only by attacking these entrenched forces and bridling or destroying them that the "radicals" within the convention hoped to balance the social structure and to strengthen the State.

The Mexican Revolution was in part coincident with the First World War, when the United States was proclaiming the New Freedom, and when, in Great Britain, Lloyd George had announced that England must become "a country fit for heroes to live in." It was a period when the hope for social betterment was running strong all over the world and was identified with opposition to "imperialism," "trusts," and "monopolies." If the delegates to the Constitutional Convention wrote a revolutionary program into the Constitution, they felt that they were merely the advance guard of the world-wide movement for the redeeming of man from injustice. These consciously expressed objectives were written into Article 27, dealing with the land; Article 123, dealing with labor; and Article 130, dealing with the Church. The fact that these articles conflicted with such earlier concepts of personal freedom as the right to property and the right to work was compromised upon the ground that in any given case the social interest was more basic than the individual.

The ideological conflict within the Constitution was recognized for what it was, and much of the contradictory policy of Mexican governments since has stemmed from this fact. Different governments have emphasized one rather than another of these commitments. What is of primary importance is that the government of Mexico was given very extensive powers to enforce the details of the new program embodied in the Constitution, and this program chartered a policy that would change the social and economic structure of Mexico. This change was to be symbolized by the creation of two moral, social, and political agencies: the *ejido,* a semicollective landholding community, and a trade union with extensive powers prescribed in the law. It was also to be represented by the reassertion of the nation's rights over the subsoil, the power to control monopolies, the sharp reduction of the institutional powers of the Church, and the limitation of foreign rights in the country. How much of all these future developments was foreseen by the members who wrote the Constitution will always remain a question. It is my own belief, from a study of the debates and from personal contact with many of the men active in the convention, that they accepted a formula, a theory, rather than a policy. It became a policy only as it worked out in practice, slowly and haltingly after many years of trial and error. But the Constitution of 1917 provided the Revolution with a program that could be called into action to justify public policy and political expediency. From one point of view the Revolution is the product of the Constitutional Convention. The social revolution that has since unfolded received prior legal sanction.

The turbulent passions evoked by the murder of Madero had now found an organizing principle and a sense of direction. The nature of the conflict had at least been defined, and in the future the argument would run between those who opposed and those who would attempt to live by the principles of the Constitution of 1917.

If the Constitution contained brave new principles of public policy and social justice, the instrument reared to develop and enforce them proved both fallible and inept. Carranza, who on March 12, 1917 came to power as the first President under the Constitution, was arbitrary and of another world. He had been a Senator under Díaz and was indifferent to the social issues confronting him. His lust for personal power made him an easy victim of the professional sycophants who corrupted and discredited his administration. A group of irresponsible young officers serving under him gathered in for themselves through bribery and violence what fruits they could garner from a country torn by strife. Popular turbulence was the order of the day, and Carranza met it as he could, by suppression. He used martial law against the rising trade unions, fought petty engagements all over the country, and carried on a bitter military campaign against Zapata in the south. Zapata still insisted that land be given to the people. His armed peasants melted at the approach of a strong military column and scattered to their little plots to become innocent-looking tillers of the soil, seemingly incapable of violence, only to reassemble again at the call of their leader to carry on the war they had started ten years earlier. The conflict became one of extermination.

A price of fifty thousand pesos was put on Zapata's head, and finally he was trapped. One of Carranza's officers offered to go over to Zapata and take his men with him. Zapata, suspicious, asked for a sign of loyalty, a deed against his enemies; and this officer attacked a government force and took it, so establishing his claim to acceptance, and in return begged the peasant leader to come and welcome his new adherent. With only a few men at his back, Zapata rode into the gates of an hacienda, where, in the act of presenting arms, he was fired on and killed, his white horse fleeing with his bewildered followers. The news of the assassination spread fear and sorrow among the people who had obeyed him all these years. To convince the people that he was dead, his body was exhibited in Cuautla, a large town in Morelos. That was in April 1919, but to this day they will still tell you they have seen him on his white horse riding over the mountaintops and watching over his people.

Carranza, when his term was drawing to a close in 1920, had the support only of those who during his administration had fattened at the public trough. When he attempted to impose Ignacio Bonillas, his Ambassador in Washington, as the next president, he stirred a political crisis he could not control. He suddenly found himself alone, without an army, friends, or followers. Those army generals he had most greatly favored, like Guadalupe Sánchez, commander in Vera Cruz, betrayed him. Sánchez telegraphed to Carranza: "President and Father . . . if but one remains loyal to you, I am that man." But when Carranza was fleeing from Mexico City in twenty railroad cars loaded with the public treasury and all that he could carry off, Sánchez blocked his path and tried to capture him. He escaped in the dark with a few faithful followers, but was murdered as he lay asleep in the little village of Tlaxcalantongo, on the night of May 21, 1920.

Obregón, idol of the army and popular hero of the masses, whose candidacy Carranza had opposed and who, to evade arrest, fled the city disguised as a railroad engineer, was carried to the presidency by popular acclaim. The coming of Obregón had something of the effect of a healing balm upon a people disillusioned and balked at every turn. The Revolution—the social revolution—found its first presidential protagonist in Obregón. His personal prestige with the army, which neither Madero nor Carranza had enjoyed, assured him of the authority needed to pacify the country, and his shrewd insight into the men with whom he had fought or whom he had led enabled him to bridle the hundreds of irascible "generals" who had come upon the scene during the years of rebellion. Obregón slyly took all of them into the regular army and put them all on the payroll, saying that "if a man calls himself a general, he must be one," thus swelling the regular army beyond all measure.

With Obregón a comparative peace returned to Mexico. From the day of the overthrow of Díaz it had taken ten years of civil war to re-establish an acceptable authority. Obregón won the favor of labor by encouraging the organization of trade unions, by putting their leaders in government jobs, by financing their conventions, and by giving them free railroad passes and a hundred other favors. In fact, the trade-union movement—the C.R.O.M. (*Confederación Regional Obrera Mexicana*)—acquired its first real power during the Obregón administration. He was also the first to make peace with the Zapatistas. He accepted their demand for land distribution, placed a Zapatista general in charge of troops in Morelos, and made some of their followers officials in the Department of Agriculture. This open acceptance of the popular impulse released a spirit of creative optimism and energy that seemed to flood the country as if a new spring had burst upon it. Under José Vasconcelos, Obregón's Minister of Education, an imaginative educational movement was inaugurated; the artists of Mexico appeared upon the scene—Diego Rivera, Siqueiros, Orozco, and others who pleaded for public walls to decorate with the murals that have become world-famous. They organized themselves into an artists' union and worked on their scaffolds with pistols strapped on conspicuously for all the world to see that they too belonged to the Revolution. The early years of the Obregón regime created a feeling that can be explained in the words: "At last—the strife is over and at last we may set our hands to remaking the Mexico which so many poor men had dreamed of and paid for with their lives." Obregón set up the first agrarian department to deal with land distribution, permitted representatives of the labor party in Congress, attempted to cope with the banking and monetary difficulties created by years of civil war and inflation, worked out a compromise with foreign creditors through the Lamont and de la Huerta agreement, sought some basis of understanding with the United States in the so-called "Bucareli Conference," which provided for two mixed claims commissions, and promised to pay Americans for their expropriated lands. The United States sent Charles Beecher Warren as Ambassador, and it seemed as if Mexico would at last settle down and remain at peace.

The country was once again thrown into civil war at the

approach of the next presidential election. The army divided between the two presidential aspirants, Adolfo de la Huerta, a former Governor of Sonora and friend of Obregón, and Plutarco Elías Calles. Obregón sided with Calles. When de la Huerta led a rebellion (1923–4), a large part of the regular army deserted the government, and Obregón won only because he was able to call upon the loyalty of the agrarian and labor groups. An important element in his victory was indirect help from the United States. Calles was therefore elected President, but only after the country had once again been torn by civil strife.

The Calles administration survived on the brink of catastrophe and in the midst of a profound inner stress that threatened to snap at any time. That the country survived those four fateful years (1924–8) will remain a seeming miracle and an evidence of inner vitality. In spite of his many faults, his arbitrary temper, and his complete ruthlessness toward political opponents, Calles crystallized the ideas of Mexican nationalism and saved the Mexican social revolution from internal disintegration and external pressure. Internally, he greatly strengthened the trade-union movement, gave the C.R.O.M. what amounted to a monopoly over labor, pushed the distribution of land, and, through his Secretary of War, Joaquín Amaro, disciplined the army with an iron hand. It was under his administration that the Mexican road and irrigation programs were launched, the rural school system pushed ahead, and the National Bank of Mexico founded. He became involved in a bitter struggle with the Church, however, and in a contentious argument with the United States over oil and agrarian legislation that brought the two countries to the edge of war. The attitude of the United States Ambassador, James R. Sheffield, seemed to lead to an impasse. President Coolidge's appointment of Dwight W. Morrow, toward the end of 1927, in place of Sheffield, greatly changed Mexican-American feelings and opened the road toward the subsequent understanding between the two nations.

The presidential election of 1928 stirred the country to a

new revolution. The supporters of the Church, the opponents of the brittle Calles rule, the men who stirred the "*cristero*[1] rebellion," the landowners who hoped to see the land program reversed, the foreign investors who saw in the growing trade-union movement the hand that would throttle their enterprises, and the oil industry, unsuccessfully resisting the application of Article 27 of the 1917 Constitution, all saw in the coming election a possible turning point in their fortunes. The air was filled with stress, and the bitterness in Mexico was such that any political aberration seemed a possibility.

The Constitution of 1917 limited the presidential term to four years and prohibited re-election. In 1927, however, to make possible the candidacy of Obregón, the Constitution was changed to permit his return to office after the passing of an intermediate term. Obregón's candidacy provided the pretext for a rebellion by Generals Gómez and Serrano. But Calles was forehanded. Francisco Serrano, the most popular army candidate, the intimate barracks companion of Obregón and his former Secretary of War, was taken from a banquet in Cuernavaca with eleven friends and shot without a hearing while being transported to Mexico City. Their bodies were carried to Mexico City and exhibited. That did not put an end to the rebellion. Arnulfo Gómez led his followers into a revolt against the government. He was defeated and killed. Thus once again the election of a new president was possible only after the suppression of a military rebellion specifically organized to prevent the choice of the candidate supported by the government. Obregón was now elected against great popular feeling, fanned by the trade-union leader Luis N. Morones, among others. Obregón was elected, but he too was killed, on July 17, 1928. A young religious fanatic shot him in a restaurant where he was surrounded by friends and henchmen.

The death of Obregón created a moral and political crisis

[1] Operating chiefly in Jalisco, Michoacán, and Colima, beginning in 1927, the *cristeros,* were armed marauders who harried the government and committed widespread acts of depredation, purportedly in defense of the Church (their rallying cry was "*Cristo Rey*"—"Christ the King"). The movement died out in 1929.

that might, once again, have thrown the country into the spasmodic convulsion so frequent in Mexican history. The vacuum created by his death had to be filled, and it could be filled only by Calles. No other leader could have kept the country from splintering into factional strife. The qualities of self-restraint and political authority exhibited by Calles in this crisis challenged the admiration and induced the prudence even of his bitterest enemies, for Calles himself was suspected of being implicated in Obregón's murder. People said openly that now, with his only possible opponent out of the way, he would have himself elected president and re-create the personal tyranny seemingly so congenial to the Mexican atmosphere. Instead, however, Calles did the one thing no one expected him to do. He placed all of the police authority in the hands of Obregón's most intimate friends to follow the trial of conspiracy to its end. All they uncovered was a small group of fanatics led by a nun, Madre Conchita, and a few insignificant boys fascinated with the idea that the times required the sacrifice of Obregón.

After taking from the lips of all men the rumors and accusations against himself, Calles dramatically announced that he would never again occupy elective office and that the day of the *caudillo* was over. It required the self-confidence of one sure of his own complete control over the hurricane in the making for him to say that he would not permit anyone else to move into the seat he was vacating, which Obregón's death had left empty, except one who, in the emergency, was a legally chosen representative of Congress. He would use this moment of tension and strife to attempt a bridge between the tradition of the *caudillo* and political democracy. The moment was tense with implicit tragedy, for the logic of political tradition required either a tyranny or a convulsion. That neither came to pass is to the credit of Calles, and it must be recognized as the beginning of that change in the political atmosphere which has since brought relative peace to the country.

That the promise proved greater than the fulfillment, and that ingrained political instability forced Calles to suppress an uprising by General Escobar, were consistent with the Mexican mores. But the fact that he never again occupied the presidential chair is of more than symbolic significance. It is true that his influence remained decisive up to the early days of General Lázaro Cárdenas, but politically he had no choice. In the scheme of Mexican politics he was forced to make decisions or see the country thrown into a new civil war.

This is not the end of Calles's story. His later career was clouded by a retreat from his earlier belief in the social program of the Revolution. His friends played upon his vanity, proclaimed him *jefe máximo* of the Revolution, and endowed him with a seeming omnipotence, while they gorged themselves in his protecting shadow. An all-engulfing mood of political cynicism took hold of the country. As if by magic, a new aristocracy of gilded "socialists," who turned public gambling into a national industry, appeared on the scene. Having lost their earlier faith in the people, they salved their consciences by a systematic persecution of the Church, as if that were sufficient to save them from the charge of having perverted a popular movement to corrupt ends. Calles fell a victim to his insidious friends, who first ruined his reputation and then destroyed his influence. The Revolution itself became a mockery and a delusion in their hands.

Between the time of the death of Obregón in 1928 and the coming of Lázaro Cárdenas to the presidency in 1934, three men occupied the presidential chair, each placed there by the will of Calles and maintained in office by his influence. Emilio Portes Gil was chosen as Provisional President by the national Congress for the years 1928–30. He was former Governor of Tamaulipas, a convinced agrarian, a civilian, a lawyer as well as a skilled politician. He carried forward the previously initiated agrarian, road-building, irrigation, and rural education programs. He organized the National Revolutionary Party as a means of compromising the conflicting ambitions of Mexican political leaders in the hope of avoiding a military rebellion at every change in office.

In the next election it proved necessary to suppress a new

rebellion, this time against General Gonzalo Escobar, when nearly seventy per cent of the army deserted the government. Calles, whose power was still at its height, defeated the armed uprising with the support of the agrarians and the unions, and, with the implicit support of the American government, Pascual Órtiz Rubio took office in February 1930.

Órtiz Rubio was chosen because he had been in diplomatic service abroad for so long a time that he had no enemies at home. By the same token he had no friends and did not understand the immediate situation. Administratively inept and a promising tool in the hands of those who would have formally called a halt to the agrarian and labor program of the government, he soon proved unacceptable even to the corrupt clique that surrounded Calles. He was forced to resign in 1933. It is significant that the presidential change could occur in mid-term (he had been elected for a four-year term) without a revolution. But Calles was then still strong enough both to compel the change and to pick the succeeding first magistrate.

General Abelardo L. Rodríguez took over in 1933 and served until the next presidential term, which began in November 1934. Rodríguez, as a soldier and an intimate of the clique around Calles, found the going easier. He steered clear of the errors of Órtiz Rubio and managed to combine interests in public gambling and social welfare. He thus fitted in with the mood of increasing cynicism and corruption in public office without repudiating the commitment of the Revolution to social welfare.

This period (1928–34) between the murder of Obregón and the election of Lázaro Cárdenas is most perplexing. If it were possible to discover what had taken hold of the leadership of Mexico in those debased and clouded years, it would illumine much of Mexican history. Here was a group of new men, most of whom had come from the ranks of the Revolution and had risked their lives in a hundred battles for the redemption of the people from poverty and serfdom. If called upon, each would have declared (and honestly so) that to be his primary aim, and yet, at the first opportunity, each fell an easy victim to pelf and power. That they repudiated their commitments is certainly true, but most of them could not have described the repudiation that had, in fact, occurred.

Their difficulty lay in the fact that they had come to power suddenly and without preparation, either morally, psychologically, politically, or even administratively. They were taken from their villages as barefooted youngsters who had slept on the floor and could barely read, and after a few years spent on the battlefields found themselves tossed into high office and great responsibility. This new world was filled with a thousand temptations they had not dreamed of: gold, women, houses, carpets, diamonds, champagne. They had arrived on the scene in the big city with their boots muddy and their faces unshaven, their manners uncouth, and the memory of their friends and families in little mud huts, living on *tortillas* and beans. Here, at no price at all, just for a nod, all their hearts desired was offered them in return for a favor, a signature, a gesture, a word. It was a world of fable, and in their innocence and hunger—or greed, it does not matter—they succumbed to it. They succumbed to it because they had no moral fortitude. They had no philosophy and no faith, no system of values, no sense of the big world. The big world, especially the big city, was too much for them. They had, or at least most of them had, some notion that the people wanted land, that they were fighting against foreign influence, that they were defending Mexican nationalism. But somehow those things seemed unrelated to the immediate opportunities for self-aggrandizement, had no relation to the pleasures of the flesh.

A violent revolution made by people come from the poverty and moral insufficiency of the Mexican rural background proved incompetent, except in isolated instances, as if by a miracle, to mold men who appreciated the larger world and their responsibility to it. If they became corrupt, it was because they were corruptible, and if they were corruptible, it was because the world they had been reared in was barren of moral, spiritual, or political values. They did not even have the ordinary integrity that comes from habituation to an efficient administrative organization. Those of them who remained in the country, in the little villages, close to the people and to the soil, escaped the moral devastation that overtook the successful leaders who, at the age of twenty-one or twenty-five, found themselves governors of states or members of the cabinet, when all of their previous life had been that of a poor peasant, or a gallant leader of a small personal following with a bit of luck and shrewdness to boot.

It was against this background that Lázaro Cárdenas came to power. The times called for a reassertion of faith in the common people. The Calles group needed, it was clear, a spokesman free of the moral turpitude that had enveloped the leaders of the Revolution. But none of them, least of all Calles himself, could have suspected that this man whom they had chosen for the presidency would repudiate their system and break their hold upon the country. After all, like most of them, he too had risen from the ranks, had served in one office after another, and had shared their earlier hardships even if he had not taken on their habits of peculation or fallen victim to their disillusionment and cynicism.

What distinguished Cárdenas was his simplicity, his complete devotion to and identity with the common people of the country, especially the Indians, the peons, and the little farmers. He had escaped the corroding impact of the army barracks, its vulgarities, its loud sarcasms, and its disregard for human life. In an unpretentious sort of way, the thing most precious to him was the dignity of the common folk, and he spent long days listening to their complaints, needs, aspirations. His energy and patience in their behalf seemed unending. "They need so much; patience, at least, I can give them," he said. His respect for human life was such that he is not known ever to have ordered the taking of life. When I commented upon his recklessness in traveling around the country without a guard, he said: "It is better to die trying to do good than to keep oneself alive by doing evil." His energy seemed inexhaustible, and he spent his years in office going over the country from village to village to attend to the needs of the people, taking the government to them personally.

There was also a kind of method in this close association with the people. If he was to reduce the hold of the clique that had ruled and filched for so long, he would need the people, for the challenge to the Calles clique was in Cárdenas himself. That they did not know it is an evidence of their self-confidence and of his habit of silence, his long-headedness, and his seeming concern with little things—a school here, a few cows there, a small bridge or road, or something individual—a chance to be sent to a hospital if sick or a bit of money if in need.

Cárdenas came to office on December 1, 1934 for a period of six years, for the presidential term had been extended with a "six years' plan" elaborated by the National Revolutionary Party. His first act in office was a challenge to the Calles group. He closed all gambling places operating under federal concessions. He moved the presidential residence from the Chapultepec Castle to a modest home, and opened the national telegraph system to the poor for an hour a day for any complaint or request to the President. Accepting the principle that the land ought to belong to the people—for, as he said, in the end the government would belong to those who owned the land—he speeded the distribution of land among the villages. This problem he would solve so that no future government could undo his work.

As with the land, so with labor. He supported the trade unions because he saw in them a moral as well as a political principle: that the men associated in labor ought to have an instrument that would represent their interests and needs. He also felt that the industries, especially the foreign industries, had been indifferent to the human needs of their workers and had denied them standing as moral persons. It was on similar grounds that he ultimately expropriated the oil industry, to bring to an end its interference in the internal politics of Mexico. In his own words, it was done to keep it from deciding the next presidential election.

The oil expropriation in 1938 over a labor dispute that was on the verge of compromise was politically motivated. When the oil companies declared that they would not obey the decisions of the Mexican Supreme Court, they impugned the dignity of the President and assumed a position that amounted to rebellion. When they did this by announcing in public advertisements that from then on they were not responsible for what might happen to the country, they precipitated a political crisis that, morally speaking, could be met in only one way. Cárdenas acted in defense of what seemed to him the essentials of national dignity, and the response from the people was such as to unify the country as it had never been unified before. Cárdenas became a national idol, even to his opponents. At last a President had come upon the scene who was not afraid to bridle the foreign interests and to assert that the national estate and dignity had to be protected at all hazards.

The flood of popular enthusiasm was so great as to be almost pathetic. Men felt as if a new day had dawned. Simple Indians in their bare feet brought their pennies, or even a chicken or a pig, and offered them to the President toward the payment for the expropriated industries. Even the Church permitted collections in front of its doors for the payment of this debt. Cárdenas remarked that this was the first time in many generations that the Church had publicly supported the government. He was pleased with having finally broken the impasse between the Church and State. Two years earlier he had used his influence to bring the persecution of the Church to an end.

The flood of strikes that followed Cárdenas's inauguration was the occasion for a bitter attack by Calles. The confusion of a house divided against itself was evidenced by the behavior of Congress, whose members first flocked to Cuernavaca to offer their allegiance to the lord of yesterday, only to discover that he had lost his power, and then, the next day, marched themselves to the National Palace to offer allegiance to the

President. Cárdenas carried out the turnover of internal power slowly, by gradually consolidating his control over the military through shifting the younger elements in the army. It had to be done unobtrusively at first because a direct challenge to Calles might have been fatal, but when Cárdenas felt himself strong enough, Calles was put on a plane and shipped to the United States.

Cárdenas nationalized the railroads and turned them over to the workers to run, only to discover, as in the oil workers' unions, that neither their leadership nor their integrity was equal to their responsibility. But unions had his support because he believed that people must ultimately learn from their own experience and have the opportunity to govern themselves in the light of changing needs.

With the Calles influence eliminated, with internal peace and great popular support, Cárdenas could devote his seemingly endless energies to the details of the administration. He tried to do it all himself. Each little detail, no matter how small, came to him and was handled through him. People flocked around him by the thousands wherever he went, each with a petition in hand, a demand, a need. Something that they could get in no other way they would now receive from the hands of the President. Cárdenas would spend hours and days visiting, listening, and then, in the night, classifying the innumerable papers he had collected, writing on each one of them what was to be done, and forwarding them to Cabinet ministers, many of whom he dragged along, much against their will, in his constant travels over the country. He attended to the larger issues, too, as best he could—the establishment of the National Credit Bank for the *ejidos,* the pushing of the road and irrigation program, the creation of a Polytechnical School, the promotion of a railroad that would finally connect the Isthmus of Yucatán with the rest of the country, the organization of special schools for the children of soldiers, and a thousand other things such as the gathering together of hundreds of abandoned children from all over the country and founding a home for them. No personal need that he saw in his travels did he fail to attempt to take care of, even such things as going to a small country hospital and ordering cork legs for those who needed them. In fact, he played the role of a great father to the people, a role that taxed his energy and time, but gave him the loyalty and support of the common people. It seemed not only that everyone in Mexico had seen him and shaken hands with him, but that he remembered the first names of almost half of the people who crowded upon him.

There was something of a folk hero in Cárdenas, and his peregrinations were popular parades filled with banners and bands and shouts and cheers. Many a night there would be a dance in some little village, in a small house with a dirt floor, lit by candles, and when the time came, they would see the President off in the early dawn when the moon was setting over the horizon.

All of these personal virtues and this devotion, however, failed to save him from the Mexican milieu. His aides in office, with a few conspicuous exceptions, were true children of the Mexican bureaucracy and at least mildly corrupt. The well-trained men at his disposal—again with some conspicuous exceptions—were few, and he was not a good judge of the character of his own immediate associates, especially among the civilians. He knew the military better and, curiously enough, expected the civilians to be less honest and to have less integrity. They had been brought up in the corrupting environment of the large cities, he explained. The attempt to do everything himself—for what else could he do?—cut under the administrative organization, but did not change it. Politics, petty politics on a state and national level, burdened his conscience and sapped his energies, for he, too, had to maintain his political fences; no one in Mexico is immune from that. The weight of centuries stood between him and his objectives.

Cárdenas had governed the country without resort to force, had played down the military, saying: "These people must learn that they can be governed without terror," and he hoped that a new way of peaceful political accommodation would come to Mexico. What Mexico must have, as he saw it, was internal peace and legal non-violent successions in the presidency. When the end of his term would come, he would retire, so completely that the new man in office could govern without constraint or wire-pulling. He would, if he could, bring the tradition of the *caudillo* to an end by his example and in his own person.

The Second World War was in the making during those years (1934–40) and cast its black shadows over the Cárdenas administration. The passions of race and class and the heightened national hatreds found their echoes inside Mexico and attracted adherents who sought to turn them into instruments of local politics. The Spanish Civil War brought an active Falange movement into being, and the Nazi propagandists bribed, promised, and cajoled for place and power and influence. Through it all, however, Cárdenas saw clearly that Mexican interest lay within the democratic tradition, and his personal predilection associated him and his government with the side of democracy. In the Spanish rebellion he aided the Republican forces, and later, after their defeat, made a home in Mexico for many Spaniards in exile. In the shadow of the Nazi threat, and in spite of the deep differences with the United States, he never was in doubt where his true allegiance lay. Long before America was involved in the war, he sent word to our State Department that in case of a war with Japan we could count on every human and material resource of the Mexican people, and before leaving office he offered to sign a defensive military treaty with the United States. His quarrels with the oil companies in Mexico seemed to him a private affair that did not in any way involve the basic identity of the two nations against a common threat of propaganda and force steaming from outside.

Many people in and out of the government did not share Cárdenas's views and sought to find in the moral confusion that came as a by-product of the increasing fury in Europe a means of salvaging their own interest, or a means of imposing their own political beliefs. The Cedillo rebellion in 1938 was not entirely unrelated to these darker elements, and the coming of the presidential election in 1940 brought them to a head.

General Juán Andreu Almazán gathered about him all of the dissident elements in Mexico, and his able campaign aligned a powerful political force against the government. Although the election came off without a formal rebellion, it did not take place in peace. There was much isolated and organized violence, and many were killed in street riots and in personal feuds. A rebellion did not take place because Almazán knew that in the end he would be defeated, and not because he did not have a following that could have greatly embarrassed the government. Cárdenas's personal popularity, his hold over the people and the army, especially the soldiers and young officers, combined with the friendship of the United States, would, in the end, have doomed any rebellion.

General Manuel Ávila Camacho, who served as President between 1940 and 1946, proved a kindly and well-intentioned chief executive who, according to his own words, wished to govern without damaging any section of the population. The continuing support of Cárdenas made it possible for this to be the first administration since the fall of Díaz in 1910 that was not forced to meet the challenge of armed revolt. Without pushing the social program forward, Ávila Camacho supported what had been accomplished, and Mexico settled down to an internal peace it had not known for a long time.

The sudden attack upon Pearl Harbor by the Japanese brought into being the explicit as well as the implicit commitment of Mexico to stand with the United States against outside aggression, and Ávila Camacho's ability to take Mexico into the war without, it must be said, any great enthusiasm among the Mexican people, and somewhat to their surprise, reflects a profound shift in the feeling of the people of Mexico toward their powerful neighbor to the north.

Cárdenas assumed the role of Secretary of War, but kept from meddling in politics. The war greatly increased Mexican industrial activity, opened many opportunities for the investment of foreign and Mexican capital, and spread the feeling in Mexico that now, at last, it was a partner in the great world, playing a role in keeping with its dignity and relative importance. The war, among many other consequences, brought inflation in its wake, reduced the country's powers to acquire the needed raw materials and equipment from the outside, greatly increased Mexico's economic dependence upon the United States, and tended to make it easy, after a time, with rising prices, to throw upon the American government the blame for Mexico's economic difficulties. But never during the war was there any danger of a real strain developing between the two countries.

The election of 1946 proved much less agitated than usual. The fact that the candidate of the official government party, Miguel Alemán, was the first civilian since Madero to be elected to the presidency is symbolic of the changed political atmosphere. Time alone will reveal how permanent this change is. That the election proved as quiet and peaceful as it was is in no small measure due to the refusal of Cárdenas to back any candidate for the presidency. His mere presence in the background proved a tower of strength to the government. The present administration is committed to the industrial and economic development of the country, without, however, attempting in any serious fashion to challenge the programs written into the law as a result of the Revolution that began in 1910.

The release of energy and emotion evoked by the popular upheaval that began with the overthrow of General Díaz has worked its way in many directions and greatly changed the Mexican social and political design. An encrusted feudal landholding society has been shattered, the older political oligarchy destroyed, and the power of the military caste reduced. The common people, both on the land and in the cities, have been called to participate in the shaping of their own destiny. In a measure a new basis for the government has come into being. Peasant leagues, trade unions, and a growing native middle class are all now conspicuously vocal in political affairs, and the role of the intellectual as spokesman and participant has been much enhanced. The old fear and oppression that hung so heavily upon Mexico have evaporated with the promise of internal peace, as the idea of a common destiny in a common nation has replaced the bitter divisions between caste, class, and race. The foreign interest has been reduced, and the feeling of the Mexicans that they are masters in their own house is greater now than it has been, perhaps, since the Spanish Conquest. A feeling of equality and democracy is the prevailing tone. Education has increased, and for the mass of the people there is a seeming promise of greater opportunities for the achievment of the good life. There is at least some presumption that they can live without violence and be governed without terror.

Against these very important gains stand the continued brittleness of Mexican politics and occasional local violence, such as was shown in the cities of León and Tapachula. The fact that the government still uses a single officially supported political party to put its own candidates in office is further evidence of continued political instability. Political opposition is still fraught with the prospect of armed rebellion. Perhaps worst of all is the *mordida*—graft (literally bite)—that has grown in a widening circle from official to unofficial persons and is now perhaps the greatest single impediment both morally and politically to good government and economic progress. The extortions for the privilege of staying in business, organizing any economic activity, or securing the necessary legal permission for carrying on the work of the day have become so burdensome as to weaken the economy and the moral substance of the nation.

It is a curious fact that this blight has spread from public officeholders to inspectors, to clerks, and from them to petty labor leaders, and even to private employees, who on occasion can and do exact a special payment for a service they are already hired to perform. The long agitation against capitalism, imperialism, industry, and foreigners, and the belief that the individual ought to exact all that the traffic will bear, have imposed an impediment even on the working of governmental enterprises, or enterprises controlled by the workers themselves. Every manager, employer, and foreman is in some measure cast in the role of an enemy, and every enterprise is a succulent root to be sucked dry, if possible.

The decline in the personal integrity so essential to the new responsibilities thrown upon both government and private industry as a result of the changes of the last forty years is the greatest single moral failure of the Mexican Revolution. In so far as the Mexican Revolution has failed to instill a sufficient sense of responsibility in the new generation it can be said to have encrusted it with a moral disease that may prove its ruin. The Revolution has also failed to satisfy Mexico's basic economic needs. The Mexican economy is burdened by poor natural resources and a rapidly growing population, and while the people have achieved greater freedom and self-esteem, their meager supply of food, clothing, and shelter has not been commensurably increased. The pressing preoccupation of the day is how to enlarge the real income of a growing people. The persistent stress of conflicting interest is deepened by the continued subversion of public needs to private ends.

CHAPTER 5

Politics and Government

THE CONSTITUTION of 1917 was designed to strengthen the Mexican government, always weak because it had no moral hold upon the people. It had always rested upon force, even terror. The government had always leaned upon the army, or that part of the army upon which the government of the day could depend, but because the army was corruptible and the military leaders ambitious, the government was at the mercy of recurring military rebellions. For half a century the one political certainty in Mexico was that any government, regardless of party or announced purpose, would be overthrown. Only two governments in all this time lasted through their prescribed periods, and those only because they had the good luck to defeat numerous efforts to overthrow them.

The Díaz regime produced the great political miracle in

modern Mexico, stability. It overcompensated for the previous instability and disorganized violence by imposing tyranny and organized violence. It is probably true that neither in matters of justice nor in equity was the Díaz regime more commendable than the previous unruly and improvised political administrations. It did provide order. At least, everyone knew that power rested in the person of General Porfirio Díaz. By controlling the army he controlled the country. It was under this regime, more than at any time before, that Mexico became a nation with a sense of destiny and coherence.

Before that, almost every part of Mexico at one time or another either threatened or attempted to set up a separate government. The country was in a constant state of imminent dismemberment, and the miracle is that only Texas carried the threat to fruition. Even where separation was not carried to its logical conclusion, entire regions were independent of the federal government for years at a time. It was only under Díaz that order was finally established. Under this order an extensive program of internal development was possible—of railroads, ports, and telegraphs—and these in turn contributed toward political consolidation.

The Revolution of 1910 returned the nation to the previous state of chaos. Between 1910 and 1917, or, perhaps even more accurately, between 1910 and 1930, the country was either torn by revolution or in active preparation for revolution, with the reappearance of the local *caudillo* whom the federal government did not dare challenge for fear that he and his friends —or that he and the government's numerous enemies—would prove stronger than the government itself. The governments lived upon sufferance or upon the hope that further violence could be avoided. It required all of the astute ruthlessness of Obregón and Calles, with the deliberate killing of leaders of any uprising, to give the political situation a semblance of stability. Even under Cárdenas there was a revolution, as late as 1938—a revolution by the last of the revolutionary *caudillos,* Saturnino Cedillo. But no one could be certain the civil strife was at an end, for in the election of 1940, when General Ávila

Camacho succeeded to the presidency, there was active talk of an uprising. This violence evidenced the narrow basis upon which Mexican government rested. The relative peace of the last twenty years may be taken to mean that the purpose of the Constitution of 1917 to strengthen the government has succeeded. It brought into being the agrarian and labor organizations upon which the government could fall back in time of crisis.

It is still true, however, that the army is the chief source of the government's power. As Cárdenas once expressed it, "When the land belongs to the villages, the government will also belong to them, but," he added, "now the government depends upon the army." That day may come, but it has not yet arrived, and it has not arrived because the very machinery of the government is self-defeating. The government of Mexico is the President. There is no other way of expressing it. If the President is not strong enough to be the government, then he is overthrown, as was Órtiz Rubio. Or if he is not strong enough to be the President, then the real power is some *caudillo,* the great man who can and does control the government. In recent history that was Calles. He did not wish to be a *caudillo* in the beginning, but was forced into the position of dictator to prevent the recurrence of chaos. The leaders accepted his will because he could enforce it.

I recall one day in a train when I met a general in charge of troops in one of the northern states. We were on the way to Tehuacán, where Calles, long after he had retired from the presidency, was recovering from an illness. I asked him where he was going, and he replied: "Well, yesterday I saw the President in the City of Mexico, but now I am going to see '*el mero jefe*'—the real chief."

A story is told of Órtiz Rubio that when there was a rumor of an uprising against the administration, he called Calles on the telephone and told him that he, the President, was joining Calles in a revolution against the government. The story does not have to be true to indicate the political reality. If the President could not prevent a revolution, or defeat it, he could not stay in office, and he who could do either one or the other was the real ruler.

To prove that he was in control, Cárdenas found it necessary to put Calles on a plane and ship him out of the country, and he could do that only after he had made sure of sufficient support among the masses and in the army. The President is the government, and all discussion of Mexican politics must assume that fact. It is possible to discern other trends; and the time may come when this will no longer be true. For the present, however, the President has in his hands the military, political, administrative, legislative, and judicial power. That is a great responsibility—too great, in fact.

The legislature takes its policies and its laws from the President, and there is and can be no effective opposition in the Congress. The judiciary takes its views from the administration. One has only to read the decisions of the courts under Carranza, Obregón, Calles, and Cárdenas in matters of land and labor to be convinced that the court tends to reflect, as a matter of course, the political predilections of the head of the State. He is the effective chief of the administration; the members of the Cabinet are simple instruments of his will, and if he is an energetic and hardworking man, he keeps track of even the minutest details of their labor. He is also the active head of the army, and it is he who decides where and at what post this or that general is to be placed.

Under these circumstances, the President must make sure that the political machine works smoothly, that all of the elections go right, that all of the governors are his friends, that the members of the Chamber of Deputies and the Senate are his true and trusted followers, and that the government is staffed by trusted political allies. That is his primary job, because if he cannot trust the members of his government he cannot trust anyone else. Traditionally speaking, the President of Mexico must be able to do everything he wants or he will be unable to do anything he wants. He has either all power or no power; there is no middle ground. The constitutional formula for a division of powers between the legislative, judicial, and executive is merely a formula. It may represent an aspiration for the future, but it has no immediate reality. This is so because aside from the army there is really no effective body politic upon which the government can rest. True enough, the thousands of *ejidos* and the numerous agrarian leagues have a new importance and in times of crisis can be of great aid to the government. But for all practical purposes they are creatures of the State, created, financed, supported, and protected by the State. They are not merely beholden to the government, they are dependent upon it. It is still true that an unfriendly government could do them great damage. The day may come when these peasant organizations will become an independent political power and a true source of real strength upon which a government might rest.

What is true of these peasant organizations is still more true of the labor unions and the labor movement. They have proved important because their leaders are tied to the President, but the tie is personal. They are essentially creatures and instruments of the government, they are strong with the strength of the administration that breathes the breath of life into them. There is no independent trade-union movement of any consequence in Mexico. There are unions that have outlived government opposition, but they are not strong or numerous. The great movements in labor are not self-sustaining. In the time of Calles the C.R.O.M. (*Confederación Regional Obrera Mexicana*) was a child of the Obregón and Calles governments, and the C.T.M. (*Confederación de Trabajadores Mexicanos*) was a creature of later administrations. The government has financed, protected, and nurtured the trade-union movement as a stick to lean upon or to be used against its political enemies in and out of the country, but the stick is only as strong as the arm that wields it. The trade-union movement may in time become politically independent. Today its importance lies in its being the vehicle of the policies of the administration—that is, the policies of the President. The unions and the *ejidos* serve one important function; they give the President a seeming and, in a measure, a real support among the people. That fact has political significance for the future.

For the present the administration—that is, the President—must be its own architect of political security. The government is unstable except in so far as the President can stabilize it, and all of his efforts are bent in the direction of giving it permanence, by surrounding it with friends in every office, every post, every organization, every significant grouping. Those whom he cannot control are enemies. If he cannot control his friends, they too become enemies. No one can be elected governor of any state who is not acceptable to the President. The charge that Díaz had puppets in the state governments was true enough. For the most part this has always been true, but it is now easier, legally, than ever before for the central government to determine who can be elected, who can stay in office if elected, and who is to be removed. The excuse can always be provided, the machinery to eject him is permanently available, and the fiction of state sovereignty remains a fiction, The Constitution of 1917 has made it simpler than it used to be for the President to be a dictator, which he has always had to be.

There was once a man who was one of the large group that always accompanied the President on his trips through the country. This man suffered from the heat and from the difficulties of living in a train or traveling on horseback over the mountains. He was obviously uncomfortable. I inquired: "What is he doing here?" The reply was: "He is acquiring merit." "What does he want merit for?" "He wants to be governor of Chihuahua." This man did not acquire sufficient merit and did not become governor.

Under the Constitution the Senate has the duty of deciding upon the legality of a state government or of breaking off all federal relations with it. The Senate, therefore, ultimately decides who has been elected governor. But the Senate, like the governors of the states, is a creature of the President, and the Permanent Committee of the Senate, which acts when that body is not in session, is hand-picked by the President. So it is he who finally decides who has been elected governor of the state.

The question of the legality of a state government comes before the federal government in many ways, most frequently because two and sometimes three governors, each with his own legislature, claim to have been elected by a huge majority. As the local legislature must decide who has been elected and then must have the count accepted by the federal government, it always follows that each candidate for state governor has his own legislature elected with him. After the election, two or three state legislatures announce that their candidates have been elected, establish themselves as near the state capitol building as possible, organize a government, and bombard the President, the Secretary of the Interior, and the Senate with telegrams announcing their candidate's election. It is a little difficult to believe that three candidates have each been elected for the office of governor at the same time. It therefore falls upon the Permanent Committee of the Senate to decide who was really elected. Once the issue has been settled, the local military chieftain is instructed to see to it that the properly certified governor is permitted to take office and to enter the state capitol. The President has to make the decision. If he did not, there would be civil war in the state.

I recall an instance in Aguascalientes when after an election for governor the President arrived and was met by a large crowd in an organized parade, armed with banners, demanding that their candidate be recognized, insisting that he had been elected. There was much shouting and yelling, and strong words, and speeches to the President while he was on his way to the state capitol. Finally the President came out on the balcony and made a statement to the people in the square below. He said that the central government had no interest in the local election provided a good man was elevated to the office of governor. Two men could not occupy the governor's chair at the same time. If the candidate the crowd was clamoring for had really been elected by a majority, the President would see to it that he was put in office in spite of the fact that the other man had already been declared legally elected. But if the man they were opposing was really the properly chosen official, *he would take the responsibility of keeping him in office.* The President had to make a decision or there would have been civil strife in the state.

The powers of the federal administration do not end here. The Constitution authorizes the central govenment to see to it that democratic governments prevail in the states, that the Constitution and the federal laws are published and executed by the state officers, that individual liberties guaranteed by the Constitution are not denied, that peace is maintained between the different powers within the state governments. The federal government can interfere for any one of these reasons, and does. A local governor suddenly finds himself attacked in the Mexico City press. He is accused of having violated individual rights, of suppressing the local legislature, of having become an arbitrary tyrant. It is asserted that democratic government has disappeared in the state. The charge may or may not be true. That is not really important. What is important is that a new election is coming—federal or state—and that the local or national politicians are not certain of the governor's political fealty to the federal administration. The governor will issue long statements denying the charges and accusing his accusers. The papers will be filled with advertisements appealing to the President, to the public, to the Senate, on behalf of one side or the other. The Senate, or its Permanent Committee, will decide to investigate the charges, and the results, when announced, will determine the fate of the existing state government. If the Permanent Committee of the Senate decides that the charges are true, it cuts relations with the state by declaring that the federal powers in the state have disappeared. The President then instructs the local military commander to eject the governor and appoints a provisional governor, usually the local chief of the army. A new election is then held, and the new governor, if he is the right one, receives the approval of the Permanent Committee. Political peace and harmony are re-established between the state and federal governments.

Within a single year the federal government often has removed a number of governors. Thus in 1935 the Senate removed the governors of Sonora, Sinaloa, Guanajuato, and Durango. President Alemán removed two governors in the first two years of his administration. The governors, in spite of the federal system established by the Constitution, are the instruments of the President.

This is further illustrated by what has happened to the municipal governments. Under the Díaz regime the elected municipal governments had been suppressed and replaced with a *jefe político*, a direct tool of the old dictator. The *jefe político* became, in fact, a little Díaz in his own province. This petty tyrant had become a symbol of the worst aspects of the Díaz dictatorship. The revolution re-created the free municipal government.

The state governors, however, have arrogated to themselves the powers to nullify municipal elections. They, like the President, want only friends in office. But under the powers granted to the President to preserve the constitutional liberties of the municipalities, the central government has on more than one occasion interfered within the states to protect the local governments against the arbitrary acts of the governor.

The continuous fence-building so essential to the preservation of the President's political power takes another form. He controls the election of deputies and senators. No one can be elected without his consent and approval. It is another instance of the necessity for "acquiring merit."

I have seen a man who thought himself elected senator, and whom everyone else thought to have been elected, arriving in Mexico City flushed with victory, living in the best hotel, and spending money freely, suddenly turn crestfallen and move out of the hotel, counting his pennies. "What has happened?" I asked. "The old man says I was not elected." "What are you going to do?" "The old man has given me a good *chamba*. He has made me collector of customs in Matamoros. He really is a good person and knows what is best."

A friend of mine in Mexico, a young and devoted attendant of the President, told me one day that he wanted to be a member of Congress. I asked him if he had talked with the President. "Oh, yes," he replied. Two months later I learned that he had been elected. "Tell me exactly what happened. I want to know how you were elected." "Well, it was this way. We had an election, but my opponents stole all my ballots." "What did you do?" I queried. "Well, you can't go before the committee without ballots, so my friends and I sat down and made up the ballots. We knew everyone had voted for me." "And you were elected?" "Yes, unanimously." Two years later he had been elected Senator. I said to him: "I hear you have been elected Senator." "Yes," he replied, "unanimously."

There is no effective independent political conscience and organization upon which a government can rest. To survive in peace, the government must control its own party, the governors, the members of Congress. The alternative is chaos and rebellion. It is not necessarily true that this system in the hands of a good man fails to represent the interests of the people, but it does not rest upon "effective suffrage." It is no one leader's fault. It is not even the fault of any one historical period. Nor is it easily remediable.

It will not be easy for the reader to understand the significance of these controls unless he recognizes them as part of the technique for passing on the administration from one president to the next. If the machinery were to break down, the next election would be settled by violence and civil war. The most important decision that the President has to make, and that fairly early in his administration, is who is to be his successor. If the President cannot or will not make it, he will either be faced with a revolution or become a mere puppet of the group surrounding the new candidate.

Watching Mexican politics closely, one begins to discern the drift of the new alignment by noting changes in the Cabinet and asking: "Whose friends are they?" This is true because in

Mexican politics there is a kind of unconditional personal identification that is self-revealing. The elections of new governors, or the removal of incumbents from governors' chairs, and the election of new members to the Chamber and the Senate reveal the drift. The Congress counts the final vote and decides formally who has been elected to the presidency. The seating of the candidates by the credentials committee is the best indication of what is going on, and members of the credentials committee are and must be either creatures of the President or, if he has lost control, of the candidate most likely to be successful. The election, therefore, is decided long before the electorate is invited to vote.

What is true of members of Congress and the Cabinet is true of the army. Who has been promoted or retired? Who has been shifted in command from one post to another? All such changes are evidences of political maneuvering. An unreliable general is suddenly shifted to a state in which the President feels absolutely sure of the lower officers; in a crisis they will remain loyal. The general knows it and his hands are tied.

This was not possible a few years ago. It used to be customary for the general to move with his own troops. They belonged to him. He had raised them and trained them, and they were his people. It took three unsuccessful revolutions after 1920 and the purging of hundreds of army officers to establish the principle that the troops a general commanded did not belong to him and that he could be moved without them. This was one of the essential conditions to the peaceful passing on of power.

It is true that election campaigns, speeches, and propaganda go on at the same time. They are part of the play for the alignment of popular opinion for or against a prospective candidate. At the same time they tend to strengthen the conviction that the right candidate has been chosen. The signs and symbols of popular election mean more, however, for they are an evidence of a drift toward popularly based governments. But the election will be determined by the administration, even if it does not raise a finger; its friends and associates will determine it on their own account without specific orders. No government has ever lost an election unless it was first driven from office by force. The cases of Carranza and Obregón, of de la Huerta and Calles, are in point. Revolutions tend to occur before elections because the only way of assuring that the candidates will receive an official majority is to control the government.

A political campaign in Mexico is in the nature of make-believe. The candidate who has official approval is certain of election. Tradition and popular expectation ask for a campaign, and in cases like that of Cárdenas the campaign gives the candidate an opportunity to travel into every corner of the country and visit the humblest villages in the mountain regions. But the outcome of the election is never in doubt. The opposition candidates, in spite of an active campaign, have no expectation of being elected. They know that their people will not be permitted to vote; that if they do vote, their votes will not be counted; that if counted and sent into the final test in Congress, they will be disregarded; and, finally, that if elected by some strange accident, they could not govern. An opposition candidate elected to the presidency could not, if he took power, name even his own private secretary. In fact, the election is decided by those who are going to count the votes officially; and their count was determined in advance.

What, then, is the purpose of the opposition candidates, parties, and campaigns? The answer, I think, is clear: it is to build up the moral justification for a revolution. No one is fooled by the process; no one expects the opposition to win. What the opposition does expect is that it can so work on the popular discontent, so stir up political passions, and so confuse public opinion that it can win the allegiance of large masses of people to its side, and especially that of the army. There is always some hope that parts of the army can be won over—sometimes the whole army, or nearly the whole army, as in the electoral campaign of Obregón against Ignacio Bonillas in 1920. If the army or a part of it can be won over, then the electoral campaign may have helped to provide the moral environment within which rebellion can be successful.

Violence is an accepted and expected political instrument. Luis Cabrera has suggested that there were more than a thousand *pronunciamientos* between 1812 and 1921, but only three revolutions. The distinction is important. The military uprising is an electoral device, a way of changing the authorities in power, of replacing one government with another. A peaceful election is frequently regarded as an evidence of imposition. When in the past the government was strong enough to assure the election of the official candidate without violence, as in the long Díaz regime, it was a sure sign of tyranny. A rebellion, therefore, has the respectable dress of an attempt to give the opposition an opportunity to secure office. The fact that, if successful, it will play the same preponderant role as the current government in electing the next candidate is beside the point. If there were no rebellion, the government in office would perpetuate itself by imposing its chosen candidate. Rebellion, therefore, is an accepted instrumentality in an electoral campaign. If it does not occur, it is sometimes because of fear that the United States will side with the government in power. That was certainly so when Almazán was defeated for the presidency.

While rebellion is an electoral device, revolution is an accepted instrument of social and economic change. This kind of revolution may have the approval even of the conservative elements in Mexico. A revolution that ultimately becomes legal because it succeeds in imposing its desires upon the nation by force and rewriting the law to fit its program is considered necessary "in such countries as ours." The political philosophy of Mexico is saturated with the belief in violence, both for electoral purposes and to effect social change.

The creation of the *Partido Nacional Revolucionario,* the P.N.R., by Calles in 1928, and its reconstruction by Cárdenas in 1938 and by Ávila Camacho in 1945, did not really affect the political tradition. In its earlier form it was financed by an amount withheld from the wage of all government employees. When this proved too objectionable and involved too much criticism, the formal withholdings were changed to "voluntary" contributions. Cárdenas abolished the imposition of the burden upon government employees, but the party is financed by the government. The head of the party is appointed by the President, and if the head of the party and the President disagree, then a new appointee replaces the old one, as happened when Portes Gil was replaced by Barba González, a lifelong friend of Cárdenas.

In effect the official government party has become the recognized electoral machinery of the administration. Although other parties are in existence, free speech is unrestricted, and political activities and organizations go on, the effective electoral control is organized by the government through this new instrumentality, and it has tended to reduce violence in elections. The elections would be no more a reflection of popular suffrage than now if there were no official party, but they would be less free from local violence.

The conservative and dissident factions out of power complain that the government party is merely a device for distributing offices among friends of the President. That, of course, is true. But if the conservatives were in power, they would behave in the very same way. The conservatives forget that a revolution of twenty long years was fought over the issue of who should govern Mexico and in whose interest, and would have the people who won the revolution turn the government over to those they defeated. The agrarian and labor groups are under government control and behave as they are expected to. As soon as it becomes evident who the official candidate is, the unions and the agrarian parties hasten to nominate him unanimously before the government party holds its convention. That happened before the nominations of Ávila Camacho and Alemán.

The political outcome of the revolution of 1910 has, clearly enough, greatly strengthened the power of the central government and of the President. The older Díaz tradition of control by disregard of the law, for it has been truly said that the Constitution of 1857 was forgotten in his personal administration, has been replaced by a constitutional mandate to control the state governments.

To some extent the difference is between open and secret control. Both the constitutional provisions and the government-party system tend to make the centralized control of political life matters of public knowledge. Their very legality and publicity tend to have a restraining influence upon the too arbitrary use of the powers at the President's disposal. With all their shortcomings, these changes must be recognized as, on the whole, a stabilizing and democratizing influence in Mexican political life.

What was the alternative? The Revolution left the country armed to the teeth, with hundreds of local *caudillos* in control of military bands of greater or lesser strength, with each *caudillo* an irresponsible autocrat in his special state or region, holding absolute dominion over the property, the fortunes, and the lives of those living in his jurisdiction. He was subject to no law and independent of any central authority. It required four revolutions between 1920 and 1938 to discipline the military *caudillo* and convince him that the central government was more powerful than any one individual military leader.

But the tradition of the *caudillo* is an old one in Mexico and dies slowly. The older habit of violence returned with the Revolution, and in spite of the great power of the President and the unbroken hold of the government-party system, violence is still a matter of course in most elections, local, state, or federal. But on the whole the violence is sporadic, personal, unplanned.[1] The deliberate throwing of the nation, or even of the state, into an upheaval because of a coming election is less likely; and a kind of peace is returning to Mexico after all these years of rebellion. The *caudillo,* the absolute ruler of a region, is passing away, though slowly. As long as the army is disciplined and control over it firmly in the hands of the President, there

[1] The election of deputies in July 1949 passed without a single report of violence.

is little likelihood of its again becoming an acute problem in a military sense.

One of the last of the military *caudillos* who ruled an entire state—in this case San Luis Potosí—was Saturnino Cedillo, a big, semiliterate man who had risen to power in local fighting. He was unillumined by any political doctrine except a greed for power and personal aggrandizement. At one time, during the *cristero* rebellion, he had control of over eight thousand men who belonged to him and whom he had armed and brought into the field. He traveled, even when on horseback, with armed guards with sawed-off machine guns right behind him, and his automobile, in which I once rode, was crowded with arms, machine guns, and ammunition—a fort on wheels.

I heard him say one day to a man who had some grievance: "I ought to have you strung up." In San Luis Potosí his will was the law, the rule, and the way. There was no higher authority to appeal to, for even the federal government, unless it wished to stir up a rebellion, preferred not to interfere too much. The Governor of the state, a nondescript little man in black, with a squeak in his voice, once said in reply to my question who he was, when he made an unexpected visit to the home of Cedillo: "Who, me? I am the Governor of the state. It is a job the old man gave me."

One of the members of Congress from the state was a citizen of another, and when I asked him how it happened that he represented San Luis Potosí in the Congress, he replied: "The old man wanted me." "Did you ever visit the district you represent?" "No. What for? The old man told the committee and they did all the rest."

Such a situation made rebellion inevitable, and revolution the natural beginning of any election. As it turned out in this case, Cedillo rose in rebellion hoping for revolution and was at last killed in the mountains.

In a subtle sense the mass of the rural population, Indian or *mestizo,* illiterate or schooled, expects the President of the country to play the part of the great father. There is an implicit submissiveness—a bending of the head, an attitude of acceptance and compliance—which unconsciously forces upon the President the exercise of arbitrary power. Like a father, he must rule personally and cannot delegate his authority. If he does, he will risk losing it. Men, big and little, sit for weeks in the antechamber to be received and heard over an unimportant detail that any clerk might have disposed of. But a clerk is a poor shadow of the great father, and so is a member of the Cabinet. The personality of the President must be part of every minor transaction between the rural folk and their government. Time matters not at all. Years may be spent in securing an audience just to have the judgment come from the only source whose authority is not only political but also moral. It is in this situation that administration breaks down. Like an indulgent father, the President cannot say no; and if he does, the no is not final. Surely the father's heart can be mellowed, his kindness reawakened, his true virtues as the father of his children brought to bear upon the issues in hand. These issues are so small, so unimportant, and the President is so great, so all-powerful, that only bad advisers stand in the way of his doing the justice the people ask for. And if he refuses, then he is no true father, he is no true leader, he governs arbitrarily and without moral authority. He is a step-father, a tyrant, a usurper, a villain, or he has no power, being a tool of unfriendly and inimical forces. It becomes essential to drive him from office. There is no alternative between personal government and revolution. Inefficiency, corruption, cruelty—if they be personal—are all acceptable. What is not acceptable is cold, impersonal, efficient government.

For the *criollo* and the urbanized and semiurbanized *mestizos* the President is the military chieftain. His authority is derived from the military, rests upon the military, and can be removed only by the military. Government means military government. It is always arbitrary, always unjust, always based upon force. The President is always feared and therefore respected. If not feared, he is not respected and is therefore held in contempt and overthrown. To be respected he must be strong —a *presidente macho* (stallion president)—and as such he is irresistible and obeyed out of fear and out of a kind of automatic submission to the inevitable. Personal bravery is the prime essential; all else will fail the executive if there is a suspicion that he is a physical coward. As a military leader he must have valor evident to the whole world.

The Mexican complex is such that the alternative to highly centralized power is anarchy, and for the time being, anyway, the Revolution has tended to move in the direction of centralized temporary power. For the one clear gain, politically, is the principle of no re-election. Obregón succeeded in being re-elected, but was assassinated before he could resume office. The President, within limits, can perpetuate his policies by throwing his influence toward the election of his successor. In fact, he must do so. But he can neither succeed himself nor be a candidate again at any time.

This development has not eliminated the army from politics, but it has to some extent changed the character of the army's participation. The individual general probably can no longer impose himself upon the nation because he happens to have a group of friends who will follow him in battle; but as long as the central government has to use the army for its own political purposes in controlling the states, the army is bound to continue of great political influence, and no man could reach the presidency against its will.

In a crisis, as was shown at the time of the de la Huerta and Escobar rebellions, the labor unions and especially the agrarian communities proved of very real military value. The rebels found that they could hold only the land they physically occupied because the agrarian communities were hostile to them and actively supported the government.

It is hard to see how the agrarian communities can emancipate themselves. The government's participation, especially in the large co-operative *ejidos,* is such that in a measure it has replaced the old plantation-owner. The Banco Ejidal extends credit to these communities between crops. It does not pay wages. The credit is a weekly allowance to be repaid out of the yield of the crop. The profit is divided between the members of the *ejido*. But the bank, for its own safety, must exercise a degree of supervision that makes the federal government an integral part of their every activity. Presumably in time—but not at any foreseeable time—these communities will accumulate enough savings to become their own credit agency. They could then become an independent influence in politics. For the time being, they are part of the governmental machine, but that still gives the government a wider base than it had before. Somewhat the same is true of organized labor.

With the widened base for the government to rest upon, there has come an increase in the range of its responsibilities. The federal government, both by constitutional mandate and by legislative provisions, has assumed a supervising interest in all mining, the moving-picture industry, commerce, banking, the electrical industry, public health, public education, labor, land distribution, and agricultural credit. In addition there are other activities that are now largely in the hands of the federal government, such as road-building, aviation, the railroads, the oil industry, coastwise sea transportation, the tourist industry, telegraphs, and, through the control of labor or credit, textiles, sugar, and cotton.

Thus the centralized government has assumed the burden of managing the greater part of the economy of the nation. The President has become the arbiter of the economic activities of the people. The burden of governing is infinitely greater than it was when the Revolution began, and the political instrumentality has not grown to equal the new burdens. The idea of a directed economy has taken increased hold of the government, while the character of the political machinery has changed but little in comparison with the new administrative responsibilities. Nor has the efficiency of government or the integrity of the politically dominant bureaucracy kept pace with the increased powers of the government over the national economy. Graft had a kind of traditional sanction when most of the economy of the nation was in foreign hands, when government officials shared through special favors some of the profits of private concerns. But when the government itself is the major economic entrepreneur, through direct or indirect control, the problem is of a different order, and there is not in sight the growth of that kind of devoted and selfless public servants whom the situation demands.

The new burdens of government have made the President the key figure in the economic as well as in the political situation; and the political psychology is such that he must make all the decisions. He is the great man on a white horse. He is the new *caudillo,* the only real *caudillo* left. How clear this is may be seen in the extraordinary powers that the Constitution permits him to receive from Congress. Under these powers he becomes the effective legislative agency of the nation. Instead of his submitting a law to the Congress, the Congress passes a resolution empowering the President to issue a decree law in a specific case. In the last thirty years a large part of the controversial legislation in Mexico was thus issued by him under his extraordinary powers rather than by Congress.

There is only one thing to be added. The political disequilibrium in Mexico lies in part in the nature of the tax system. Most of the taxes collected go to the federal government. The states receive a pittance and the municipalities an even smaller one. It thus turns out that all other political divisions in the government are dependent upon the federal government for favors, for they have no resources of their own. I have seen townspeople build their schools with their own hands, and then wait for years for the state or federal government to give them the money to buy the windows or doors they could not make. What is true of the school is true of a bridge, of pipe for a water system, of an engine to turn a mill. There is really no prospect of giving Mexico a vigorous democratic government resting upon a broad popular base without first redirecting the flow of income from taxes so that the towns, the municipalities, and the states can enjoy financial independence. But this change, and it is probably the most essential, is the least likely to occur. Without it the central government and the President must remain the dominating influence in the politics of the nation.

The Revolution has certainly increased effective democracy in Mexico. It has also increased, both legally and economically, the dependence of the people and of the communities upon the federal government and the President. The older tradition that the king rules has survived in modern dress: the President rules. He rules rather than governs, and must do so if he is to survive in office and keep the country at peace. The issue, in political terms, is the absence of effective political opposition. In Mexico all opposition presumes eventual revolution. If and when there develops in Mexico the tradition of "His Majesty's loyal opposition," loyal to the government even if opposed to its policies, then party government, rather than personal government, may become the rule. That day is still distant.

CHAPTER 6

A Theory of Property

THE INCREASED POWERS of the Mexican government, as we have seen, stem from the Revolution of 1910 and are partially symbolized by a theory of property. This theory is not new. At least, the Mexicans can point to ancient precedents to support their claim that the doctrines written into Article 27 of the Constitution of 1917 are consonant with good legal traditions derived from Spain. But if the theory is not new, the specifications are. There has come about in Mexico such specific definition of the rights of the State over the form, content, character, amount, and kind of real property that may and may not be held by specified persons or corporations as to provide the government with a legal instrumentality for molding private real property in any manner it considers desirable. The concept of private real property has become flexible; it can be made to mean many sorts of different things, and may be defined differently for different purposes.

The Constitution of 1917 was a revolutionary document, an attempt to legalize changes imposed by violence and projected for the future. The social upheaval was to be confined within the prescriptions of a new constitution, but the constitution was to be sufficiently broad and flexible to permit changes. The Constitution legalized not so much the past accomplishments of a popular movement as its future aspirations.

The form and content of the Constitution give evidence of its having been written in the heat of battle, and the debates in the Constitutional Convention turned not so much on legal formulas and ancient precedent as on rectifying grievances and establishing justice. The argument was replete with bitterness. The danger of internal reaction, the power of the United States, and its possible intervention are part of the atmosphere in which this legal document came into being, a document the more remarkable because it was written in a hurry by young men, only a few of whom were trained in the law, and whose greatest adventures had been on fields of battle. In spite of all this the Constitution of 1917 has become an enduring political instrument, and some of its precepts have influenced other parts of the world.

All of Mexico's previous constitutions had been inspired by ideas derived from the French and American Revolutions and from the Spanish Constitution of 1812. That was true of the Constitutions of 1824 and 1857. The Constitutional Convention of 1917 was called merely to reform the 1857 document, but what resulted from its labors was something very different. If in form the government remained the same, a democracy based upon popular suffrage, the end result proved to be something altogether unexpected. The new Constitution wrote a revolutionary concept of property and labor into the basic law of the land, and by a series of changes relating to the Church and other institutions greatly increased the power and responsibility of the State.

The formula governing private property stemmed from the

Constitutional Convention itself, as it was not contained in the draft proposed by Carranza, then in control of the government, and was only adopted after an acrimonious debate between the conservatives and the radicals. The delegates had been chosen during the height of the civil war and represented the military chieftains most nearly in control of the country at that time. Their mandate derived from a revolutionary army still in the field. In the Constitutional Convention itself party lines were not originally clear. The early discussions were concerned with the rights of the individual so characteristic of traditional liberalism. The emphasis was upon curbing the powers of the State, but it soon became evident that the convention was oriented in a different direction: to make the State an instrument of social reform and economic change. The inchoate character of the Revolution had found in the Constitutional Convention a vehicle for crystallizing objectives that had largely remained beneath the surface. How this came about still remains a mystery, for there was no reason to assume that the soldiers, the lawyers, and the few laborers in the convention had any well-defined notion of social policy. A few individuals there were who, seemingly, had a sense of that direction. Among them were General Francisco J. Múgica, J. N. Macías, Rafael de los Ríos, José Lugo, Pastor Rouaix, as members, and, as an adviser, Andrés Molina Enríquez, a lawyer by profession and the author of *Los Grandes Problemas Nacionales,* the one important book before the Revolution on the basic Mexican problems. That these few men found it possible to impress their own broader purposes upon the delegates to the convention is explained partly by the fact that the others had no purposes of their own.

Article 27, however, was not a mere accident. It was in part the result of an internal division that endangered the unity of the dominant revolutionary forces. The few radicals in the convention, with Múgica at their head, and with the advice of Andrés Molina Enríquez, made a political issue out of the program to be embodied in the new Constitution and threatened to provide a political banner for a possible rebellion by

Obregón, then head of the army, against the government of Carranza. Pastor Rouaix, a member of the convention and at the same time Secretary of Agriculture, was instrumental in achieving a compromise between the radicals and the always stubborn and self-willed Carranza. It was thus by an implicit threat of a new revolution at a time when the country was still unsettled, and when the seeming threat of American intervention was very real, that the way was opened for the newer ideas.

The first draft of Article 27 was composed by Andrés Molina Enríquez at the request of Pastor Rouaix. It was later submitted for informal discussion to a small group of delegates meeting in the Bishop's Palace at Querétaro. It was there hammered out by an unauthorized committee and laid before the convention substantially in the form in which it was adopted. There was but one day's debate on the floor of the convention. The article was accepted with only a fraction of the delegates fully aware of the transcendental character of the social and economic revolution they were imposing upon the nation. In spite of the official claim that the article was unanimously adopted, the first fifteen votes, cast after a day's discussion begun at three in the afternoon and ended at three in the morning in a hall lighted by candles, were against and not for the article.

The purpose of the article was to subject private ownership in land to broad public ends. In theory at least, individual ownership in land is not destroyed. The authors of the article sought to subordinate private property to public law in such a manner as to make the public purpose prevail without destroying either the democratic State, individual initiative, or private property. But all ownership of land was made amenable to *modalidades* (forms) prescribed by the Constitution and subject to future modification by the legislature. This, in effect, was a declaration of public policy that would retain the form of private ownership but destroy its substance. The law came to mean that the legislature could, as a matter of general policy and by specific enactments after the policy was declared, so change private ownership as to make it protean, flexible, and malleable to the will of the State. The rights of private ownership, compensation for expropriation, inheritance, sale, transfer, investment, and use were retained.

The substance of what would be inherited, sold, transferred, or used became something very different from what was called private property before Article 27 was enacted. A revolution in the ownership and use of land had been written into the law, and private real property now disappeared, to give place to a limited right of usufruct, subject to changing legal prescriptions to be laid down by future legislative enactments. There was no general confiscation.

A social revolution was thus accomplished under legal guise. It seemed the less painful and unreal because it was to be executed in the future as the power of the Revolution was consolidated and the sense of direction was clarified. Otherwise the Constitution was left substantially in its old liberal form excepting for Article 123 on labor and Article 130 on the Church, which will be discussed in later chapters.

The juridical thread that made this possible is to be sought in the nature of the Spanish colonial dominion. The theory, as the Mexicans state it, runs to the effect that the Spanish kings received the recently discovered lands as a personal donation from Pope Alexander VI. The American possessions were therefore lodged in the person of the king and not in the Spanish nation. The kings held their American possessions as personal property. Private property of individuals was created in America as a *merced,* a gift from the king. For all practical purposes, these grants to individuals had all of the characteristics of private property. But they were held at the will of the Crown. The king could in theory, at his own pleasure, recover the lands so held and return them to the original royal patrimony.

Article 27, under this juridical principle, merely reasserted the powers formerly held by the Crown, but now belonging to the Mexican State as the Crown's successor, and re-established the right of reversion over all private real property.

From the standpoint of those who held this to be the traditional relation of the State to the privately owned lands, there was nothing new in Article 27. The period of the Independence, in which another principle of property had applied, was considered a legal aberration, something that in fact was inconsistent with the basic law of the land. The validity of this view of the legal history of property in Mexico may be criticized by those who oppose the results of the doctrine; but the authors of the legal revolution in landholding considered it the true one, acted upon it, and justified their action by reference to it.

The Mexican legal tradition, so defined and justified, became the source of infinite difficulties both internally and externally, especially with the United States. But the resultant argument was almost always a fruitless one because the foreigners (especially the Americans) and the Mexicans now argued from different premises. The position of the United States seemed to the Mexicans to be beside the point, for they denied the basic principle from which our arguments stemmed. Private property as we define it was, in the light of the Mexican position, nonexistent in Mexico at any time, as all claims to such property, even those based upon legal documents issued by previous governments, were considered as not valid. For it became a Mexican contention, asserted all through the elaborate diplomatic discussions carried on for over twenty years, that no government in Mexico was ever legally empowered to alienate the national patrimony, which included all of the land of Mexico, to any individual except on the basis of a *merced* subject to reversion at the will of the giver.[1]

This concept is written into the first paragraph of Article 27. The land and the waters within the national territories belong originally to the nation, which had and has the right to transfer dominion over them to private individuals, thus creating private property. Private property becomes, therefore, a matter of public concession and, as such, is limited in later articles to the prescriptions imposed by the State. The State assumes for itself for all time, therefore, the right to impose such *modali-*

[1] For a fuller discussion see Chapter xiv, pp. 265–75.

dades (forms) on this private ownership as may be dictated by public necessity. This necessity is partially defined in the article as the need for so distributing property as to achieve equitable division of wealth and preserve the land's resources.

In Mexico the State has always been capricious and unpredictable and, as such, can change, modify, amend, regulate, and abolish any form of private property established by previous enactment. The future powers and rights of the State cannot be limited and circumscribed by any past or present act establishing a form of private right, and the owner has no prescribed claim to compensation. What he may receive from the State in compensation for damages is not imposed as a juridical obligation, but is justified on moral grounds. The State may compensate the owner when it feels that the person from whom the property has been taken has a moral claim. He has no legal claim because no private individual can limit the powers of the State and because no past act of the State can limit its future exercise of power in the name of imperative public necessity. This, therefore, is the meaning of the Revolution as it affected private ownership in land.

Article 27 also specifically defines the different kinds of property that can be held and specifies the legal persons that may or may not hold different kinds of property in land. It must be clear that if the State has such powers of limitation over private ownership in land, then other property cannot be considered immune. The State has always exercised wide powers over income and goods; and while Article 27 does not deal with this species of property specifically, it is implicit that Article 27 could be (and in some instances has been) expanded to include other forms of property.

Mexico has not established collectivism. The Mexican milieu would not permit it. There is an essential individualism in Mexican tradition. But, legally speaking, the powers of the State are so greatly enhanced that in theory, at least, it could achieve a number of variants from traditional individualism within the present legal framework. The legal balance between the individual and the State has been shifted. That this is so may be seen from an examination of the legal principles embodied in Article 27 as they affect (a) the nature of private property and (b) the persons who may or may not own private property.

Under this theory, as we have already seen, private property arises only when the State passes title to an individual for part of the territory that belongs to the nation. But by definition the State cannot alienate the subsoil and the waters to a private person except by concession under specified limitations of use. In Mexico, therefore, the purchaser acquires only the surface of the land and its appurtenances. Even ownership of the surface is not absolute. The nation retains undefined rights and powers over the surface, and these rights are subject to expansion and modification in the future. The article itself specifies a certain number of limitations. Later laws have added others and may increase their number at any time in the future. Private property is subject to expropriation for purpose of public utility by means of compensation, and the Mexican courts have ruled this to be compensation after the fact of expropriation. In practice this may mean, and in many instances has meant, no compensation. The right to private property is further limited by law to the assessed tax valuation plus ten per cent. An owner may therefore have his property expropriated at a value fixed long ago and be paid for it some time in the future.

Private ownership is further circumscribed by the right of "public interest." The State could appropriate any private lands and waters, irrigate the land, and compensate the owner by a return to him of a piece of property having the same value his had before, even if much smaller. The State, by appropriating all of the unearned increment derived from irrigation, is enabled to sell irrigated lands in small parcels on long-term credit to needy cultivators. It is, as the authors of the law claimed, a literal application of the theories of Henry George. Under the law the owner of the land is left with a right to appeal, but he is in fact at the mercy of the irrigation commission.

Enough has been said, perhaps, to indicate the tenuous character of private property as reflected in Article 27. We now turn to the definition of the kinds of property that may or may not be owned by different kinds of legal persons. Only Mexican citizens may acquire ownership in lands and waters or their appurtenances, or concessions to exploit the subsoil minerals and fuels. Foreigners can acquire such rights only if they surrender any claim upon protection from their home government in matters pertaining to these rights. For purposes of enjoying these rights and opportunities, foreigners must agree to lay no claims against the Mexican government other than those which a Mexican citizen could lay against it, and must not invoke diplomatic protection from their own governments —or must suffer the penalty of forfeiture if they do.[2] In addition, foreigners may under no circumstances have direct ownership of land or waters within a hundred kilometers from the border or fifty from the sea. No religious institution of whatever denomination can own, administer, acquire, or make loans on private real property. All such property now belonging to them vests in the nation. All church buildings belong to the nation, which shall determine "which of them may continue to be devoted to their present purposes." All other buildings belonging to or administered by churches, whether educational or charitable, belong to the nation and are to be used "exclusively for the public services of the nation or the State." All private or public institutions devoted to charitable, scientific, educational, or mutual-aid purposes may acquire and hold mortgages on private property if the mortgages do not exceed ten years. But such institutions may not under any circumstances, either directly or indirectly, be under the patronage of religious institutions. Commercial stock companies can hold only such land as is essential for their industrial or mining activities, but cannot own, hold, or administer rural properties. Their needs for land must be specifically determined in each instance. Still different is the legal provision for groups of the Mexican population who have retained their communal lands, either in law or in practice, or have had lands granted to them. These corporate groups may continue enjoying their rights in

[2] See Chapter xiv, pp. 265–75.

the land as a group until such time as the law determines how these lands are to be divided.

These varying rules and regulations do not exhaust the range of the State's power in determining the shape of Mexico's land system, for under Article 27 an additional body of law and regulation is specified for the solution of the agrarian problem. For the purpose of satisfying the land hunger of the Mexican rural population, any alienation of land by villages after June 25, 1856 is declared null and void and the land restored to the original communities; those communities that have no title and can produce none shall, under the general rule of public utility, receive expropriated lands for their needs. The only exceptions to this rule are properties not exceeding fifty hectares (about 123.5 acres) acquired after 1856 that have been held in undisputed possession for at least ten consecutive years. All properties larger than fifty hectares must be returned to the original communities. The states are required to break up the large plantations, limit their size, and impose forced sales under specified conditions of payment.[3]

The Mexicans, it must by now be clear, have written a new theory of property into the law. The principle of private property has not been abolished, but it has been so modified as to leave something very different from the unlimited rights contained in the older theory. The concept has become flexible and changeable, subject to adaptation to varying needs. The formula is broad enough to contain the varying forms of ownership that have always, in fact, existed in Mexico: the rights of the migratory Indian groups who have no notion of private ownership, but who have from time immemorial made use of given areas for their own purposes; the collective ownership of communal agricultural villages that have always owned the land in common and still do; the small landholder—the *ranchero*—who works his few hectares as an individual; the large corporation engaged in mining or oil; the bank giving mortgages; and the charitable institution or educational foundation that invests funds in property. The formula has to be

[3] For a discussion of the agrarian problem see Chapter ix, pp. 136–53.

broad enough to cover all of these existing types. But Article 27 makes possible new forms of ownership for the future; every law, every administrative provision, makes for a new type of ownership. The law is broader in scope than most, or perhaps all, other property concepts. It permits communal ownership and makes certain kinds of property immune from lien and mortgage. It favors the small owner. It is neither socialism, nor communism, nor collectivism, nor simple private ownership. Ownership of property has become conditional, subject to use and to the requirements of public interest, and variable in form and content.

One illustration of this is indicative of the whole concept. The lands given to the villages as *ejidos* belong in theory to the villages, but these lands may not be sold, mortgaged, leased, or placed under any type of lien. They are to be used by the villagers directly for their own purposes. While the village owns the lands, it must pass on to individuals what is tillable. These in turn may neither sell, nor mortgage, nor hire others to work on such lands. They must be worked directly by the recipient, and if they are neglected for two years, they revert to the village, not to be held, but to be turned over to another individual to be worked.

Here, perhaps, is a good example of the underlying concept of the functional notion of property: it is given to the village for specific purposes, and under specific conditions for use, and these must be fulfilled. It is interesting to observe that the *ejido* lands have perhaps greater legal protection from administrative or legislative interference than any others in Mexico. For a village cannot be deprived of its property for any reason whatsoever by any agency, except by specific order of the chief executive, and then only when he replaces such lands by another area capable of serving the needs of the community, and as near as possible to the village. Without destroying private property as a principle, and without forcing a collectivistic program upon the country, the formula, it seems, has accepted the dictum that, "given the protean right of property, all forms of exploitation are possible."

CHAPTER 7

A Theory of Labor

THE MEXICAN REVOLUTION, as embodied in the Constitution of 1917, specified not merely a theory of property, but also a theory of labor. Here again the new doctrine greatly enhanced the powers of the State and endowed it with such detailed powers for controlling the activities of labor and industry as to make it a party to every contract, every bargain, every dispute, every rule and regulation. Article 123, the constitutional formula for this increased role of the State, has made it possible for the government to define the character and the content of Mexican industrial life.[1]

In the sight of the law, the trade union is given the status of a "moral person" with special rights and privileges. The law

[1] So important has "Artículo 123" been deemed that streets have been named after it in many places, Mexico City included.

promotes the growth of these "moral persons," provides directives for their activities, makes them an obligatory agency in every industrial enterprise, protects them against destructive competition, and shapes the range of their interests and activities. The trade union has become an instrument for the reduction of the power of private industry and for making the State the arbiter of the nation's economy.

It is worthy of note that this law was written for a predominantly agricultural country, with little industry and less native capital, without either a large middle or industrial laboring class, and with nearly all important enterprise in foreign hands. It is this last fact that helps explain the sudden adoption of so ample a body of labor and social legislation; it also indicates why it proved acceptable. The absence of Mexican capital in industrial, mineral, and commercial establishments made the new law a nationalist program on behalf of the native workers against the stranger in their midst. It affected no important local interest and provided the State with a leverage against foreign capital. This broad law could be enacted only in a political vacuum, where the interest most affected had neither voice nor representation.

The Mexican trade-union movement is a creature of the State, for it must always be remembered that in 1917 there was no significant trade-union movement in Mexico. Perhaps not so many as thirty thousand workers in the whole country belonged to unions, and in the Constitutional Convention there were only two labor leaders, one from Yucatán and another from Vera Cruz. Yet the convention wrote into the Constitution the most comprehensive and detailed labor program then in existence anywhere.

The numerous and detailed privileges with which the law endowed the workers and their unions were, as in the agrarian program, something to be fulfilled in the future. Whereas there was an agrarian problem of great proportions, there was no labor problem of similar importance. The theory upon which the labor law was elaborated may not have been new, but it was foreign to Mexican experience. It was a sudden application of imported doctrine unrelated to Mexican conditions. It was a future aim written into the law.

The aim projected a national working class to counterbalance a foreign industrialist class. It was an effort to develop new sources of national political power based upon workers' organizations. In a sense, a limited syndicalized state was foreshadowed, wherein the union, with the support of the State, would become not merely a protective agency in defense of the worker, but also an instrument of the newly discovered nationalist policy. The important point to remember, however, is that the union was to be a creature of and subordinate to the State. The very nature of the Mexican Revolution is missed if it is not clearly seen that the redemption of the worker in Mexico from peonage and semislavery is but half the story, and perhaps the lesser half. The other is to increase the power of the State by basing it in part upon these union organizations. The unions have grown strong, but the State has grown stronger.

A partnership between the State and the labor unions has been established in the law, the first being the major partner. The improvement of labor conditions, the increase of the worker's dignity and self-respect, the creating of a feeling of power, and participation by the unions in national affairs were all to the good, but the greater by-product has been to give Mexican government an additional prop to rest upon and an additional means of fortifying itself against foreign influence. The labor legislation like the agrarian, is a phase of the new nationalism.

The struggle over Article 123 within the Constitutional Convention took much the same form as that over Article 27. Labor, as a class, was to be given privileges it did not then enjoy, which, as a matter of fact, were not embodied in any constitutional document then extant anywhere in the world. The collective rights of the group were made to predominate over the individual rights of the citizen. The individual was made subordinate to the group. The idea of "public interest" thus came to dominate the labor code as it dominated the agrarian code. The Constitution has therefore created two classes with special rights in the body politic: agrarian communities (*ejidos*) composed of agricultural peasants on one hand, and unions composed of laborers on the other. These two "moral persons," special creatures of the law, have been encased in an essentially individualist constitutional framework.

Article 123 sets up minimum rights for the workers. They are significant in the degree to which they separate the workers from other Mexican citizens and mark them out for special treatment. The itemized privileges with which the workers are endowed seem simple and innocent enough—the right to organize, to an eight-hour day, to participation in profits, and so forth—and might erroneously lead one to assume that they are static. But by making the union a legal instrument, the collective labor contract a source of industrial law, and the Board of Conciliation and Arbitration a judicial body with power, the Constitution forged an instrument for reshaping Mexican industrial life. Let me repeat, it was done by the State and not by the workers. The State, legally speaking, created the working class. The few earlier labor laws enacted in Mexico, beginning in 1904 and with greater frequency after 1914, were passed without participation by the workers. The Constitutional Convention, influenced by foreign ideas, imposed this new legal doctrine and formula upon the country. The labor program had no local antecedents, whereas the agrarian revolution was essentially Mexican.

Article 123, in its detailed enumeration of specific rights of labor, was really a collation of ideas of social legislation drawn from the world at large. The Constitution drew upon New Zealand, England, France, Belgium, and the United States. The ideas of Justice Higgins of Australia and of Justice Brandeis and Father John Ryan of the United States were made use of, as were earlier Mexican efforts at labor legislation. These included the first law, passed in 1904 in the state of Mexico under Governor José Vicente Villada, and dealing with industrial accidents. A similar law was enacted in 1906 by General Bernardo Reyes in the State of Nuevo León.

With the beginning of the Revolution a number of different projects made their appearance, the most important of which was a proposal for a labor law developed in Vera Cruz under the auspices of Carranza. This led to a study of similar legislation in other parts of the world, and José Natividad Macías was sent to the United States to gather information and ideas on this subject. It was he who at the Constitutional Convention proposed a body of law that in committee was finally hammered into Article 123 and adopted by the convention.

In detail, Article 123 prescribes the hours of labor, a minimum wage, participation in profits, and protection of women and children; regulates discharge and requires three months' pay for unjustified displacement; allows organization of labor as a right; and by implication makes way for collective bargaining. It legalizes the strike as a means of establishing equilibrium between diverse factors of production and as a means of harmonizing the rights of labor and capital. It limits the right of suspension of work in a factory to the necessity of limiting production to maintain prices, and this can occur only with the consent of the Board of Conciliation and Arbitration. It imposes upon industry the responsibility for accidents, regulates matters of hygiene, makes place for social security, and, as reformed in August 1939, makes social security obligatory for invalidity, unemployment, accident, and sickness. It imposes upon the larger industries a series of obligations in matters of housing at a fixed price and makes provisions for schools. Large corporations are also required to maintain infirmaries for their workers and to provide specified public services in communities made up of their laborers. Among many other specified items, the law establishes the Boards of Conciliation and Arbitration, to be made up of representatives of labor, the employers, and the State.

These boards are essentially independent of the regular judicial powers of the State, and upon them falls the responsibility of settling differences between capital and labor. As a majority is always created by the State's vote, whatever the State favors in the matter of labor rights prevails in these boards. The State has in fact become the arbiter of the issues between capital and labor, and as long as the State feels, as it has felt, that it is to the interest of the nation to strengthen the unions, it can increase the range of the unions' powers. These boards supervise the execution of contracts, decide the legality of a strike, and execute the public policy.

By implication, the Constitution recognizes that contemporary Mexican society is divided into classes, and that it is the function of the State to protect one class against another. The Constitution is therefore not merely a body of rules equally applicable to all citizens, but also a body of rules specially designed to benefit and protect given groups. The community is not made up of citizens only; it is also made up of classes with special rights within the law. What has in fact happened is that the old idea of the "estates" has been re-created in Mexican law. The pattern of the older Spanish State, divided into clergy, nobility, and commons, has been re-created in modern dress, with peasants, workers, and capitalists replacing the ancient model. This is not done formally, but it is done sufficiently well to make it evident that a very different kind of social structure is envisioned in the law, even if only by implicit commitment, than that in a liberal democracy.

It is true, of course, that within the Constitution there is an inner conflict between the older tradition of individualism and the newer notion of class. That, however, merely means that the Constitutional Convention was not fully aware of the implications of its own labors. It has required a long series of judicial decisions to bring the issues to the surface.

Deliberately or not, the State has created "moral persons" who, in the law, stand between the individual and the State. It is, I think, impossible to understand Mexico's labor philosophy, its attitude to foreign corporations, its readiness to carry out a policy of expropriation in specified instances and to turn over to the workers the operation of certain industries or individual industrial units, without recognizing this subtle and almost unconscious drift in Mexican law. Under the Mexican constitutional provision that the "State . . . shall make laws

. . . relative in general to every contract of labor," the distinctions between laborers working for a wage or salary or as agents of commercial and financial companies, and those defined as intellectual workers, such as engineers, actors, and artists, have in fact been obliterated in the law. There is a tendency to think of the "liberal professions" as part of the laboring class and subject to the principles of labor legislation.

The encouragement of labor unions is evidenced in many ways: only Mexicans may be employed in certain jobs, the laborer is expected to be a member of a union, the employer may not discharge a worker who has a case pending before the Boards of Conciliation and Arbitration, no new workers may be hired during a strike, collective contracts must be signed with a majority group, and the benefits of these contracts apply to the minority as well. The collective labor contract, while in force, is recognized as the law operating between the two parties. All disputes must be taken for settlement to the Boards of Conciliation and Arbitration. Trade unions are further encouraged by limitations against laying off workers, by the requirement for three months' pay in case of discharge, and by many other specific items in the laws. All of these provisions are enforceable by the Boards of Conciliation and Arbitration and by the courts. In fact, the decisions of the Mexican courts almost make organization a prerequisite for both labor and management.

Article 123 governs all labor contracts. A labor contract that failed to fulfill its specifications would be in violation of the Constitution. Other provisions of the contract may increase, but cannot reduce, the privileges prescribed in the Constitution. There has also come into being a *Contrato-Ley*, a form of collective contract applicable to all units in a given industry or economic realm. When once accepted by two thirds of the companies involved, it becomes obligatory upon the rest and enforceable against any new establishments that may be organized in that industry.

If the labor law does not repudiate the individual liberties consecrated in the Constitution of 1917, it gives them a new direction. Numerous examples may be cited. Thus the rights of society are declared affected when an employer attempts to replace a laborer before the Board of Conciliation and Arbitration has decided that the discharge is legal. The same is held to be true when an employer attempts to replace a worker who is sick, or when a legal strike exists. Under the ægis of the State, the local unions have been formed into federations, and these into national organizations. While absolute unification of all working-class organizations in a single union has never been accomplished, the State, by its support of the majority union, by the use of the police and the army to protect the rights of the workers on strike, by favoring the members of the majority union in matters of employment opportunities, and by other means, has in fact made out of the union an official organism for the effectuation of its own purposes.

The Boards of Conciliation and Arbitration have gradually been endowed with increasing jurisdiction by the Mexican Supreme Court until they have become judicial agencies in the matters that pertain to their competence. They are sovereign in determining the facts of a dispute, and the subject matter of their deliberations is derived from the collective labor contracts, which are presumed to exist even if not written down. Their decisions are obligatory, and all labor controversies must be submitted to them. Their judgments cannot be suspended, because they are presumed to reflect the public interest. What they decide is compulsory law for the matter under their purview, and failure to enforce judgment violates Article 123. Their procedure is not subject to the limitation of legal proof in courts of justice, and their judgments are based upon the facts developed and upon their conscience. No authority can substitute for their powers to determine the facts; any refusal to comply with their decisions terminates the collective contract and brings into being the consequent financial sanctions it involves—that is, the payment of damages and three months' wages for unjustified discharge of workers. The only recourse against the decisions of the Boards of Conciliation and Arbitration is an appeal to the courts on the grounds of violation of the individual rights guaranteed by the Constitution, but such an appeal does not act to suspend the decision of the boards in matters of fact or judgment upon the controversy derived from the collective labor contracts.

The collective contract is obligatory and subsists during a discussion for its renewal. If the employer puts impediments in the way of conclusion of a new contract, it can be promulgated by the executive, and the company may be fined up to fifty thousand pesos.

As can be seen from the above, the law has created an instrumentality for erecting and expanding the rule of organized labor within the industrial system and for making the labor contract a protean source of increasing power for the unions. The State in the meantime, by always being able to decide which way the majority of these boards shall go, has retained its control over both the union and the industry. A special system of class legislation, deliberately conceived as requisite for the maintenance of the special position of labor, has become a normal characteristic of contemporary Mexican policy.

While Article 123 leaves to the states the right to legislate in matters of labor within their province, the federal government has arrogated to itself by amendments to Article 123 the following industries over which federal labor law is made to rule: textile, electric, movie, rubber, sugar, mineral, oil, railroad, air and sea transport; all companies directly or indirectly administered by the federal government; all work in the Federal District, territories, zones, or territorial waters. It also operates in conflicts that affect more than one state; collective contracts that have been declared obligatory in more than one state; and all matters pertaining to education required from industrial, commercial, or agricultural establishments. The federal government, as can be seen, has taken over the greater part of the area of industrial activity as its province, and the powers of the federal government can be made to reach into almost any significant activity in the nation.[2]

[2] The economic aspects of Mexican labor legislation and practice are discussed further in Chapter xiii, pages 222–8.

CHAPTER 8

Church and State

THE ENIGMA of Mexico is reflected in the persistent strife between Church and State.

The Church in Mexico, as old as the Conquest, represents the spiritual values that men from the Old World had to offer to those of the New. The speedy conversion of the Indians seemed like a miracle to the friars and provided the conquerors with a moral justification that salved their consciences. The Church was also a challenge to their rapacity. Its defense of the Indians as human beings possessed of souls and capable of redemption saved the Indian from the infamy of being branded a soulless creature incapable of a life of the spirit, to be identified only with the beast of the field.

One need not deny the delinquencies of individual priests or the frequently mistaken policy of the Church. But the Church, in the early days at least, stood out as the protector and friend of the Indian, as the only advocate and well-wisher he had a claim upon. The lives and labors of such men as Bartolomé de las Casas, Vasco de Quiroga, Fray Juán de Zumárraga, and Sebastián Ramírez de Fuenleal, who bearded King and Viceroy and damned and excommunicated officials and *encomenderos* in their efforts to implant the rule that the Indian, too, is a man, equal to his master, and not merely deserving but possessing the rights of a being endowed with spiritual substance, represent one of the great glories of the Church.

The identification of the Indian and his master as children of the same God in a measure saved the Indian's faith in himself. It gave him a claim upon life that he could not otherwise have asserted or believed in. He may have become a pariah and an outcast, but he remained a human being with a right to the sacraments and a claim upon justice. If the State offered the Indian a circumscribed status as a subject and protected him in his limited rights, the Church identified him as one of the faithful and cast the mantle of the Christian faith over him.

Both the Crown and the Church labored against the immediate interest of the conquerors, who wished to garner the fruits of their labors in ostentatious wealth, a luxurious life, and untrammeled power over their subdued Indians. In the long run the Church succeeded in identifying the Indian with the conqueror, and, more than that, it saved his sense of identity with the unseen universe, for the Indian was and has remained deeply religious. The Catholic doctrine, its forms of worship, its sense of the fallibility of the human creature, its many saints, its embellished ritual, its persistent surrounding of the details of life with symbolic meaning, and its elaborate churches captured the imagination of the Indian and gave him a temple in which to express his feeling of dependence upon the unseen gods. How much of the Catholic doctrine and theology the Indian has ever understood is a debatable question—probably very little, even to this day. But the Church was the house of God and of the infinite forms in which he revealed himself, and the saint was the particular representation of the faith. It proved easy for the Indian to keep in the Catholic Church the faith he had had so long and to identify his own deep religious sense with the newer forms that adorned the temples, often built upon the places where the older idols had rested. On the days that custom and tradition had sanctified, the Indians gathered to sing and dance and pray and weep in front of the new saints, as they had in another day before the older ones. The mystical thread that tied them to the unseen and mysterious universe was not broken and obliterated, and they became good Christians for the same reasons that they had been deeply religious before the Catholic Church arrived.

An essential link between the past and the present was preserved and gave life a sense of continuance and a sense of direction. The Indians worked for the Church, built its temples, adorned and embellished its walls, tilled its lands, knelt before the Host, and obeyed the Fathers of the Church, because that was the kind of religious life they had always known. The confessional, the fasting, the penance, and the tithe were not alien to their former experience, and they gave their loyalty to the one institution brought from Europe that seemed somehow closer to them than anything else the strangers had to offer. The faithful were early counted by the millions, and the rapid conversion of the Indians was ascribed to a miracle.

The Church grew rich and influential and became an important handmaiden of the government. It became part of the Spanish colonial administration, with a bishop upon occasion exercising the role of viceroy. The entire system seemed an organic whole, and by the right of the *patronato* granted to the Spanish Crown by Alexander VI in the year 1493, the Crown ruled the Church as a matter of right. The State picked the archbishops, bishops, priests, and deacons—even the poor sacristan had to be nominated by the Crown or its representative. No church, convent, monastery, hospital, or school could be built, no parish laid out, no tithe collected, no letter written to Rome or received from the Holy Father, except by permission of the Crown. The Crown claimed all Church properties as its own, and required and received—irregularly—inventories of the Church's possessions. The Church, as we can see, had become great and rich, but dependent; it had become an arm of the Crown, its spiritual arm, but subject to the will of the royal master who ruled from Spain.

The very success of the Church was to prove its undoing. It was too closely identified with the Crown and could not, when the test came, escape from some of the evil days that the Crown fell upon. It was not possible to drive the Spanish power from Mexico without at the same time attacking and weakening the Church: the thousands of little Mexican villages never fully shared the larger universe that both Church and Empire represented.

The Mexican village was parochial. It knew nothing of Spain, Rome, or even Mexico. Viceroy and bishop, governor and priest, might think and feel themselves a part of a universal Empire and a universal Church. They might belong to the big world and represent a European aspiration for empire in politics and religion. The parochial village knew the humble church that it adorned and the sacred image of the saint that it guarded and worshipped. The saint was the very particular saint of that particular village, the center of its life and faith, and the priest might be a stranger who came upon occasion, and, in some instances, was admitted to the church only with the consent of the village elders. The very idea of a great universal Church was alien, unknown, and beyond conjecture to the simple folk who prayed in a non-European tongue and who had retained in their forms of worship many of the older patterns belonging to an older faith, now transmuted into Catholic practice by time and the intermittent teaching of the priest. While the Church was permanent, the priest was often transient. There were never enough priests in Mexico to fill the needs of the thousands of little villages.

Cathedrals, convents, monasteries, colleges, and hospitals were mainly in the big cities and larger towns. The poor priest and friar traveled on muleback from one little village to another to carry the word of God and to perform the holy offices for the Indians, gathered on special feast days in honor of the local patron saint. To the little villages, with their hundred barefooted Indians, the world was limited to the horizon, and the saint within the church was the symbol of the faith that had replaced their older gods. The Indians were in their own way Catholics, and they were counted by bishop and viceroy as members of the universal Church and the universal Empire. But only those who did the counting were aware of the Empire with which they were identifying the Indians.

The religious conflict in Mexico is part of the particularism of the little village that never belonged to Rome, Madrid, or Mexico City. At the time of the Independence the Indians worshipped God in a hundred tongues, and were literate in none. When the battle between Church and State came to a head, it was fought out by the literate in city and town, between the middle-class intellectuals, mainly lawyers on one side and priests on the other. The lawyers won the battle. The mass of the Indian communities remained at the margin, without understanding what the strife was about unless their immediate church and immediate saint were violated. That alone could make the conflict a real one for them; and, on the whole, the war between Church and State never took that form, for even in the bitterest days of the conflict under Calles, when the churches were closed in the cities all over Mexico, they remained open in the little villages, where the priests were, as always, in only occasional attendance. Anticlericalism in Mexico has always been a middle-class doctrine of European origin, just as the ideal of a universal Church is, in Mexico at least, middle- and upper-class and European.

When the movement against Spain began, the Church was riven into warring factions. The ecclesiastical hierarchy remained loyal to the Crown. They were Spanish-born, and to them the continuance of the colonial tie with Spain seemed essential to true and Christian government. The *patronato* (patronage) had for so long tied the Church to the Crown that for most Church dignitaries no other relationship was conceivable. The Crown, too, was the bulwark against the tide of new and heretical ideas that, originating in France, was flooding the world and threatening to engulf mankind in heresy. The power and influence of the Church were intertwined with the colonial system. The churches, schools, hospitals, and charitable institutions were part of the social and political structure. Even if it had occurred to the Church dignitaries to deny the validity of the Spanish Crown's title to its American colonies, they were in no position to act upon such an assumption. The loyalty of the ecclesiastical hierarchy to Spain was part of the order of nature as then given.

It was different with the parish clergy, however; there was hardly a battle in which priests were not found as officers of the rebels. These were mainly Mexican-born, often *mestizos,* by origin and experience close to the Indian, as poor as their parishioners, and identified with them. The ideas of nationalism, liberty, equality, and fraternity, when they became aware of them, did not seem beyond reason or unacceptable. As parish priests they had become conscious of their own inferiority in the hierarchical scheme, and the woes of their poor parishioners gave the ideas of "progress" a seeming inner validity. It was, as we have seen, Hidalgo and Morelos, both parish priests, who became the first great leaders of the Mexican struggle for independence.

The achievement of independence brought the question of the relations between Church and State to a head. Was the newborn State to inherit the rights previously enjoyed by the Spanish Crown? It was on this question that the quarrel developed, and the failure to find a compromise by a concordat in the early days of the Independence laid the foundations for the evils to follow. Had some way to an early peace been found, the form and substance of the quarrel might have taken a different turn. Unfortunately for Mexico, the stubborn temper of the times made peace impossible, and the quarrels have continued to this day.

As early as 1822 the assembled bishops of Mexico decided that the patronage devolved back to the Church, that it was a personal grant to the king, and that when the king disappeared the Church recovered the powers hitherto vested in him. But the exercise of the powers represented by the patronage had long been held to be political. By insisting that the patronage reverted to the Church, it seemed to lay claim to the political prerogatives exercised earlier by the Crown.

The Church thus came to be considered a rival political power within the State. This power was for the most part officered by Spaniards. It was rich in worldly goods, and possessed, according to the Catholic historian Lucas Alamán, half of the land in the country. It controlled education, held mortgages upon a large part of the land it did not own, and was freed by its privileges from the ordinary jurisdiction of the courts. With Independence, the Church was faced by a demand for a renunciation of its ancient prerogatives.

The Church, for its own survival, required a strong and friendly government. Yet every effort on its part to influence the creation of such a government identified it with the opposition, laid it open to the charge of political meddling, and multiplied its enemies. Its power and wealth, its immunities and privileges, its hold over the imaginations of men, and the numerous host that followed its banner made it a danger to every government that came to power against its will. Every government it supported was subject to the charge of being Church-controlled. The patronage merely symbolized the early conflict. The war was really about something else—survival. Under the circumstances, the Mexican governments could not prosper with a society presided over by so preponderant a church, and the Church could not continue in its ancient role if liberal doctrines from France ruled the policy of the new, irresponsible, and weak governments, whose very poverty and instability made the strong and wealthy Church an enemy to be feared and despoiled.

In addition, a new theory came to rule the minds of men. The very idea of a guild or corporate body seemed in some way contrary to liberty and equality. Property owned by the Church was said to be held by a dead hand. The dominant theory made a fetish of competition, the price bargain, free trade, and equality of taxation. The conviction that these new values would open the way to human felicity made the struggle with the Church more than mere competition for power. A new description of the nature of the social order was involved. The opposition to the existence of corporate bodies led to a repudiation of the monastery, the convent, the ecclesiastical courts, and the special immunities and privileges of the priesthood. Anticlericalism was of a philosophical character and part of a new description of the role of man upon this earth.

There really was no room for compromise once the issues were defined in philosophical terms. Over the patronage an agreement might have been reached in time if the Church in Rome had been able to shake itself free from the influence of Spain in shaping its early American policy and had recognized the independence of Mexico. But the influence of the Spanish Crown at Rome was very great and rested on many centuries of close co-operation and understanding. At best, the Church in Rome was not well informed. The early opportunities for an agreement passed away, and the conflict was beyond compromise. Both sides were intransigent. The State and the Church, as ideas complete in themselves, proved incompatible.

The first serious attacks on the Church began in 1833 under the leadership of Valentín Gómez Farías, then Vice-President of the Republic. He secularized education and suppressed the university because it was under ecclesiastical control, declared that the payment of the tithe (*diezmo*) was not a civil obligation, permitted members of the monastic orders to forswear their vows and leave their retreats, and attempted to present candidates for parish vacancies as the Crown had under the patronage.

These provisions were soon followed by others. Even the irresponsible Santa Anna, who was hailed as "a brilliant star" and savior by the clerical party, prohibited the sale of Church property without previous consent of the government and, during the war with the United States, imposed a forced loan upon the Church. The way the wind was blowing it revealed by a proposal for a law by a member of Congress, Vicente Romero, to the effect that only the spiritual jurisdiction of the Church should be recognized and that all of its property should be confiscated because it derived from alms and should therefore be distributed among those in need of alms. These various proposals culminated in the Ley Juárez in November 1855 and in the Ley Lerdo of June 1856 for the suppression of special courts for churchmen and military, and for the disentailment of church properties by assigning them to the lessees at current rentals, capitalized at six per cent. Juárez, on July 12, 1857, in the midst of a bitter civil war, promulgated the laws that have in fact set the pattern for State and Church relations ever since. He confiscated all of the Church's properties, suppressed the religious orders, and empowered the governors to designate the buildings to be used for religious services. The books and objects of art of the religious communities were turned over to the public museums and schools. Nuns were allowed to leave their convents, and no more novices were admitted. Juárez also withdrew from Rome the Mexican representative, who had not been received by the Pope.

The Maximilian adventure was partly the result of the battle between Church and State. The idea of monarchy in Mexico was not dead. The hope of achieving stability in the faction-torn country and securing for the Church and the army their ancient privileges gave the conservatives considerable support and helped to drag on the conflict until Maximilian was shot in Querétaro on June 19, 1867. The Church party has never recovered from that defeat.

The position of the Church was further weakened by President Lerdo de Tejada's decrees of September 24, 1873 and December 14, 1874, incorporating into the Constitution of 1857 and expanding the laws previously issued by Juárez. He made marriage a civil contract, prohibited religious institutions from acquiring real property or lending money on mortgages, replaced the oath by a simple declaration, forbade the establishment of any monastic order, prohibited the teaching of religion in any of the governmental establishments, suppressed religious holidays, stopped any manifestations of religion in public, regulated the ringing of church bells, denied priests the right to be heirs or legatees, prohibited the use of any special religious dress in public, and nullified any special privileges that members of the priesthood might have enjoyed under law. The use of churches was regulated. The Church was stripped of all its ancient prerogatives and its special juridical status was abolished.

The long Díaz regime, without making any fundamental changes in the law, permitted the Church to recover a part of its lost freedom. It modified the Constitution of 1857 by amending its Article 27. The change permitted the Church to own the buildings it needed for its offices and either to acquire such real property or to administer mortgages for the upkeep of these buildings. Through the formation of anonymous companies the Church also acquired a limited amount of other property. It re-established schools and colleges in a number of states, and rural schools in numerous villages. A few seminaries were organized for the training of young aspirants for the priesthood. The Church re-entered the field of public service, establishing a few asylums, hospitals, lying-in institutions, and poor houses. A number of papers were published in the interest of Catholics in Mexico City, and in some of the states as well. Without changing the law, Díaz permitted the reappearance more or less openly of the religious orders.

The Mexican Revolution of 1910 brought the conflict between Church and State to the surface again. The conservatives and the foreign influences in Mexico bitterly fought the revolutionary movement, and the Church, fearing the recrudescence of the older anticlerical principles, found itself aligned against the popular movement.

Unfortunately for itself, the Church became identified with the foreigner in the eyes of the Mexican politicians. It shared its opposition to the Constitution of 1917 with outsiders and with the large landholders, and the behavior of the Catholics in the United States—especially the Knights of Columbus, who openly urged the American government to intervene in behalf of the Mexican Church—did not help matters. Had the Mexican Church identified itself with the social program of the Revolution, had some Mexican priests emulated the earlier role of Hidalgo and Morelos and become proponents of the social and economic redemption of the Mexican peon, the story might have proved different.

The Mexican Church sided with the Díaz regime, was hostile to Madero, proved friendly to Huerta, and later opposed the Constitution of 1917. Finally it found itself publicly proclaiming that it could not obey those articles of the Constitution which affected the life of the Church—that is, Articles 3, 27, and 130. This merely tended to identify the Church with other enemies of the Revolution at the time when Mexico was struggling with its back to the wall against foreign, especially American, pressure. Unfortunately, the Church could not state its case without being classed with other enemies of the government. The conflict with the revolutionary governments simmered throughout the entire period after 1910 and came to a head under Obregón and, still more clearly, under Calles in 1926.

On February 5, 1926 the Mexico City newspaper *El Universal* published an account of an interview with Archbishop Mora y del Río (he declared that it did not fully represent his views) in which he expressed his objections to the articles in the Constitution that dealt with the Church, saying that the Mexican priests would not obey them and that he would support them in this attitude. The formal declaration by the bishops on April 21, 1926 that they were opposed to Articles 3, 5, 24, 27, 130, and others, and that the Catholics should organize to change the Constitution, precipitated a great political crisis and led Calles to issue a law requiring all priests to register with the government and giving the government powers of repression. The Congress rejected an appeal from the bishops on the grounds that they had lost their citizenship when they refused to obey the Constitution.

The Mexican political atmosphere had become extremely tense, and an explosion was possible. Early in 1926 Monsignor

George J. Caruana, a naturalized American citizen and a Maltese by birth, who had served as chaplain in the American army, was sent to Mexico in an effort to work out a compromise with the government, but he found it impossible to harmonize the conflicting interests. His American citizenship proved a handicap. The Mexican conservatives were in no mood to make their peace with Calles. Caruana was advised by both Mexicans and Americans that the Calles administration was weak and would not endure, and that a settlement would merely strengthen it and prolong its life.

So tense was the situation that a meeting arranged between Caruana and a member of the Cabinet with the consent of Calles had to take place in the middle of the night in the Cabinet member's office after all employees, including his private secretary, had been sent home. I was under the impression then that with a little more firmness on the part of the Papal delegate, some working agreement could have been reached, but the insistence of both Mexican and American advisers that the Calles government should not be placated under any circumstances proved too strong. When the government realized that the conversations would be allowed to drag on and that the spokesman for the Church could not moderate the opposition, he was expelled on May 18, 1926, on the pretext that he had entered Mexico under false pretenses.

On June 24 Calles issued a decree putting the religious laws into effect, closing all religious schools, expelling all foreign priests, and ordering all priests to register. In reply the Mexican episcopate ordered all priests to abandon the churches on the date that the law came into effect, July 31, 1926. A rebellion on behalf of the Church broke out in some of the states, especially Jalisco, Nayarit, and Durango, and dragged on for three years, costing many thousands of lives.

It was during this time that the American government was reaching a point of extreme tension with the Calles administration over the agrarian and subsoil legislation. Once again it seemed to the Mexican liberals and anticlericals that the Church was abetting and even applauding the threat of foreign intervention. All through the end of 1926 and in 1927 rebellion was in the air. Bands held up trains. In one instance, in April 1927, a band held up a train between Guadalajara and Mexico City and murdered the crew and most of the passengers. While the bishops disclaimed responsibility for the brewing civil war, the government implicated individual priests and took the opposition of the Church as an excuse to lay the whole blame upon it. The Gómez-Serrano military revolution against the Calles administration toward the end of the year did not help matters. This impasse dragged on for three years, until it was broken by the good offices of Ambassador Morrow.

The foundation for the agreement was laid at a secret meeting between Calles and Father John J. Burke on April 4, 1928 in Vera Cruz. Later negotiations were continued under the friendly influence of Morrow in 1929 with the new President, Portes Gil. The agreement provided in substance that the law requiring the registration of priests did not empower officials to register any except those who had been nominated by the Church, that religious instruction could be given in the churches, and that Catholics retained the right of petition.

The peace did not prove a lasting one. The *cristero* rebellion simmered on. The states, exercising their powers under the Constitution, passed laws limiting the number of priests. Some of the states limited the number to one priest for every fifty thousand inhabitants others made it impossible for any priests to stay in the state. Tabasco, for instance, required all priests to marry before they could exercise their functions. The churches were closed, clandestine religious meetings in private homes were persecuted, and individuals had their homes confiscated on information that private chapels in them had been used for the holding of religious services. The position of the Church deteriorated, and the amendment to Article 3 dealing with education, requiring that all instruction, in addition to being in the hands of the State, should also be socialistic and anti-religious, again brought the issue to the boiling-point. The persecution of the Church had become a matter of political agitation, and the Mexican revolutionists, many of whom had forgotten their older doctrines and had grown rich from the exercise of public office, held onto their anticlericalism as the only remnant of their earlier faith. For many of them this was the one point of identification with their zeal of 1917.

These conditions lasted until 1935, when Cárdenas quietly used his influence to modify the situation in favor of the Church. His desire for inner unity and his wish not to embarrass President Roosevelt, under pressure from American public opinion to do something in regard to the difficulties of the Church in Mexico, all combined to influence his change of policy. He also acted to quiet the conscience of many Mexicans afflicted and torn by being denied the consolation of their faith. He did it without changing any federal law, for such a change would have roused the agitation all over again. The state governors, under his advice, gradually modified the oppressive state laws, and peace returned to the Church for the first time in a quarter of a century. The results of this change of policy made it possible for President Ávila Camacho to declare that he was a believer and to institute a greater tolerance for the activities of the Church. The recent revision of Article 3, dealing with education, by removing the most objectionable features as seen by the Church, has further improved Church-State relations in Mexico.

CHAPTER 9

The Agrarian Problem

The chief cause of the Revolution of 1910 was the uneven distribution of land. In fact, many of the country's difficulties were the result of the large haciendas that came to dominate the Mexican countryside. With the disappearance of the king and the viceroy, the governments born of the Independence proved weak and ephemeral, and by default surrendered control of the sparsely settled land to the local *hacendados*. Who better than the *hacendado* would protect his followers and servants, make and enforce what law he needed, keep order in his own domain, and survive in a world where all else seemed to be dissolving? One thing is clear: the hacienda had great survival value. It outlived the Spanish Crown, which had given it its original start, garnered new strength during the Independence, and accumulated the lands taken from the Church.

The systematic destruction of the Indian villages after 1856, thitherto partially protected by the older colonial legislation, merely added to the haciendas' fortunes, and the long dictatorship of Díaz seemed especially designed to favor the carving up of the entire nation into huge principalities. Such were the power, prestige, and comparative size of the hacienda that the country seemed divided into a small number of isolated domains. Three haciendas occupied the 186 miles between Saltillo and Zacatecas. The properties of the Terrazas family in Chihuahua were comparable in extent to Costa Rica. In the state of Hidalgo the Central Railroad passed through the Escandón estates for a distance of about 90 miles. In Lower California foreign companies owned seventy-eight per cent of the land, an area greater than Ireland. The haciendas of La Honda and Santa Catalina in Zacatecas contained about 419,000 acres. The state of Morelos belonged to thirty-two families, and the census of 1910 recorded only 834 *hacendados* in all of Mexico.

This situation had developed slowly during the colonial period and was greatly accelerated after the Independence. The Church began losing its lands during the colonial period, when the Jesuit Order was expelled in 1767 and its 128 plantations were expropriated. This was followed by Charles IV's *cédula* of September 19, 1798, depriving a whole series of religious institutions of their properties. These included those owned by the Pious Funds, houses of the poor, houses of charity, orphanages, religious guilds (*cofradías*), and the orders of lay brothers. All of these lands soon found their way into the hands of the large landowners. This also occurred with the lands expropriated from the Inquisition on February 22, 1813, and with the Church lands expropriated by Juárez in 1856. The hacienda as an institution became the beneficiary of the changing pattern of landholding.

In their zeal for the destruction of corporate landownership, the reformers of Juárez's day decided that the communal village lands needed to be broken up, deeded to the individual villagers, and reduced to private ownership. The Crown had measurably protected the Indians against persistent pressure from the encroaching haciendas and had defended their lands by prohibiting their alienation. The Indian was innocent of a price bargain, knew nothing of the meaning of a contract, and saw no virtue in a paper called a deed. The sudden removal of this protective legislation under the guise of good intent broke the legal restraint that had kept numerous Indian villages intact.

The enforcement of the law led to so much violence that the State was forced to modify it. But the damage had already been done. Under the Díaz dictatorship the way was opened for a systematic destruction of the village lands. The philosophers of the regime sought to convert Mexico into a modern industrial nation. They looked with envy at the growing population of the United States, and it occurred to them that what Mexico needed was large-scale immigration, which they hoped to get by colonization.

There were a number of difficulties in the path, however. One was the fact that the Mexican government never knew what land it owned, land titles being notoriously bad. They had always been bad. During the colonial period the Crown repeatedly ordered the revision of titles, never, it must be said, to any purpose except to make the smaller holdings less secure and to maintain the tradition that the State could at will deprive people of what seemed a good title and had been held for considerable periods. The theory persisted that large parts of the territory belonging to the Crown were held by people who had no title to them. In all such proceedings—and they were frequent—it turned out that the large property-owners who had friends, power, and prestige came off well. In their zeal to colonize the country, the advisers of Díaz turned to this ancient device to recover the lands belonging to the nation and to make them available to new settlers. To this end they assigned large areas to individuals by concession, giving them the power to exact a presentation of the original titles and to take back for the nation what was being held without a valid deed. But the poor *ranchero* had no title, or could not find it.

His claim was age-old occupancy by his family. This was even more true of the Indian. In the end this procedure turned into a general attack upon the holdings of the Indian communities.

This theory of a recovery of the national lands was influenced by another belief. The idea of "progress" had been affected by a perverted social Darwinism, which held that in the struggle for survival only the fit survive, and the Indian was assumed to be unfit. The Indian was described in official publications of the Department of Agriculture as *un lastre*, a burden upon the economy of the land. It was believed that he ought to be displaced, his communities destroyed. The sooner the Indian and his ways disappeared from off the face of the land, the better; for with so great a burden upon it the country would not "progress" and become a modern state. A systematic campaign to destroy the Indian communities, and with them the Indian too, it was hoped, was initiated. The fact that at the time the Indian represented more than half of the total population was considered evidence of the need for the change rather than an argument against the enormity of the undertaking or the social hazards it involved.

These political ideas led to the granting of concessions to favorites of Díaz to form *compañías deslinadoras* (surveying companies) under a law passed in 1883 and amplified in 1894. These favorites, usually Mexicans, generally transferred their rights to foreigners, and it thus came about that a small number of foreign companies had a free rein to roam the country and examine the titles of all property-owners in Mexico. The companies were allowed to retain one third of all the "national" lands they discovered, and to purchase the rest at a pittance. It is true that they were required to colonize the lands they acquired, but, as a matter of record, they rarely did so. What in effect occurred was the transfer of a large part of the territory of the nation to a few companies, most of them foreign, many of them American. By the end of the Díaz regime 72,-335,907 hectares (a hectare is equal to 2.47 acres), nearly a third of the Republic, had been surveyed. This was so great an upheaval in Mexican rural property that it has been called the New Conquest. Seventeen of the largest surveying companies acquired 38,382,923 hectares.

Many of the properties that later became objects of diplomatic controversy had their origin in these transactions. During this process the Indians of many villages were driven from their lands or saw themselves encased within the boundaries of some neighboring plantation that had long aspired to subject them to its rule. At the time of the Revolution there were haciendas that had as many as seventeen villages confined within their boundaries and subject to their will.

It has been estimated that in 1910 less than 3 per cent of the agricultural population owned any land at all. As late as 1923, thirteen years after the Revolution began, less than 2 per cent of the haciendas held 58.2 per cent of the area, and 110 of them owned 19.32 per cent of land in private hands. In some states the haciendas occupied over 90 per cent of all the privately owned land. The hacienda was the ruling influence.

In contrast to these great holdings, 59 per cent of all proprietors in Mexico had less than five hectares each. It is enough to note that of three per cent of the population who did have land at this time (for as we have noticed, the other 97 per cent were landless), the vast majority had not enough to make a bare living.

The Mexican Revolution cannot be understood without an insight into the irritation produced by the foreign ownership of land in the country. The Mexicans who wrote the Constitution of 1917 were under the impact of the Díaz policy in agrarian matters. They could not escape the fact that a very large part of the lands of the country had been permitted to fall into the hands of foreign companies. Holdings by foreigners were to be found in all parts of Mexico, and as late as 1923 they owned 20.1 per cent of the privately owned lands of the Republic, or 32,044,047 hectares, an extent equal to the combined areas of all the New England states, New York, and New Jersey. The foreign-held lands were chiefly in the sparsely populated states in the north and on the coasts, as, for instance, Chihuahua, where 42.7 per cent of the land was held by foreigners, and Nayarit, 41.9 per cent. In Mexico and Querétaro, two of the thickly populated states, foreigners held 16.1 and 14.0 per cent, respectively.

Americans owned by far the greatest proportion, 16,558,000 hectares, or 51.7 per cent of all foreign holdings. The Spaniards came next, with over 6,000,000 hectares, or 19.5 per cent; then the British with over 5,000,000 hectares, or 16.6 per cent; and the rest was scattered among others.

The hacienda system and the extensive foreign ownership set the problem that the Mexican Constitutional Convention of 1917 had in mind when it wrote Article 27. To appreciate the social milieu within which the Mexican Revolution was fought, we need still further description of the hacienda economy. In 1910 nearly one half of the total rural population resided within haciendas. Many others not on haciendas lived in villages near them and were tied to them by necessity. The hacienda communities were more numerous than the free villages, in 1910 there being 56,825 plantation communities and only 11.117 free agricultural villages. Nearly 82.0 per cent of the total rural communities were located upon haciendas in 1910. In other words, Mexico was a country of hacienda communities. The free villages, though larger in size, were fewer in number and concentrated in states where the population was dense and the hacienda of comparatively lesser importance.

We can now see why the hacienda was the preponderant institution in Mexico. It controlled more than half of all the land in private hands and contained within its boundaries approximately 50 per cent of all the rural population, and 82 per cent of all rural communities in the country.[1]

This institution laid a deadening hand upon the land. Born in conquest and nurtured on injustice, it gradually absorbed the living substance of a people, only to nourish pride and arrogance in its beneficiaries, permitting them to live idle lives in distant cities and to waste their inheritance with little sense of the human and cultural tragedy their career exemplified.

[1] As late as 1940 the census listed 5,069 hacienda communities, with a total population of 811,169 and an average population of 160.

They continued blind to the doom that lay in store for them and for the institution they exemplified, until their fate was upon them, and even then they could not believe that their day was done. It did not seem possible that something that had lasted so long and seemed eternal should suddenly and without warning pass away. And least expected was it that it should pass away at the hands of the very men who had served it as peons.

The owners are not to be blamed for their ignorance or for their lack of insight, or even for their lack of charity. They were their fathers' children, reared to play a grand role with hands of clay. For this hacienda, this all-embracing institution, was neither creative nor enterprising. It was constructed for security and not for progress—not even for increasing profit. Its owners, at least toward the end of the nineteenth century, left the management of the estates to hired administrators, mainly Spaniards, from whom they asked only a fixed income to be delivered in some distant city—the capital of the state, or Mexico City, or preferably Paris. The administrators shifted the burden of the plantation to subrenters, and these in turn to still others, who might in their turn sublease parts of their leasehold, until the poor *aparecero* or *mediero,* species of sharecroppers who supported the entire load, was barely able to eke out the poorest sort of subsistence, his food being maize, beans, and, with a special blessing, a few *chiles* (peppers). His wages, when he received them, had remained stationary. They were, in fact, a formal and nominal accounting rather than a payment in specie, and they had remained for over a hundred years at *dos reales* (25 centavos), or, in other areas, *tres reales* (37½ centavos). But the wages were nominal, paid in token coin if paid at all, or recorded as a kind of symbolic notation in the *tienda de raya,* the hacienda store, usually kept by a poor relation of the owner for the owner's profit. What the peon received in token coin he spent in this store, for there was no other, and the hacienda was so large that he could not trade anywhere else even if he wanted to. His token coin would not have been acceptable in any other place, and he was not permitted to leave the hacienda if he was in debt.

The relationship between the peon and the hacienda had, in time, and perhaps imperceptibly, become so organized that the *acasillado* (the worker living in the hacienda community) was in fact living on credit. He was living beyond his means even at his low level of subsistence, and the hacienda store carried him on its books for his whole life, and his children after him. Special advances for the recurrent cycles of birth, baptism, marriage, death, and the perennial saint's day were given in kind: a couple of bottles of strong drink (*aguardiente*), candles, sweets, firecrackers, and other items for decorative and exhibitionary purposes; for even a peon must have his day in the sight of his fellows, and tradition required that these be made possible through the good offices of the *patrón.* There was no other place to go and no other person to ask. The *patrón* was the father or godfather of his own people. From him all blessings came, from him favors could be asked with hat in hand, and from him protection could be expected. These folk huddled in little miserable huts about the big house of the hacienda, a castle built of stone, with narrow windows, and slits in the walls for defense against marauding bands or revolutions, guarded by armed men, and surrounded by a high wall with strong gates. It was not just a house; it was a fort. From this fort emanated the rule that governed the hacienda, and the hacienda might be and often was greater than a province in France.

The hacienda can be described as a social, political, or cultural institution. It is more difficult to describe it as an economic enterprise, for its economy was peculiar to itself. It had been inherited, but not purchased. It represented no investment by its current owners. It yielded an income, but not a profit. It paid few or no taxes. It expended as little as possible on its internal operations. The system of wage payments has already been indicated. Other expenses were similarly covered without the investment of ready cash. If the hacienda was large enough, differing areas would supply it with water for its own irrigation, with forests for its own construction, with pastures for its own herds of oxen, sheep, horses, and cattle. The hacienda would supply lime, sand, and stone, the mill would grind the flour, the small *trapiche* would provide the dark sugar and the *aguardiente* so important in the lives of the peons. The blacksmith, carpenter, mason, and woodcarver would, by ancient rote, do all the building. They would make the primitive tools, repair the wagons, provide the horsegear from saddle to bridle, and embellish, repair, and maintain the castle and its appurtenances with the minimum expenditure of money. Blankets were woven on the place, ropes were made from local fiber-growing plants, and clothes were homespun. Little came from the outside, and little was paid for in cash. If all of the work could not be done by the people on the hacienda, it was done by the neighboring or half-surrounded villages dependent upon the hacienda.

But these villagers supplied their labor in return, not for money, but for a piece of land to till: one day's work each week during the year for the right to plant a hectare, two days' work for two hectares. Thus if the plantation was large enough and had many villages, hundreds of laborers were available without cash outlay. These men often worked as sharecroppers. The owner provided the oxen, the tools, the seed, and the land, while the peon gave his own and his family's labor. The contract varied, but it was not on a cash basis, and the supplies offered by the hacienda had been raised and stored by these very men during the preceding year. The animals they had grazed, the horses they had broken, and the wagons they had built were now lent to them for the new season's work. In return the hacienda received a fourth, a third, a half of the yield from each little plot, depending upon the prevailing custom and the crop under consideration. The operation was by rote and a kind of local common law known to all concerned. The peons lived in a world of their own and considered themselves part of the hacienda. The owner was a beneficent or malevolent spirit, depending upon time, temper, and circumstance.

The church, if there was one, stood by the big house. A school, if there was one, was by the church. The hacienda had its own jail and stocks and administered a kind of rude and accepted justice traditional upon the place. All roads upon the hacienda led to the big house, and almost none led off it. The storehouses within the great wall were stocked from the yield of the lands and from the labors of the peons. They brought loads of corn or beans from the distant fields without any cost to the hacienda, and if the *hacendado* lived in the neighboring town, he was similarly supplied.

The hacienda also secured, without cost, domestic service for the big house and for the house in town. The *patrón*, if at all concerned with his princely holdings, would pay at least an annual visit to his hacienda, preferably on his saint's day. Then the entire populace would gather at the big house to do him honor and to receive in return such gratuities in *aguardiente* and sweets as the munificence of the owner or an ancient tradition sanctioned.

On its own account, the hacienda worked only the lands under irrigation or those in perennial crops, leaving the dry farming or the lands dependent upon the irregular rains of Mexico to the renters and sharecroppers. The accumulated surplus beyond the needs of the hacienda was carried to the nearest town or railroad in oxcarts, on the backs of mules, or on the backs of men, and sold. It was in this way that the ideal of security for the *hacendado* was achieved, but even this security was not fully realized, because the *hacendado's* family traditionally lived beyond its means.

Like their own peons, the *hacendados* spent their substance before they received it, and for very much the same kinds of luxuries and necessities, only at very much higher prices. And once mortgaged, the property could not be sold, for all of the possible heirs had to agree to the sale, and the *hacendado* never had the money to pay off the mortgage. If anything, the mortgage increased with each generation, and for this reason alone, if not for many others, the hacienda remained a routine economic organization.

It is no accident that Mexican agriculture remained stationary or declined. Fertility fell steadily all through the nineteenth century, prices of agricultural products increased greatly, and the hacienda system was saved from complete bankruptcy by a tariff on agricultural products, which squeezed the poor consumer and progressively reduced the real income of the rural population. It is one of those curious political phenomena which would not be believed if the facts did not stare one in the face. In a century of falling agricultural prices the world over, agricultural prices in Mexico were rising.

It was this institution and the economic and political milieu it created with which the Mexican Revolution grappled. That the Revolution should have been successful indicates weakness within the hacienda system, which proved incompetent to meet the changes wrought by a growing industrialism.

It must now be clear what the purpose of Article 27 was: to recover the land granted to large companies by concessions, to make it difficult for foreigners to acquire agricultural rural properties, to break up the hacienda system, to encourage the development of communities, to free the population from peonage, and to return to the villages the lands taken from them. But Article 27 contains a great deal more than what was dictated by a desire to break the hold of the hacienda upon the nation. These other elements are partly reminiscent of an old Spanish legal system, and partly responsive to the demand to fortify the State against its traditional enemies in Mexico: the hacienda, foreign influence, and the Church as a political power.

A review of the initial revolutionary aims and published legislation does not reveal, however, that what has since occurred was in the minds of the people who initiated the movement. The broader program has the appearance of an afterthought. Madero proposed a very mild program in regard to the land, speaking only of the restitution of lands to the small owners who had been deprived of the properties through the abuses of the laws regarding *baldíos* (uncultivated lands). Carranza, when he issued the decree of January 6, 1915, seemed to have no general land program. He, too, would merely return the lands taken by fraud or force from the village; and where a right to restitution could not be established, lands would be given to the villages by donation. But there was no general idea of reconstructing the landholding system in its entirety. In fact, there is some reason to believe that no one, not even the drafters of Article 27, had this objective clearly in view, and certainly the governments of the Revolution up to the time of Cárdenas (1934–40) resisted the growing pressure to make the law mean what it has since come to mean, the implicit destruction of private landholding in Mexico and the substitution of communal village ownership as a dominating, even if not an exclusive, pattern.

The purpose in the early years was to satisfy those villages which could prove titles to lands of which they had been deprived. The emphasis was upon restitution. The complicated legislation governing proof, the definition of the villages entitled to lands, the enumeration of the heads of the families in each village, and the need for establishing political category by the villages before they could benefit from the program implied a definite desire to confine the process within the narrowest limits. In addition, the Mexican courts took it upon themselves to review every step in the execution of the law and fostered endless litigation. Under the circumstances, it is no wonder that the Carranza government's record of land distribution is confined to the granting of lands to 213 villages between 1915 and 1920. In 1920 the next important step was taken by declaring that, if it was impossible to establish the right of restitution, outright donation could take place. The limitation regarding political category remained, however, and the majority of Mexican rural communities had no such political category. This limitation was finally removed in 1927.

By the end of 1926, lands had been granted to 1,892 villages. It was not till 1932, however, that the Mexican courts wrote a self-denying ordinance to the effect that the agrarian program was not subject to judicial review and was to proceed by administrative measures without right of appeal to the courts except for the purposes of evaluation and compensation. These changes opened the road to a greater measure of land distribution under later administrations, and by 1930 lands had been granted to 4,104 communities.

With all these changes there was still one great impediment in the law. It automatically excluded the *acasillados*—that is, the villagers confined within plantations—from the right to petition for lands. That this should have been so was a logical consequence of the original purpose of the program. It was not aimed at the destruction of the plantation. In fact, the theory was that the *ejidos* granted to the agricultural communities would supplement the income they derived from laboring on the neighboring haciendas. But actually, on the basis of the 1921 census, there were 46,391 resident hacienda communities excluded from the right to receive lands, and only 13,338 agricultural villages that under certain circumstances might be solicitors for land. Worse still, the free agricultural villages were preponderantly located in a few of the southern states, where the hacienda system was least developed. In other states where the vast majority of all rural communities had been absorbed into the hacienda system the agrarian program was to have the least effect. The fact is that in some of the states the vast majority of all the rural communities were located on haciendas, and the greater part of the rural population as well. In the rich agricultural state of Guanajuato there were 3,629 plantation communities and only 118 non-plantation agricultural villages, and the plantation communities contained 79.1 per cent of the total rural population. In contrast, in states such as Puebla, for instance, where the villages were preponderant and where the agrarian movement was having the greatest effect, the haciendas had less than 10 per cent of the rural population.

In fact, for historical reasons too complex to explain here, Mexico was divided into two rather sharply different areas in so far as the location of the rural population was concerned, and the agrarian movement was accentuating the division between these two areas, perpetuating the hacienda system with the *acasillado* in one part, mainly the center and the north, and creating semicommunal villages in the other part. If the agrarian program was not to have as its main result the development of two distinct and antagonistic Mexicos, it was essential to change the law so that the *acasillados* also had the right to receive lands. This was finally done by Cárdenas in 1935, after which the agrarian movement may be said to have taken on a national character rather than a regional one. As a result of all these changes in the law and the growing insistence for land by the villages, the movement was greatly speeded up under Cárdenas.

The conviction grew upon government personnel that the elimination of the hacienda as a system of agricultural organization was to be sought for the good of Mexico. By the end of 1945 land had been given to 20,179 communities. The number of peasants benefited by 1945 was 1,812,936, and the program has continued, even if at a slower pace, since 1945. It is clear that at least a third of the total population of Mexico has been thus benefited. The average grant of crop land per family is 4.6 hectares, and up to the end of 1945, 30,619,321 hectares had been allocated. By 1940 the *ejidatarios* were 51 per cent of the agricultural population and had 47 per cent of the crop land of Mexico.

A very large part of the best lands in Mexico has thus changed hands in the last thirty years, and the process is continuing. Among the more than 20,000 *ejidos* there are some 500 co-operative communities where the hacienda was expropriated as a unit, and is now being operated co-operatively. These are some of the largest *ejidos*, such as the Laguna region in the states of Coahuila and Durango and the Yaqui Valley in Sonora, located on the best lands and engaged in growing commercial crops.

The original theory, it must be clear, has broken down. What began as a minor land reform to satisfy a few needy and injured villages has become a profound agrarian revolution. A semicommunal land system, reminiscent of the older corporate ownership, has been established. The lands given to the communities cannot be sold, nor can any lien be placed against them.

The agrarian revolution has revealed a definite trend toward the substitution of semicommunal for private ownership of land as a dominant pattern for the nation. Large landholding has not entirely disappeared, and the hacienda in modified form still persists where the population is sparse, or where special presidential decrees have temporarily permitted its survival, particularly as cattle *ranchos.* But these large plantations live under the shadow of the Constitution, which authorizes their dismemberment. Legally the large hacienda has no standing. With the increase of the rural population, no large or medium-sized property is immune from dismemberment for *ejidos.* The law sanctions only two types of property in Mexico, the small holding and the *ejido.*

The small property had no defined area marked out for it in Article 27. The administrative and judicial agencies have at different times changed their minds as to its size. It was at one time defined by the courts to mean a property just large enough for one family to work by itself. Until recently the law defined the small property to be 150 hectares (just over 370 acres), but the pressure of the increasing population in the villages has made for constant pressure against the "small private holding." The conflicts between these small holdings and the *ejidos* are a constant source of friction, with their attendant violence; for it is a fact that these issues of landownership in Mexico, in spite of the law and because of the law, have in the last resort been settled by violence. In so far as the *ejido* has the protection of the State and is politically important, it is the stronger and more persistent institution and will in all probability win the battle by attrition.

The recent amendment to Article 27, defining the small property as 100 hectares of irrigated or 200 of temporal land, does not resolve the question. There is no likelihood of peace and quietude in the rural districts. It is doubtful whether two such types of economy, one semicommunal and the other private, can in the long run subsist together, either in the law or in practice.

There are, in fact, three different and insistent tendencies in the agrarian program. One of these is individualistic. The small property sanctioned by the Constitution has a long tradition among the independent *rancheros,* numerically small but important in the north.

In the northern states the population is predominantly *mestizo,* and the traditional pattern is individualistic. The *ejido* is not the typical pattern in these communities, and the recent irrigation projects that have been developed in the northern area have tended to take the form of individual holdings; so, too, have the titles granted to national lands under the decree of August 27, 1923. There is a measure of individual holdings in other states, and the small property sanctioned by the Constitution fits in with that pattern. Against this traditional individualist agricultural middle class, there is the equally old, or even older, tradition of communal village holding.

This communal village antedated the Conquest, persisted all through the colonial period, was strengthened in certain ways by Spanish colonial legislation, and is now sanctioned by the Constitution. But this communal organization has taken a new turn. The men who wrote the law of 1915, which is the original agrarian platform later embodied in Article 27, believed in individualism and wrote their program accordingly. Recognizing that it was the communities that were clamoring for land rather than the individuals within the communities, the law of 1915 decided that the lands should be given to the community in perpetuity, but that the tillable land was to be divided among the villagers. The result of the law, therefore, was that the village owned the waters, pasture, and woodlands, and operated them as a collectivity, but the tillable lands were to be allotted to individuals for private cultivation.

It must be remembered that these little holdings, from one to five hectares, are transmissible by inheritance, but are neither salable nor subject to any kind of lien, must be worked by their possessors themselves without depending upon hired labor, and revert back to the community if not tilled for two years in succession. In effect, however, this application of a modified individualism has created a new influence within the communities that may make collective utilization of credit, machinery, working gangs, and so forth difficult or impossible, and may make agricultural efficiency, implicit in certain kinds of co-operative farming, more difficult. The parcels ceded to each individual are simply not large enough to make possible an increasingly high standard of living upon an individualist basis, and reduce the possibility of securing the benefits of such efficiencies as are to be found in co-operative agriculture. The one-time economic plantations, operated as units, have thus, in many instances, been broken into petty fractions, with all of the dubious benefits of such a procedure.

This is not the only form of the *ejido*. Under the Cárdenas administration the agrarian law was reformed to permit the expropriation of entire plantations (excepting the small holding left to the owner, with the house, barns, and so forth) and the division of these into large collective units to be operated co-operatively. The areas chosen for this new type of *ejido* are few. They are good land, and are taken from properties where a great deal of capital has been invested in irrigation works, drainage, and wells. That is, the villages that received *ejidos* were given not merely land, but a very considerable previous investment in agricultural engineering. In some instances, they were also given partial use of the machinery needed to operate the lands, on the theory that the Constitution endowed the State with power to expropriate not merely the land but also the essential appurtenances that made the operation of land possible as well. This theory has been upheld by the courts. We thus have another influence in operation. The large co-operative is a community agricultural plant, with lands, tools, machinery, working animals, and labor under common management. Local committees representing the villages are part of the administration, and the State has usually contributed funds to the enterprise. These co-operatives have also developed other community ventures, such as hospitals, schools, and theaters.

It seems evident that the communal and co-operative tendency is the strongest, but not the only one in Mexico, and that for many generations the rural scene will show very diverse patterns. Where the population is small, individual landholdings, including the hacienda in some form, will survive to some extent; but where the older community is the persistent form of social organization and the lands are poor, and where the emphasis is upon subsistence agriculture, the *ejido,* semicollectivist, semi-individualist, will continue. In areas dependent upon commercial crops the co-operative, large *ejido* has been established and will survive.

The large *hacienda* has been outlawed; the agricultural corporation has been eliminated; the foreign owner of agricultural lands has, in law at least, been driven from the soil; the medium landholder is tolerated for the time being; the small landowner is accepted under the law, but is in theory and in practice on the defensive wherever the population of the village is increasing; and the *ejido,* semi-individualist or fully co-operative, has achieved the only sure sanction under the present agrarian legislation. Some years ago, in a conversation I had with General Calles about the direction of the Mexican agrarian program, he made the following significant remark: "In the past Mexico was divided into *latifundios,* with the big house (*casco*) in the center; in the future we will organize it around the village, with the school in the center." That was in 1933, long after Calles had acquired the reputation of being a reactionary. In some degree this is the present pattern of the land, and in some measure this is the change that has occurred in Mexico. I say "some measure" because the design is still unfolding.[2]

[2] The economic aspects of Mexican agrarian legislation, reform, and practice are discussed further in Chapter xi, pages 182–92.

CHAPTER 10

Education

SOME YEARS AGO Manuel Gamio, Mexico's distinguished anthropologist, published a volume of essays under the title *Forjando Patria—Forging a Nationality.* Nothing could better describe the objectives of Mexican education.

At the end of the Díaz regime only 2.9 million out of a population of 15.1 million were literate, and there were rural areas where no one could read. Of all Mexican projects in recent years, the creation of a national school system has been the most generous. Its most serious handicap lay in the sparse offering the city folk had to make to the rural people. Their ways were so far apart that it was difficult to find a basis for co-operation.

The new start in Mexican education dates from 1920. It was not until Obregón came to power in 1920 that a change occurred which, to the backward glance, gives the Mexican social upheaval seeming direction. Violence diminished. The armed bands under self-appointed generals declined, organized labor was encouraged, distribution of land to the villages was speeded, and the new direction of the Revolution was signalized in education by the appointment of José Vasconcelos as director of the Mexican National University.

Strongly influenced by Tolstoy, Vasconcelos was theoretically a pacifist and an equalitarian. He denied any difference between Indians and Europeans. He once said: "They all have souls, all human beings are equal. After all, that is the doctrine of Christ, and I am a Christian." Moreover, he was a "Latin-American" citizen, preaching against "imperialism." Mexico was to be the example of how to destroy tyrannies, of how to organize liberty, of how to develop the true spirit of the Latin-American nations. Within a few days after his appointment he announced that he had not come to assume the rectorship of the "monument of ruins" in order to cultivate foreign patterns. He came as "a delegate of the Revolution," to organize "a rapid, intense, and effective educational system for all of the sons of Mexico." It was not sufficient to teach French in the university while the city streets were crowded with abandoned and neglected children. To educate and protect the young was the government's first responsibility. To this end a Federal Department of Education would have to be established; he called on all to "bring their grain of sand" and assured them a role in the new enterprise. This was the beginning of a campaign that made out of education something of a new missionary movement in Mexico.

Education was broadly conceived: art and music were to be brought to the people. A popular chorus was organized, and, to prove that music knew nothing of caste or class, one was also started in the federal penitentiary, composed of "gentleman and lady prisoners" to serve the ends of "moralization." Night courses in choral mass singing as well as in instrumental music were established. The newer nationalism was made manifest by a visit to the Aztec ruins for the purpose of "feeling pride in belonging to a race capable of constructing monumental works whose like is found nowhere else in the world, with the possible exception of Egypt."

An active campaign against illiteracy was launched. "Honorary primary teachers" were enlisted, and anyone, "even the devil," who could read and write or show that he had passed "three primary grades" could join the company. The place was preferably the home of the teacher, and the time Sundays and holidays. The honorary teachers "can delicately and with proper circumspection also give advice about cleanliness and hygiene, food, and other essentials of a better life." These teachers were to fight the prejudice against "bathing during certain days or months of the year when the weather was not considered favorable," and to suggest that it ought to be done at least "every Saturday."

Hundreds of volunteers soon responded. Evening and Sunday classes were opened. As there was no time to await the building of schools, classes should be held in "patios, gardens, public squares, or on the street corners." The teacher must seek out the humble and illiterate folk. "What we need are not geniuses but workers." The campaign began to bear fruit in small unobtrusive ways. One man wrote that he was teaching the Indians on the slope of Ajusco Saturday afternoons and Sunday mornings, and that he had as pupils "two adults, seven boys, one woman, and six girls." The Railroad Dispatchers and Telegraphers, with their seventeen locals and fifteen hundred members scattered all over the country, volunteered as a body to serve as honorary teachers.

From Tejamen, Durango, came the news that a group of "honorary teachers" had formed an institute and now had fifty-four pupils. They were using "a sheet of zinc for a blackboard, the open air for a schoolhouse," and their classes were "flourishing with enthusiasm." The first impulse toward "incorporating the Indian" was evidenced at this time. In the little *ranchería* of Umeni, in the state of Hidalgo, some Otomí Indians were being taught the Spanish language, and it was "hoped that similar efforts would be initiated" for "incorporating the Indian masses, ignorant of the national language." One woman was "teaching the servant in her house," as that was the only person she could find at her "disposal."

The campaign evoked widespread interest. The editor of *Excelsior*, one of the conservative papers in Mexico City, described his surprise on visiting the "humble" districts of Tlaxcapan and Santa Julia to discover improvised schools in the homes of workers, "a multitude of little ones and laborers" receiving instruction, and people giving as much as four hours a day to teach the illiterate without compensation. He noted that in the Federal District alone there were 379 such improvised classes. The teachers were given some advice on reading-matter. The three great masters who ought to "inundate the Mexican spirit" were Benito Pérez Galdós, Romain Rolland, and Leo Tolstoy. All of their works ought to be read, those of the first because he is the "ultimate genius of our race," of the second because he gives "an explanation of our social problems," and of the third because he represents in modern times the nearest "incarnation of the spirit of Christ."

The National University took over the schools in the Federal District. This was the first step in the creation of a Federal Department of Education. The directors of the professional schools were elected by "all of those who had an interest in the schools." The National Conservatory and the School of "Arte Teatral" were united, and the Symphony Orchestra began giving regular public concerts. The School of Fine Arts was organized and the first open-air school was established. In addition, the first public libraries were being founded. The National Preparatory School was brought within the fold of the National University.

The campaign for the federalization of education was translated into law by Congress when it reformed the Constitution, providing for federal responsibility in education. Early in 1921, within a few days of the passage of this law, Obregón created the Department, and Vasconcelos became its first Secretary and a member of the Cabinet. The states and counties (*municipios*) were allowed to retain the schools that they then supported, and private schools were allowed to continue. The Department's activities were to be an addition to the existing school system of Mexico.

The project for federal education was drawn on a grand scale, for that was the tradition in program-making. "The rural schools, the primary and technical schools, will be developed even at the expense of the universities." In the future, education was to begin at the bottom. "If there be not money enough to establish rural schools, then the Department will send forth ambulatory teachers to preach the good news of the regeneration through work, and virtue to all the hamlets in the mountains." These "ambulatory teachers" later became the "missionary teachers" who gave the rural school its flavor of adventure, idealism, and play.

It is significant of this period that there is little talk of the community. The emphasis is upon instruction, upon improvement. The talk is about reaching the Indian and the poor, the isolated and the neglected. But we are still in a world where literacy in the older sense is the important thing to be stressed. The Mexican rural school, as we now know it, came later. The leadership for that new departure was to be developed by experience, and the newer rural school was to find its advocates in such men as Moisés Sáenz and Rafael Ramírez. The school is not enough. A country without books is a country without a culture. Libraries scattered over the country where all may have access to them must be a part of the program. A printing press, an editorial department, and a section of translations must all be incorporated into the Department of Education if it would "awaken a people that has lain dormant and subject to the outsider, even in the things of the spirit."

In addition, no culture can be developed that does not provide adequate support for art, hence the Department must have a section of fine arts, not to supervise and judge the artists —"The State cannot judge the work of the artist. No one can judge his work except himself." But the State can encourage him. Such encouragement "will exalt the national spirit." That was the beginning of the fever for covering the walls of Mexican public buildings with murals. Diego Rivera, José Clemente Orozco, David Alfaro Siqueiros, and many others responded, and spread the fame of Mexico abroad.

Education became free, secular, and compulsory up to the age of fourteen. A clear distinction was drawn between rural and primary urban schools, and special schools for Indians were authorized. In reporting to Congress at the end of his first year in office, Obregón was able to describe an unexpected advance during so short a time. Within the year, twenty-five model schools had been established, as well as twenty-two night schools and a commercial school, and a large number of private schools were receiving federal aid; 20,000 books had been distributed and small libraries had been founded in 198 different places. There were still available about 20,000 books for further distribution. A summer school for foreigners had been created. School breakfasts for the poorer children were provided, 8,000 a day being served at a cost of about 9,000 pesos a month. A million copies of a primary reader were being printed, of which 100,000 had already been issued. The federal budget for education, including both university and primary education, increased from 4,000,000 pesos, to 15,000,000, including the expenditures in the Federal District.

In January 1921 the government printing offices were placed under the Department of Education, and the classics were printed in sufficient number to make their general dissemination possible. Among the books published and scattered at a price of fifty centavos each were works of Homer, Sophocles, Euripides, Plato, Plutarch, Plutonius, Dante, Shakespeare, Lope de Vega, Calderón, Tolstoy, Romain Rolland, Bernard Shaw, and Ibsen, a rich offering at government expense for an illiterate folk.

The direction of a movement so broadly conceived is often unpredictable. It was not the printing of the classics, the organization of the choral societies, or even the literacy campaign in the urban communities that was to provide the impulse for the significant educational development of contemporary Mexico. It was the "ambulatory" missionary to the rural villages who was to become the inspiration of a new departure in rural education that has since given Mexico its distinctive role in modern education, a role that has influenced countries with similar problems in other parts of the world. The missionary soon discovered that he was the only representative of modern civilization in the rural community. If the wide gap between the urban and the rural was to be bridged, he had to bridge it. He had to be all things to all men. He had to bring to the rural community the medicine, the law, the hygiene, the science, the skills, the tools, the literacy, the very notion of education, for the rural villages lacked everything—a school, a playground, a library, a doctor, an agronomist, an architect, a book, a newspaper, and in many instances even the Spanish language. If the missionary was to carry on, he had to do so himself, with what courage, initiative, and imagination nature had endowed him. He could get little help from the Federal Department of Education. That was far away and too much absorbed in doing the thousand seemingly necessary things Mexico City approved and asked for, including open-air concerts and mural painting.

Here in a world that was primitive and isolated, with the folk scratching for a living in a difficult soil with primitive tools, and steeped in an ancient and non-literary tradition, education, if it was to mean anything at all, must in some way become identified with the life of the community as it was. Here there were no individuals, there was no personal ambition, and no place for it. There was only a community in which all of the people were equally poor and equally illiterate. If education was to be fruitful, it had to be for the community, old and young. It must be immediately useful to them or it would not be useful at all.

The interesting thing to relate is that the "missionaries" discovered that fact and put their energies to dealing with it. They turned to making a "people's house" for the village and not just for the children. They had at their disposal neither money nor equipment, and little preparation. Their first task was to convert the village elders to the purpose they had in coming, and, with that accomplished, to design a school and build it, as they did in thousands of cases, with the aid of the community. The men, women, and children gathered the stones, dug the foundation, and constructed the walls. It was their house. With the school built, they had to gather the funds for windows or doors—perhaps by selling a pig or two—and then to make the furniture for the school, sometimes only stumps of trees or benches made of clay; and with that done, to lay out a garden for the school, and a play yard for the children. After that they would purchase a lamp for the night school, then construct a shower bath in the schoolyard, perhaps only a tin can with holes in it, from which one boy on a ladder would pour water while another was taking a shower. The school was to be the community house, and it might need a kitchen, a sewing-machine, a barber's chair, and a first-aid kit; the children would bring a pig, rabbits, and chickens. The teacher had to serve every office from scribe to medicine man, from agronomist to architect. He had to know everything, for no one else had any contact with the modern world.

The school program had no design or tradition to follow. It was experimental. If it had any purpose, it was to enrich the life of the community by the fullest utilization of its local resources, for it had no others. The interesting fact remains that this planless plan worked. The missionaries in some way managed to bring the community into focus, group its activities about the school, and make the school the very heart of the village.

In 1922 the missionaries held a meeting in Mexico City and told of their experiences, exchanged what knowledge and insight they had gathered, and set about to spread the endeavor through the land. By the end of 1924 more than a thousand such schools were in existence, all constructed by the communities themselves, and they had 65,000 pupils. The Federal Department of Education encouraged the effort, but it did little more. It could really do little more. Its resources were not great enough for the needs it had to meet, and even if they had been greater, the Federal Department had little to give to this new development. It was something that it stimulated but had not designed. It just grew. The trained teachers in the city schools, the product of the Mexico City normal schools, were not fitted for this kind of task, could not carry it out, and would have been out of place even if they had been willing to undergo the hardships, the isolation, and the poverty of the rural community.

The Federal Department of Education paid the teacher one peso a day and sometimes provided him with a blackboard and a few pieces of chalk. The scanty reading-matter it had to offer was of little use, and the advice it gave was of even less import. The teachers had to be improvised, and once they were installed, a way had to be found to inspire them and to increase their competencies. The community activities gradually grew into a kind of program. The aim came to be to improve the community. If it lacked water, teach it to dig a well, pipe water from a distance, or purify the water it took out of a hole in the ground that during the dry season was covered with dust and in which the pigs, cows, and burros drank and waded. The teacher was perforce the only person who could inoculate against typhoid or vaccinate against smallpox. If the community wanted land, he was the only one who could write to the Agrarian Department in its behalf. Improve the community, awaken it, make it serve its best ends with such means as could be garnered from the immediate resources. The community itself became organized about the school, and various committees came into being to carry out the purpose of the communities as they developed.

The great need, however, was for improving the teachers, and there was no rural normal school competent to the task. There was no experience for the kind of instruction that these teachers required. The older experience of the rural missionary suggested the organization of traveling "cultural missions." The early missionaries were formally organized into a corps of federal rural school inspectors in 1925. A kind of formal inspection and reporting was coming into being, and the teachers gathered and trained were perhaps not possessed of more than three years of elementary schooling. It was with this inadequately trained personnel that the task had to be carried out; to improve the teacher became a prime consideration.

One must always remember the complexity of the Mexican rural scene, its poverty, its lack of resources, and its isolation from those influences which fill the urban world. If the educational program was to retain vitality, the rural teacher had to be trained within his rural environment and yet be given those things that the urban culture had to offer which were acceptable to and could be accepted by the rural districts. The first cultural mission was organized in the fall of 1923 under the leadership of Rafael Ramírez, later to become the head of the rural school system, and to whom Mexican rural education owes a great deal more than it has ever acknowledged. The first cultural mission was held in Sacualtipan, Hidalgo, and included an instructor in soap-making, tanning, health, physical education, agriculture, and music. The second was organized in 1924 and contained on its staff a soap-maker, a tanner, two agronomists, a carpenter, and a domestic-science teacher. By the end of 1924 there were six cultural missions in operation, and by 1926 a regular division of the Department of Education was created to look after the cultural missions, which had by that time become a recognized activity of the Federal Department of Education. By the end of 1935 the Republic had been divided into eighteen zones, with a definite cultural mission in each zone, and in that year 75 institutes were held under the direction of these missions, attended by nearly 4,500 rural teachers from twenty states.

As finally developed, these missions became traveling normal schools devoted to improving both the quality of the teaching and the way of life of the communities reached. They came to include a chief of mission who devoted his energies to improving such rural agencies as marketing co-operatives, an agronomist giving his attention to agricultural practices, a woman social worker concerned with the life and health of the home, a nurse trained as a midwife, a music teacher who encouraged the local popular music and folk dances and organized community bands. A teacher of the plastic arts was also included. This personnel varied with time and place as need required.

A cultural mission settled in some community for a period of from three to eight weeks and gathered together all of the teachers in the neighboring region, sometimes as many as a hundred. Once organized and acquainted with the community, it set up a model school where all the activities that the teacher is expected to carry out, each in his own town, were developed. A water system was constructed. The town was cleaned up, a system of physical instruction was gone through, new ways of agriculture were taught, a model schoolhouse was built, simple medical practices were taught. The community was encouraged to participate and share in the activities. Choral singing and dances were organized; domestic science, dressmaking, cooking, and personal hygiene were taught; and, not to be overlooked, the best ways of teaching reading, writing, and arithmetic were practiced. The entire point of the discussion will be missed if it is not clear that the school was designed as an agency for the reconstruction of the rural community, and that the cultural mission was merely a means for bringing together the experience of the teachers in the rural communities and exchanging among themselves the lessons of their own experience, and for picking up what the "experts" had to add to the sum of their knowledge. The school was for the community; in a sense it was the community itself.

The cultural missions were abolished in 1938, only to be reestablished in 1942. They now remain in the same community from one to three years and place their emphasis upon the more permanent reconstruction of the specific town in which they are located. The training of teachers has been surrendered to the rural normal schools. The program of the new missions is substantially the same as that of the older ones, except that the locality receives a more effective stimulus toward new ways of life. In 1945 there were thirty-seven of these semipermanent missions in the rural districts and four in urban communities.

The older cultural mission left largely unsolved the problem of training new teachers for the rural schools. The schools were growing with great rapidity; there were over six thousand by 1929, and the training of new teachers for the expanding system still had to be met. Still more acute was the need for special teachers for the Indian population. Even in 1925, however, Mexico City was skeptical of the possibility of educating the Mexican Indian. The Indian, it was held, could not be civilized. This belief was so strongly held that Calles in 1925 felt it necessary to set up a special school of Indian education in the very heart of Mexico City to establish finally the point that even the pure, most primitive Indians were capable of being "civilized."

The "House for the Indigenous Student," established in Mexico City at the end of 1925, was to prove that. It was to bring to Mexico City the most primitive students, taken from the mountains and forests: Huicholes, Lacandones, Otomís, Yaquis, Chamulas, Coras, Mayos, students from all of the tribes in Mexico. It was to bring them to the city from their native pueblos in their native attire, barefooted, Huicholes dressed in their feathers, or Lacandones in their long shirts, or Tarahumaras with nothing but a loincloth, speaking their own languages, not understanding one another's, never having seen a city, never having slept in a bed, never having eaten with a spoon or read a book or seen an electric light. It was going to take these children of nature and immerse them suddenly in the caldron of a sophisticated world and prove to the incredulous and contemptuous that the quality of the Indian was good. The Indian was to prove his adaptability to civilization by becoming civilized. He was to prove that he could learn the external marks of city life: the clothes, the haircut, the shoes, the eating with a knife and spoon and fork, the learning to read and write and listen to a radio. In fact, the Indian boys who were brought to this school proved it so well that they beat the city boys at their own literary exercises and were declared good students.

The school demonstrated the obvious: that there is no reason for assuming an innate differential in basic abilities between the Indian and the city dwellers. It was so successful a demonstration that even the scoffers and the skeptics were satisfied. The Indian was proved as good as his white and semiwhite compeer who wore a stiff collar and went to the movies. But its very success was its failure. It succeeded so well that the students, after being "civilized," preferred to remain so, as scholars and mechanics, as clerks and bartenders in the city where the great experiment had been carried out. They had been so successfully torn from their own culture that they acquired a contempt for it and preferred to be "successful" at menial levels in the city. The demonstration proved that it would be easy to dislocate the country folk completely, even the most primitive ones, and in a very short time spoil them for anything but a poor and meager city life. These newly civilized "Mexicans," with modern clothes and the Spanish tongue, were not distinguishable from the others and had so well learned to love the movies and the lighted streets, the soft beds and the clang of the streetcars, the bull fights and the jazz, that they refused to return to their villages or, if they returned, proved to be out of place and a disintegrating influence. The problem of converting a static rural civilization into a creative one was no farther advanced than before. The school had proved its point, but it was only the ignorant and prejudiced who required a demonstration that was known to the rest. Only Mexico City needed to be convinced, and, at the cost of uprooting and spoiling some few hundred young Indians, that was achieved.

A consciousness of their initial failure dawned upon the educational authorities, and the school was given a new purpose. It was to be made into a rural training center. To it were to be brought students from all parts of Mexico. As of old, the students were to come from primitive Indian groups, to be trained as rural teachers, and to return to their villages as leaders and educators. A few years again proved the obvious: that rural teachers can be trained only in a rural environment, and that the gap created by the removal of young people from a primitive community to a modern and highly sophisticated one is so great that it defeats the purpose of trying to make them into rural leaders. Rural teachers must be trained in the environments in which they have lived and must continue to live. Teacher-training must be in terms of the culture pattern of the total environment within which it will continue to function, undisturbed by removal and immersion in a sudden sophistication that will make later adequate functioning impossible. The way to produce a rural teacher is to make a rural person more competent within the mores of his group, rather than to make him self-conscious and possibly contemptuous of his mores.

In 1932 the fact was at last realized that the school had failed, and it was abolished. Its high budget was given over to the creation of ten centers of indigenous education in the indigenous centers themselves.

This lesson merely reinforced what had already been learned from the earlier experience of the rural school. The best teachers came from those close to the rural environment. If rural teachers were to be trained for the expanding school program, they would have to be selected from the local regions where their activities were destined to be focused. They must be kept as close to their own mores as possible. Local tradition, custom, food, and ways of life must be improved; there are no substitutes for them. The teacher must be able to do the things that are traditionally done, but better than they are being done. He can be a carrier of the newer elements only if he can adapt them to the older ones, and to do that he must be part of the older tradition.

That was a great lesson in education, and it required great insight and experience to learn it. The experience of the missionary and the cultural mission had provided the basis for this lesson; but, even so, the lesson was hard. Under Calles an attempt was made to establish well-furnished modern agricultural schools. Six of them were actually set up and fitted out with a program that made them too good for their purpose. Like the school of the indigenous student, the agricultural schools were expensive. They educated agriculturists too sophisticated for their own primitive environment. The attempt to copy American agricultural schools, with all their modern methods, tractors, high-powered machinery, blooded cattle, and expensive equipment, broke down. The rural primitive Mexican peasant working his few hectares could not adapt himself to so sudden a change, even assuming that it was economically a feasible project, which is to be doubted.

These agricultural schools, too, were finally reorganized and identified with the rural normal schools, which have since become the regional rural schools that train for both agriculture and teaching at a level fitting the needs of the rural environment. They are larger, better-equipped, better-staffed rural schools, training the personnel to serve in the smaller ones, and also providing a means by which the more competent children in the rural districts can begin their professional education in agriculture. By 1944 there were nineteen rural normal schools, seventeen schools for agriculture, and twenty-three special schools for the training of children from Indian groups. These attempt to meet the need for rural teachers and for special agricultural vocational training. There are also three agricultural colleges. The effort has been a great one, and the achievement notable.

The rural school is an acceptance of Mexican reality. It has surrendered the quixotic notion of attempting to pattern Mexico upon European models or to make out of the Indian and the *mestizo*, with his peculiar heritage, his parochial ambitions, his limited economic opportunities, his half-mystical, half-mythological faith, his peculiar identification with the community, a modern individualist bent upon personal achievement and personal success. It required courage and a measure of intellectual frustration to do that. The school must be practical; that is, if it is to have any value, it must leave behind it a usable residue in habit and knowledge. By the same token, the school must be for the entire community. There is not that distinction between the elders and the children which is characteristic of an urban sophisticated world. In the rural community all of the people share a common fund of knowledge and experience, and the children become participants in this common fund at a very early date and participate in it for the rest of their lives.

The school has no way of suddenly changing the environment. If the school is to be useful, it must accept limitations and build upon them. It must define as its purpose the development of the good life within the particular environment, with the available resources, for the purpose of making the fullest use of what can be made useful in the very place where the community is located. It has no alternative and can have no other plan. It is the discovery of this limitation upon rural education and the acceptance of it, not as a defeat but as a challenge, that makes the Mexican rural school the unique institution it is. Its objectives are limited to the community, but its efforts are infinitely variable, and its possibilities as flexible as the physical and human materials with which it has to work. In that sense the Mexican rural school is not merely creative, it is also practical, in some measure the most "practical" endeavor derived from the Revolution. Mexico in its school system and in its philosophy of education has developed something that has meaning far beyond its own borders.

More than that, the endeavor represents the acceptance of the fact that a native Mexican culture can be derived only from Mexican reality. That recognition is evidence of native wisdom and realism. The rural federal schools have grown to approximately 14,000, and in 1947 there were more than 20,000 primary schools of various types in the country. Illiteracy had been greatly reduced since 1910, and the number of children in primary schools in 1944 was well over 2,000,000, though school attendance fell far short of registration, and 71.3 per cent of the pupils reached only the second grade. The federal school budget had risen from 8 million pesos in 1910 to 262.7 million pesos in 1948.

Striking as is the achievement, the task remains unfinished and must remain so for many years to come. In 1940, of the 19.6 million people accounted for by the census, only 6.8 million could read and write, and 51.6 per cent of those over ten years of age were illiterate. Of the 6.9 million literate people, only 1.6 million had attended school to the fourth grade, and, all together, only 2.8 million had actually gone to school. The interesting fact remains that 3.5 million, or more than half of those who could read and write, had not gone to school. There are at present some 120,000 rural communities in Mexico. The 16,467 schools are located in the larger ones. Most of the country villages are small, and to fulfill the promise of educating all the people, the country needs at least 50,000 rural schools served by 100,000 teachers. It does not have them. The crying need for expanding the influence of the Mexican rural school, both in number of schools and in years of attendance, will remain unanswered for years, perhaps for generations. It is part of the basic tragedy of Mexico, poverty. While the illiterates of ten years or over equaled 7.2 million in 1930, they mounted to 7.5 million in 1940. The growth in the population had outstripped the educational effort.

When one turns from the creative endeavor of the rural school to urban education, one goes from one world to another. It has proved difficult to break with the formal and routine tradition. It would be inaccurate to say that no new influences have crept in, but it would be misleading to suggest that real modernization in urban education has occurred, though the influence of such conspicuous educational leaders as Jaime Torres Bodet has made a strong impression on the primary schools in the urban centers. The formal unification of the urban and rural schools under a common primary-school program may mean an easier accommodation of the urban schools to the creative impulses of the rural school, but it is still too early to tell.

What is true of the urban primary school is true of the secondary school, the normal school, the National University, and the six regional universities in Mexico. They are poorly equipped and understaffed. Their teachers, with a few exceptions, have to make their living working at other tasks. Their libraries are poor, their scientific laboratories are even poorer.

The resources at their disposal are meager, and politics—both faculty and student politics—have greatly disturbed the academic peace so essential to good scholarship and good teaching. The happy idea of university autonomy and student participation has not worked to the scientific or scholarly improvement of these institutions. The students are too much preoccupied with university politics and too easily manipulated by university and outside politicians to devote themselves fully to their work. Student disturbances and riots have marked the coming and going of university rectors.

These are hard words, but the best friends of Mexico, and the Mexicans themselves, are concerned about the present role of the university in Mexican intellectual development. Fortunately, two recent institutional developments are of very real promise. The Polytechnical School, under the Department of Education, was established and designed to do what the universities should be doing in scientific education, and has shown great promise. But the Department of Education is not immune to politics, and every new Secretary of Education may presage a change, and often has done so both in the program and in the moral atmosphere of this very useful new establishment. Of greater, perhaps of greatest, significance is the Colegio de Mexico, a graduate school not under governmental auspices, staffed by competent scholars and teachers, with a sense of academic values and traditions. It is in this school, small and poor as it is, that there is the best hope of a revival of the older scholarly tradition of Mexican higher educational institutions.

This is not the complete story of Mexican education in full detail. One would have to add that there are over 1,500 public libraries, 33 museums, a number of open-air art schools, night classes for workers, a workers' university, 273 secondary schools, and a school of tropical medicine, an important movement in Indian linguistics, and an excellent school of anthropology. A number of academic journals are published regularly, and the publication of all manner of books has greatly increased, especially stimulated by the recent Spanish immigrants and the important Fondo de Cultura Económica, which has become one of the great publishing houses in Latin America. Of some significance, too, is the popular movement for *alfabetización* (abolishing illiteracy), initiated and encouraged by President Ávila Camacho. In spite of all these movements, however, the hope of educating the mass of the people is still far from an accomplished fact, and the rural school is still the most interesting educational achievement of Mexico.

The Conditions of Economic Progress: I

1. The Parochial versus the National Market

For the Mexicans the primary problem bred by the Revolution is how to escape from the dilemma of a nation divided between those who live in a modern world and those who live in a primitive world. It has become clear to them that this hiatus impedes both the economic and the cultural unity of the nation. As matters stand at present, a large part of the people of the country are beyond the reach of the benefits derived from modern science, and the perplexity lies in the fact that the task so clearly seen appears greater than the competencies and the resources of the nation. In the cities modern ways of life, technology, and industry have greatly changed the older pattern. The people have electric lights, sanitation, public-health services, schools, universities, department stores, automobiles, railroads, books, newspapers, imported luxuries, fashionable clothes. All the sophistications from Freud to Einstein are to them an inherent part of the way of life. Away from Mexico City and a very few other urban centers, however, even only a few miles away, all of these seeming essentials to the good life are nonexistent and most of the people are steeped in a primitive routine that even the Revolution has but slightly altered.

In fact, for the rural folk the economy represents an ancient design upon which modern innovations have made little impression. Most of the people live much as they did at the time of the Conquest; they use primitive tools, till the soil in a manner little changed in hundreds of years, grow corn as they always have, live in adobe or reed huts without windows, furniture, or covered flooring, and subsist on the rim of the modern world.

Mexico is therefore divided internally between the modern and the primitive, and the cleavage is deeper than that between the urban and the rural. The sense of value seems to be different, and what the urban community has to offer lies beyond the ken of the rural folk and may prove unacceptable to them. The impulse to improve the living standard of the folk who live at the primitive level is the projection of a new economic and social revolution. What the leaders are trying to do is to make all of Mexico into a modern community embraced within a national market, and to do it under the handicaps of poor resources, a parochial economy, ancient traditions, and inadequate training. We must always remember that Mexico is a poor country, comparable to the Balkans or to India, and that the poverty is not merely in material goods. It lacks the skills and habits of modern industry, and its thousands of isolated little communities are too small and scattered to be easily fitted into any government program.

In 1929 the average annual income per inhabitant equaled 123 pesos, or 34 centavos per day—in American money then approximately 17 cents. While the national income has since increased, the value of the peso has declined and the population has expanded. Real income has probably only kept pace with the increase in population. In 1940 the average annual income per inhabitant was estimated at 340 pesos, but the purchasing value of the Mexican peso had declined by 77 per cent since 1930.

These details are descriptive of Mexico as a whole. If the present generation is to bridge the gap between the primitive and the modern way of life, it must face the still greater relative poverty of the rural population: unless it can raise the level of the rural folk it cannot hope to bring either economic or cultural unity to the nation.

Most of the little villages scattered over the width and length of the land have mainly a non-pecuniary economy and remain almost completely outside the national market. The villagers raise their own food, build their own houses, construct the little furniture they use, in many instances make or weave their own clothes, and satisfy the few needs that they cannot provide for within their own village in the parochial market from products made in neighboring towns. The modern national market has little inner connection with the parochial one. The task the reformers have in hand is to make this parochial economy a part of the whole and to give to the rural folk the wherewithal to purchase those essentials of the good life which modern industry makes available through a national market. The difficulties are innumerable.

The average daily money income of those employed in farming is about one sixth of that earned by those employed in non-farming occupations. In the 1930's those employed in agriculture had a cash income of 0.43 centavos as against the average of 2.60 pesos per day from non-agricultural employment. This relative poverty is reflected in a thousand different ways. The 1940 census showed that more than 2.4 million houses, or 70.2 per cent of the total number, sheltering 11.1 million residents, mostly in the rural districts, lacked running water and sanitation. The vast majority of these were built of adobe, reeds, or planks, had one or two compartments, and were occupied by an average of 5.11 persons, or 2.57 persons per room. We have already noted that most of the people live on *tortillas,* beans, and chile, drink little milk, and eat but little meat. Between 1934 and 1943 the average annual consumption of meat per person, if the statistics can be trusted, varied between 8.3 kilos (about eighteen pounds) in 1937, the highest, and 4.8 kilos (about ten and one half pounds) in 1943, the lowest. Mexico City, with 9 per cent of the population, used 38 per cent of the meat slaughtered in the country. Of the total population, five million go barefooted, four and a half million wear sandals, four million sleep on the floor, and two million sleep on mats.

The rural population (64.9 per cent of the total) is estimated to have produced about 30 per cent of the national income in 1929 and only 17 per cent in 1943. Because of the relative increase of industrial production, nearly two thirds of the Mexican people must therefore divide among themselves approximately one sixth of the national income. This poverty is an impediment to any attempt to industrialize Mexico.

The peasant of Chiapas does not spend for the purchase of manufactured products more than two or three pesos a year, of which only one is expended upon foreign goods. He buys nothing from the national market. From the foreign manufacturer he gets his ax, machete, and needles; from local trade he purchases his salt and occasional coffee, tobacco, firecrackers, and candles. All of the rest he produces or acquires by barter. Many other Mexican groups live at comparable levels of income. In many places they still burn down the forests, make holes in the ground with a pointed stick, and use a hoe for hilling up cornstalks. Many farmers have no plows and leave the land to rest for six or seven years to recoup its fertility after one or more crops.

The 175,000 palm-hat weavers in the Alta Mixteca, representing a population of 425,000 people, occupying parts of the states of Puebla, Oaxaca, and Guerrero, earned 16 centavos for a ten-hour day in 1939, when a kilo (2.2 pounds) of corn was worth 12 centavos in the local markets. In 1944, by government intervention in both the purchasing and the marketing of their products, their daily wages were raised to around 40 centavos. A study in 1938 showed that the average daily expenditure for food of fourteen different Indian groups was only 26 centavos. Even in the Tarascan country, in the very heart of Mexico, in villages crossed by the Pan American Highway, wages in 1940–1 were between 40 and 45 centavos per day during the harvesting season, with the right to glean and in some instances with a midday meal.

It is difficult to translate the real income of the rural population into money terms. In addition to agriculture the average villager often has other occupations: weaving of hats or blankets, the making of hammocks, the manufacture of firecrackers, of pottery, or the hundred local specialties in different villages. These, however, are subsidiary to agriculture. Much of the agricultural production remains outside the money economy, and even the non-agricultural products are usually bartered or exchanged in neighboring markets. In the village of Atzumpa in Oaxaca, for instance, every family is engaged in the manufacture of earthenware. The people bring in the clay on Monday, form the pots on Tuesday, bake them on Wednesday, prepare the coloring and paint them on Thursday, rebake them on Friday, carry them to market on their backs on Saturday, and rest on Sunday. The next Monday the cycle starts all over again. Every family also has a piece of land that it tills, owns a house, has an animal or two and a couple of fruit trees, and uses the little money income from the sale of pots for the purchase of articles made chiefly in the neighboring villages. Few things indeed come in from beyond the immediate neighborhood.

The parochial market will attract traders from long distances. The *arrieros* drive their mules or burros laden with goods, fruits, and vegetables for days, or even weeks, over narrow trails, going from one village market to another, bringing products from distant places and different climates. The market in one of the towns in Michoacán was found to have venders from about twenty different communities. At this market the following items were offered for sale: sweet water, avocados, rings, garlic, earrings, ropes, embroidery, broth, cooked sweet potatoes, onions, cherries, baskets, apricots, peppers, cabbages, cauliflower, candy, peaches, palm leaves, beans, guitars, broad beans, cooked green corn, figs, woven sacks, roots, lettuce, sweet lemons, pottery, cloth, aprons, apples, crab apples, beads, furniture, oranges, nuts, bread, cake, potatoes, straw raincoats, pears, dried fish, bananas, cheese, shawls, blankets, sarapes, citrus fruit, grapefruit, seeds, straw hats, tomatoes, prickly pears, long nuts, violins, herbs, mint, and shoes. This market had 138 venders. All of the products originated in the various localities represented in the market. They were part of a local parochial economy and had little bearing upon the behavior of the national market. This example could be multiplied by the hundreds.

There are some items locally produced that find their way out into the large world, but they are few, depending upon the particular village resources. Palm hats made in the Mixteca and the blankets from Oaxaca are sold in many parts of Mexico. Charcoal and railroad ties prepared individually by peasants, wheat and corn sold from their surplus by little farmers, may also reach the national market. But the mass of the rural population is almost outside the "economy" of the nation. This is suggested by the typical items available in stores of the larger communities, those of four thousand or over in central Mexico. These include in addition to the locally produced goods: salt, sugar, chocolate, rice, lard, coffee, soap, spaghetti, cigarettes, candies, paraffin, canned chile, vegetable oil, olive oil, creosole, wax matches, soda, soap, orange drink, spool thread, hats, mats, India silk, blue jeans, brooms, ribbons, muslin cloth, brocades, material for shirts, and flat silk, but it is clear that even some of these are regional products.

It need only be added that the possessions of the individual peasant reflect this same economic isolation. Few of the things in the rural household come from the outside: the iron tools already mentioned, the sewing-machine, and the likeness of the saint. The rest are locally made or purchased in the neighboring market. The possessions of a family will vary from community to community, and from climatic area to climatic area, but the following are typical enough: sleeping-mats, a small table, a couple of chairs or stools, sarapes worn by men during the day and used as blankets for man and wife at night, a chest for extra clothes, saints' pictures, candles, candle-holder, flower-holder, ladder, and crossbeam for hanger. The kitchen will contain a wooden hook to hang things on, a stump and flat stone for burning pitch pine, cornhusk mats for holding pots, pottery pans for frying, several round or oblong wooden bowls, a grass-root brush, a strainer, cane baskets, pottery jars, a broom, a paring knife, bowls for serving broth, a charcoal-burning flatiron, gourd containers, china plates, cups, and bowls, a teapot, wooden spoons, a tin can for water, a chocolate-beater, a *tortilla* basket, a pitcher, two-handled pots, a clay fireplace, a firepan, a metate for grinding corn, a table, small chairs, a machete, and occasionally a few forks, a table knife, and even a can-opener. The yard will have a smooth rock and a wooden paddle for washing clothes, a hollowed log for feeding pigs, a wooden pitchfork, a wooden hook, a carrying crate, a clay oven, and a hoe.

This assortment of movable possessions, varying as it does from household to household and from climate to climate, still reflects the relative independence of the family from purchased goods manufactured in the larger cities. The real and money income of the rural population, it must by now be clear, is locally conditioned. What we have, in fact, is a description of thousands of little agricultural communities, containing the larger part of the Mexican population, which at their own level of income have struck a kind of balance between the "state of the arts," the local resources, and the local population. Embracing these microscopic bits of society, each in its little place, is a whole culture peculiarly identified with every separate community or group of communities. The peculiar culture of "the place" includes family and marriage customs, local government, special social hierarchies, feast days, church and religious organization, custom, belief, superstition and taboo, particular arts, songs, dances, and music. So it has always been. The balance of births and deaths had kept the population from growing too rapidly and placing too great a strain on the local resources and the local organization. This equilibrium between the "state of arts," nature, and man was first upset by the incipient industrialism and "progress" of the Díaz regime, with its railroads, ports, and textile factories.

From one point of view the Revolution of the last generation was a violent reaction against the disruption of an ancient equilibrium.

The effort to re-create a stable world once more by fostering the *ejido* is now being threatened by unseen but persuasive forces that may well submerge the Mexican community and overwhelm the nation itself. These forces are the rapidly increasing population and the rapidly eroding soil. The first is overflowing the natural boundaries of the community, forming itself into thousands of new rural groupings, crowding the cities; and the second is washing away the very basis upon which the Mexican population depends. The government's program, conscious and unconscious, is formulated to meet the stress and dangers of these joint influences. It would meet them by converting the parochial economy, which has kept these communities locally supplied with their accustomed standards of living, by creating a national market as a substitute. The parochial economy preserved the balance between births and deaths; the "progress" of the national market is upsetting it.

The very danger of overpopulation, which most Mexican economists refuse to recognize, is a by-product of the forces set in motion to raise the standard of living of the Mexican people. In the process the older society is being undermined, not so much by the effects of the government program as by the increased population the program has stimulated. The increased population in its turn is hastening the threat of a seemingly inescapable doom hidden in the more and more rapid depletion of the soil. That is the contemporary Mexican dilemma.

For ages Mexico had one of the highest birth and death rates in the world, but they were so nearly balanced that actual growth in numbers was very slow. Since the Revolution, and especially since 1930, when the country was pacified and modern ideas of sanitation began to be applied on an ever widening scale, there has occurred a sudden cutting of the death rate without apparent effect on the birth rate. The time will come, as it has in other parts of the world, when a balance will be re-established. In the meantime, while the birth rate has remained at the average of 43.9 per thousand, the death rate has fallen to 21.5 (1941–4), and in the immediate future we can look forward to a continuing decline of the death rate. Four easily controllable diseases—smallpox, dysentery, typhoid, and paratyphoid—apparently cause 22 per cent of Mexican deaths, but this figure, as well as the infant mortality rate of 159.5 per thousand in the Federal District during 1943, will decrease with improved sanitation and public health. These same influences will in time also affect the rural districts. How helpless the rural community has been in the face of sudden death is illustrated by the following personal experience.

Some years ago I visited a school in Guerrero and found most of the benches empty. "Where are your children?" I asked the teacher. "Well, sir," she replied, "they are all dead." "What from?" "The measles." "What did you do?" "I wrote to the alcalde in the *municipio,* but I never got an answer." Such experiences are less likely to be repeated in the future, and the immediate results of the governmental health policies are already evidenced by the rapid growth of the population.

Between 1910 and 1930 the average annual increase in population was 69,000; for the five-year period 1937–41 it was almost 450,000, and it has been estimated that between 1940 and 1946 the population rose by three million. At this rate Mexico will have fifty to sixty million people by the end of the century, or more than double its present number.

This growth in population and the rapid enlargement of urban centers describe the immediate problem. A source of livelihood must be found for the ever increasing numbers, and the emphasis is upon *must,* for the problem is a pressing one and cannot wait.

2. *Agriculture and Population*

With two thirds of the Mexican people devoting their energies to tilling the soil, their income sets the economic pattern. But the agricultural yield is low, and the rural folk can see no easy way to improving their lot.

The Mexican agricultural resources have been deteriorating for centuries. Since the Conquest the desert area has increased and the remaining soils have been impoverished. At the present rate of loss of top soil, the state of Oaxaca, it has been predicted, will be a desert within fifty years. A similar destiny, according to Dr. William Vogt, may overtake the rest of Mexico in a hundred years, for, as he points out, even if within the next century the desert area of Mexico expands only one third, the pressure against the remaining resources will be so great as to hasten their destruction. All of this is occurring while a growing population forces less fertile hillside land into cultivation, thereby hastening the erosion that is even now threatening its subsistence.

In the past the deserts were less evident, the lakes, lagoons, and marshes occupied a larger area, much of the central plateau was covered with forests, the water level was higher, and the rivers ran more evenly throughout the year. The barren mountains and the naked rock, the deep gullies and the dry, dusty, desert-like soil, so prominent a feature on the very borders of Mexico's most populated places, have increased with the years.

While it is true that the erosion had started before the Conquest because of the burning of forest by the Indians as the first step in the planting of their corn crop, it was the coming of the European that precipitated a systematic and continuous destruction of the forests and, eventually, of the very soil itself. At the time of the Conquest, the environs of Mexico City were heavily forested, but the Spaniards soon cut down the trees. Cortés alone is said to have used six thousand cedars for the buildings on his estates. Many of the places that Alexander von Humboldt described as forested in the early days of the nineteenth century are now stripped of their trees and turned to desert.

Mexico City needs thousands of loads of charcoal per day for cooking and heating. To a lesser extent, so does every town and city in the country. Also, the rapid development of mining required timber and charcoal for fuel, and the coming of the railroads merely hastened the devastation of the forests. Hundreds of thousands of trees were cut down for railroad ties, and the use of wood for fuel in the engines on some of the railroads proved a further drain upon a limited resource until oil was substituted.

The loss of the forests increases the speed of the run-off during the rainy season and threatens the future water and power needs of the larger cities, notably Mexico City itself. Mexicans, while complaining of drought one year and of heavy rains another, are adding to the destructive effect of both by destroying the forests and reducing their basic food resources.

The insufficiency of the nation's agriculture may be illustrated by a few figures. Corn, as is well known, is the basic food of the people, and over sixty per cent of the area under cultivation is devoted to that crop. Less important but increasing as an essential food, especially in the cities, is wheat. But, on the basis of five-year averages since 1930, the country produces only between 70 and 80 million bushels of corn and about 14.5 million bushels of wheat per year. The yield of corn in Mexico is among the lowest in the world. Canada, for instance, has an average yield of 37.4 bushels per acre, Mexico only 7.8. The total annual average production in all of Mexico is less than one fifth of that of Iowa in a normal year. In 1943 Iowa produced 605,454,000 bushels of corn, while Mexico produced only 69,886,000.[1] What is true of corn is true of wheat. Canada gets 18.8, Mexico 11.5 bushels per acre. Kansas alone in 1943 produced thirteen times as much wheat as Mexico, 191,660,000 as against 14,568,000 bushels.

[1] There has been criticism of Mexican agricultural statistics, and it has been argued that the annual production is twice as high as given. Even so, it would still fall below the production of Iowa.

These two basic crops set the norm for Mexican agriculture and condition the rest of the economy. The acreage under cultivation has in some degree responded to the growing population and to the stimulus of the war. With 1929 as a base, food production varied from 131.2 per cent in 1939 to 136.0 in 1943. On the whole, production of corn and wheat has barely held its own, depending upon good or bad years. The average area in corn for this period ran from 3.0 to 3.4 million hectares and in wheat from 501,000 to 600,000 hectares, but the production of wheat increased by only nine per cent in 1943. The yield per hectare is on the decline except in new lands put under irrigation. Francisco Bulnes, on the basis of figures collected by Humboldt, estimates that the present yield per hectare is twenty per cent of what it was in 1803.

The area reaped has remained remarkably unchanged over many years. It has hovered around 5.5 million hectares since 1925. The year 1930 is typical. Of the 7.1 million hectares under cultivation, 1.2 million were lost on account of frost, hail, and drought; only 5.7 were actually reaped. This stability of the area reaped is the more remarkable because since 1926 over half a million hectares have been put under irrigation. These figures would suggest that the acreage being irrigated is replacing the land with insufficient rains.

If the total area reaped has remained fairly stationary, there have been some shifts in crops. There has, for instance, been a decline in the harvest of barley, rice, beans, and henequen, but an increase in cotton, sugarcane, tobacco, and coffee. Crops grown for export have tended to expand at the expense of food crops. This trend was accentuated by the war. But the thing to emphasize is the apparent long-run tendency of Mexican agricultural production to remain stable while the population is growing.

This is illustrated by a review of agricultural production for the years 1893–1944.[2] If 1929 is taken as a base, there were eighteen years before and twelve years after 1929 with a pro-

[2] Taken from *Revista de Economía*, January 15, 1946, Vol. IX, No. 1, pp. 23–4.

duction record higher, and in some instances fifty per cent higher, than the base year. If this index is even approximately accurate, then the conclusion must be drawn that Mexican agricultural production has remained more or less stationary for half a century.

If, in spite of fifty years of growth in agricultural science, and changes in landholding, irrigation, and governmental credit, production has not materially increased, then we presume the need for either heroic measures to meet the food requirements of a rapidly increasing population or a resort to increasing imports. In 1945 food accounted for twenty-two per cent of Mexico's total imports. A growing population and a stationary or declining agriculture have called forth many plans for meeting an increasingly difficult situation.

At best, however, it will be many years, generations perhaps, before the soil of Mexico can be brought to provide sufficient food for its growing numbers. The problem is not merely physical and financial, it is also social and cultural. It involves the re-education of the mass of the people to new ways with the land. These simple people are burdened with superstition and addicted to customary ways. It has long been known that a peasant population changes its habits slowly, and centuries sometimes pass without the visible imprint of new ideas. Something will have to be done, but how much can be accomplished we shall know better fifty years from now.

Officially Mexico has become aware that henceforth it must count its forest resources like drops of medicine, for the crisis is already here. The railroads have had to fall back on governmental pressure to secure ties essential for their rails, and lines of women have formed to await their turn to purchase the charcoal without which they cannot cook their food. The Mexico City government has initiated a campaign to substitute gas stoves for charcoal-burners. But the people cannot wait for the stoves, and the railroads have to have their ties.

The National Irrigation Commission, too, has discovered that its entire program is threatened by the sediment carried down by turbulent floods, and that the watersheds on which these irrigation projects depend are being ruined by deforestation. The Department of Agriculture and the Irrigation Commission are therefore undertaking to meet this crisis, but it will be many years before any improvement becomes visible.

What has been said of reforestation is equally true of erosion. While there has been an awareness of the problem for at least twenty years, it was only in 1943 that the first official steps were taken to deal with it by organizing a number of conservation districts. The reports of these initial labors show that the task is immeasurably great. To meet even the first small efforts, thousands of small retaining dams have had to be constructed, thousands of yards of ditches and drainage canals dug, many miles of retaining walls built, terracing developed in hundreds of acres, many thousands of trees and shrubs planted, the use of the soil modified, crops changed, and an entire new technique in agricultural practice undertaken.

What is involved is the financing of a project so vast that it will prove an almost unbearable drain on the government budget. The task may not prove impossible, but to succeed Mexico will have to develop an amount of energy and purpose greater than it has ever expended in any other endeavor. If it succeeds, it will have demonstrated a capacity for great and heroic effort and for an expenditure for long-term capital investment all out of proportion to any comparable past undertaking. From a starkly realistic point of view, Mexico must prevent erosion or face disaster.

Nor have the new systems of landholding produced any important change in agricultural technique. On the whole, the same primitive methods of cultivation persist except in those relatively small areas where crops are grown for the commercial market. Little of importance in agricultural science has come to enrich the new *ejidatarios* benefited by a gift of land from the Revolution. Even the simple lessons of the selection of seed and the using of manures and fertilizers are still mostly to be learned.

In great part the Mexican agricultural and agrarian difficulties are due to the concentration of some seventy per cent of the Mexican population in seven per cent of the national territory. The peasants had to be given *ejidos* near where they lived, and the lands proved insufficient, with the natural result that the average *ejido* contains only 5.7 hectares. But in populous states such as Mexico and Puebla the *ejido* contains only 2.3 and 3.3 hectares in crop land respectively; this falls short of providing the means of even a meager subsistence agriculture. Nor is the difficulty easily remediable. The rural population is growing, and new demands for *ejidos* are being pressed. To make better farming possible, these parcels ought to be enlarged, but to satisfy the remaining land-hungry peasants they would have to be made smaller. Clearly neither of these solutions is possible. Only two alternatives have been suggested: the moving of the excess population to other agricultural areas or a rapid industrialization to draw the growing numbers into urbanized centers. But these proposals are beset with difficulties so great that ability to meet the immediate and growing needs remains to be determined.

How serious the problem is may be seen from the following considerations. By the end of 1944 over a million and a half (1,805,932) *ejidatarios* had been granted parcels of land, and with their families they constituted approximately one third of the total Mexican population. This vast change has broken the plantation system and has removed land from the market as a source of investment, but it has left a greater part of the rural population without land. There are still over 8,000 villages whose demands for land have not been considered, and there are a half million (499,271) individuals who have been adjudicated as entitled to land, but who have not received any because there was none available within the locale in which they have a legal claim. On the basis of the 1940 census, of the 3,830,781 people occupied in agriculture, 1,892,257 were laborers.

The statement of Mexican economists that of three peasants who need land only one has received it is not far from the truth. As of 1940, 28.5 per cent of the land in farms was in *ejidos,* and admittedly they had a greater share of the better lands. Even so, only 3.4 per cent of *ejido* lands were under irrigation, 1.2 per cent with sufficient moisture (*jugo*) and 18.5 per cent *temporal* (having irregular rains). The rest were pasture, woodlots, and mountains. It is said that 39 per cent of the lands are relatively useless.

The small holdings are insufficient for an adequate standard of life and add to the difficulties of supplying the urban centers. In fact, recent changes in the law look to a minimum of four hectares irrigated, or eight *temporal*. But this law, if carried out, would merely increase the number of landless peasants unless other areas were opened to them. While the undivided tract is extensive, its agricultural value is relatively small and would require heavy investments in new roads and irrigation. It would also make necessary the transfer of many thousands of families to new and distant places. The prospects of such a program are complicated by the Alemán administration's guarantee against expropriation of holdings of 100 hectares irrigated or 200 *temporal*.

To meet some of these needs the government has attempted to provide agricultural credit, but the history of Mexican agricultural credit is a sad story at best. The Caja de Préstamos was organized in 1908, with sixty million pesos. By 1914 it was bankrupt, with sixty-eight loans outstanding for a total of fifty-three million pesos. Money that was to have gone into agricultural credit had been distributed to a few individuals, some of them receiving as much as five million pesos. Thus this project added little to the agricultural development of the country. A similar experience followed another effort, begun in 1916, in which the government invested considerable funds and lost the greater part of them. One debtor alone was allowed to borrow twenty million pesos, of which nine million were lost.

In 1926 the Banco de Crédito Agrícola was organized under Calles for the promotion of credit to small agriculturists, but the bank fell into the hands of the politicians, among them Obregón and Calles, twenty-three of whom "borrowed" between 12 and 15 million pesos. This bank absorbed substantial losses and reduced its operations from 16.6 million pesos in 1919 to 2.2 million in 1933.

In 1936 the Cárdenas administration established the Banco Nacional de Crédito Ejidal. It operates through co-operative credit unions and not through individuals, and is hampered by the fact that no lien can be placed upon the *ejido* lands. The government has supplied most of the money for this bank, in sums that have reached 70,000,000 pesos a year. The *ejido* bank has suffered from its inability to decide whether it is a real bank or a social service agency to aid the thousands of new *ejidos* and their million and a half members. The bank is condemned for being a "bank" and for not being one. Its clientele is poor, inexperienced, unacquainted with the subtleties of finance and credit operations, and frequently illiterate. Having received land from the government, the peasants do not understand why they should have to pay for plows, machinery, seed, or work animals and do not appreciate the subtleties of interest, amortization, or bankruptcy.

In these circumstances the institution falls between two stools. It expends large funds in such areas as the Laguna cotton districts, where the lands are rich and a profit can be made. But that is where private credit could be had and government aid is least necessary, and the government's money might better go where it is most needed and other aid cannot be secured. On these operations it shows a heavy loss and lays itself open to violent criticism from those who argue that a bank is not an eleemosynary institution. The nature of the problem is revealed by an analysis of 4,570 *ejido* communities, which showed that 13 per cent were good creditors, 61 per cent were potentially solvent but required continued long-time support, and 26 per cent had neither present nor future possibilities of meeting their obligations.

It is no wonder, therefore, that governmental agricultural credit operations are at a high cost. It has been calculated that the Banco Agrícola and Banco Ejidal lose on an average one fifth of their annual investments, and that if cost of operations is included, they lose approximately 35 centavos on every peso.

That would be a small amount if it raised the technical competence and productivity of the *ejidos;* but the best results have come chiefly in areas of large-scale commercial agriculture. The crux of the matter is that the need is greater than the government can meet.

Another effort to improve the agricultural resources of the country is the government's irrigation program, begun under Calles in 1926, which by 1946 had placed over 500,000 hectares of new land in cultivation, and had improved another 400,000 hectares. There are now twenty-eight irrigation districts. In some of these, such as the Don Martín in Coahuila and Nuevo León, and the Delicias in Chihuahua, entirely new settlement was required. It has been the practice to respect existing *ejidos* or properties of under one hundred hectares. New lands put under irrigation have made room for some *ejidatarios* who could not find land in their own neighborhood, as well as for small landowners forced out in other parts of the country, as for example those compensated by lands in the Yaqui Valley. By the end of 1944 as many as 107,742 peasant families had been placed on irrigated lands.

The average cost per hectare as of 1942 had been 700 pesos, but in some cases it ran many times that figure, and in one was said to reach 12,000 pesos. A farmer working ten hectares could not amortize this cost in twenty-five years and keep enough for even a minimum subsistence. The government, therefore, has abandoned the effort to recover the total outlay, arguing that the increased income from the agriculture tends to benefit society at large, and hence the burden ought to be a national one. The land is sold below cost at from 300 to 600 pesos per hectare. The *ejidatarios* and small owners already in the area are freed from any payment, and their land is cleared, leveled, and turned over ready for use. The government, however, in addition to the initial outlay for construction, is losing large sums annually in the administration of the various irrigation systems. The irrigation districts under management by the National Agricultural Credit Bank lost 11.6 million pesos between 1936 and 1943. The Irrigation Commission does not publish the costs of administration for those districts under its control, but its losses have been estimated at 2.5 million per annum. Altogether the government lost 25 million pesos in the administration of its irrigation districts between 1934 and 1943. In general terms, the federal government is said to subsidize the agriculturists working the lands under irrigation to the sum of about 4 million pesos a year, apart from nonrecoverable construction costs.

On an average, irrigated lands yield three times as much as *temporal,* and a million hectares would presumably produce fifty per cent of the total now reaped from all lands under cultivation. A million hectares under irrigation would also make room for 100,000 peasants, who with their families would represent 500,000 people. Another hundred thousand people, it is argued, would find occupation as laborers, merchants, mechanics, bankers, professionals, and so forth, so that with their families they would represent an additional half million people. A million hectares under irrigation would, therefore, provide a livelihood for 1,000,000 inhabitants (representing, at the present, two years' growth of the population). Land available for irrigation on the most optimistic estimate is put at 5,000,000 hectares, but the generally accepted figure is 2,000,000, and another 2,000,000 hectares of semihumid lands can be improved by irrigation. At the present rate of construction forty years and six billion pesos will be required to complete the program. If the expenditure of 145 million pesos for 1946 is continued, and costs per hectare are held at present levels, Mexico will have, in forty years, an area under irrigation larger than it is now cultivating in *temporal* lands, and will be able to produce at least three times as much and, according to previous estimates, provide a living for seven million additional people, or, at the present rate, fourteen years' growth of population.

With even this most optimistic view of the possibilities of Mexican irrigation, the irrigated land would still represent only about 3.5 per cent of the area of Mexico, and with what is now under cultivation would barely reach 8 per cent of the land in farms. With the present rate of increase in population, the problem of providing sufficient food will remain unsolved. While raising the food in increasing quantities for its growing population may not prove an insuperable undertaking, it will certainly put a heavy strain on the financial and moral resources of the Mexican people.

CHAPTER 12

The Conditions of Economic Progress: II

1. Manufactures

THE IMPULSE behind the Mexican government's desire for increasing manufacturing has been described by the statement: "We can no longer continue subsisting on imported foods, and paying for them with our export of raw materials at a price fixed by a single foreign buyer." That really is the crux of the matter. The exports, however, have to pay for the import of semimanufactured and durable goods as well. Can Mexico develop manufactures not merely for local needs, but for a growing export as well? Only if it can do that will it meet the requirements of the Mexican economy. This will depend on many factors, including that of available resources.

Mexico is better endowed with mineral resources than most other Latin-American countries. It produces copper, zinc, lead, antimony, arsenic, tin from scattered deposits, graphite, magnesium, mercury, molybdenum, cadmium, bismuth, calcium, mica, tungsten, sulphate, iron, and coal. The difficulty lies in the relative smallness of most of the known deposits and in their wide dispersion.

In the production of lead Mexico occupies third place in the world. Lead is found in twenty-two different states, with Chihuahua being the largest producer. Under favorable conditions Mexico has produced as much as 282,000 tons of lead, 218,000 tons of zinc, 300 tons of mercury, and nearly 11,000 tons of antimony per year. Without further detailing, it may be said that the production of these metals has shown a gradual increase in recent years. Not more than ten per cent of the total has been required for local industrial uses, the rest being exported.

Iron and coal are mined on a much larger scale, and are almost completely consumed inside the country. The iron deposits are considerable, being calculated at 270,000,000 tons, distributed in Chihuahua, Colima, Durango, Guerrero, Michoacán, Oaxaca, and Puebla. Production of iron has varied between 186,961 tons in 1944 and 87,128 tons in 1946. As far as iron is concerned, if all other conditions were favorable, there is room for large-scale expansion, but many of the deposits are located in inaccessible parts of the west coast, at great distances from any available coal. In the north the only iron deposit now worked is separated by a considerable distance from coal mines.

Mexican authorities estimate their coal reserves at 1,690,000,000 tons in the northern part of the country alone, but the most that has been produced so far in any one year has been about 1,400,000 tons, in 1925. There are two difficulties. The coal, in spite of the fact that it can be coked, is unsatisfactory for general uses and is located nearly six hundred miles from the industrial center where it could be used. In fact, most of the industries and railroads have turned to electrical power and oil fuel.

Some insight into the future prospects of Mexican industrialization may be had by an examination of its present character.

According to preliminary figures available from the 1940 census, Mexico's remuneratively engaged population numbered 5,677,000, or 28 per cent of the total. Of this total, only 11.4 per cent were engaged in industry. It may help the reader to visualize the economic structure of Mexico if I show the occupational distribution figures in their entirety.

PRELIMINARY OCCUPATIONAL DISTRIBUTION OF REMUNERATIVELY ENGAGED POPULATION

According to Census Figures of 1940

Classification	Number in thousands	Per cent
Agriculture, cattle, forest, and fishing	3,830	68.6
Mines and petroleum	107	1.9
Industries	640	11.4
Communications and transport	149	2.6
Commerce	552	8.1
Public administration	192	3.4
Liberal professions	43	0.7
Other occupations	164	2.9
Unaccounted for *	—	0.4
Total	5,677	100.0

* Added by author.

This table confirms the preponderance of agricultural occupation in Mexico. It throws into relief the fact that in spite of the importance attached to mining and petroleum, they employ less than 2 per cent of the working force; that industries of all kinds, large and small, employ less than 12 per cent; and that those engaged in the servicing employments (commerce, public administration, communications, transport, and the liberal professions) are more numerous than those engaged in direct production other than agriculture—14.8 per cent of the total.

A better picture of the structure of the Mexican economy may be had, however, by a closer examination of some of these broad classifications. In the "industries," which are shown to employ 640,000 people, among whom 213,000 work for themselves as isolated artisans and 12,000 are engaged in helping their families, so that only 415,000 workers can properly be classified as employed in establishments.

A very similar picture is offered by the workers engaged in communications and transport: more than one third of this group are people who have a burro or two that they rent out for carrying goods in rural districts or who own a truck or automobile of their own and find similar employment. There are, thus, only 82,000 individuals employed by others in all of the railroad, truck, bus, telephone, and telegraph industries.

Even more striking is the structure of Mexican commerce. Of the total number of persons in this classification, 66.1 per cent work for themselves. In other words, Mexican commerce is mainly in the hands of petty merchants, peddlers, and occupants of stalls or places in the numerous parochial and public markets, and in little village stores. It is important to note that of 1,341,000 persons included under the headings of industries, communications, and commerce, 626,000, or nearly half, are individuals working for themselves. In fact, only 822,000 people are engaged in all Mexican private employment other than agriculture. This makes 14.4 per cent of the total remuneratively employed. These considerations make dubious the claim that those engaged in industry increased by 22 per cent, and those in commerce by 65 per cent, until we know whether the increase was in establishments or in self-employed artisans and ambulatory activities, or, in fact, whether an increase of 65 per cent, as given for commerce, does not represent a different classification, or better counting in the 1940 census than in the one taken in 1930.

Further light is thrown on the structure of the Mexican industrial plant by a consideration of the size of the average manufacturing establishment in Mexico. Taking only those establishments that have an annual production valued at ten thousand pesos or over, we find that in 1940 ten out of the sixteen manufacturing groups listed have, on an average, less than fifty workers in each plant, and only two manufacturing groups—textiles and the graphic arts—have on an average a little over one hundred workers.

After 1940 the war stimulated Mexican industrial activities, and the government, through fiscal policies and what amounts to a policy of inflation, has sought to further the new movement for industrialization in the country.

Total investments in all Mexican industry were placed at 1,795 million pesos in 1930, and 3,454 million in 1944. But between these two periods the value of the peso has fallen by more than fifty per cent. With 1939 as a base, production has increased from 100 to 138, but, with the same base, wholesale prices climbed to 268.4 by December 1948.

Four industries—food production, textiles, chemicals, and metals—represent 78 per cent of the 1.5 billion pesos' value of all manufactures in 1940. Of the others, the most important were clothing and tobacco.

In 1944 the Federal District was the great center of Mexican industry, with 15,027 out of 50,998 establishments. Its factories represent about a third of both the total investment and the value of manufactures. Next in order, but far below, was Nuevo León, with the important steel industry in Monterrey; next was the state of Puebla. The Federal District is the great manufacturing area; textiles predominate in Puebla and Vera Cruz; and iron, steel, and smelting in the northern states.

Mexican industrial activity consists preponderantly of the processing of agricultural products. This is evidenced by the fact that in 1940 the food industry had the largest investment and produced a higher value than any other industry. Next to food came textiles. These two industries together have about three fourths of all manufacturing establishments and over half of all the investments in manufacturing, and produce about two thirds of the value of manufactures. It needs to be added that nearly one third of all the raw materials used in Mexican manufactures are imported from abroad, and that most of the industry lives behind a high tariff. This is notoriously true of the textile industry, which has remained antiquated and unreformed for many years, receiving increased tariff protection against lower costs and more efficient production in other countries.

We have here what is almost a conspiracy by a few owners, one hundred thousand workers, and a few governmental officials to provide the mass of the population with desperately insufficient clothing at excessively high costs. In spite of the devaluation of the Mexican peso, the clothing industry enjoys a tariff increase of almost one hundred per cent given it during recent years, and the importation of ordinary cloth to Mexico has become almost impossible. A national monopoly has thus been created for an old, unprogressive, and inefficient industry that can afford the luxury of indifference to technical changes in other parts of the world.

The tariff on textiles is merely a part of a general policy covering almost every item produced in Mexico. The current theory seems to be that the country can get rich by raising the price of the goods it must have, even though it results in goods of poor quality at high cost, if only a few workers and employers are, by special privilege and immunity, given a protected place within the economy.

Among the items in wide demand on which the tariff has been raised by at least one hundred per cent since 1929 are the following: rice, cocoa, beans, flour, hog fat, wheat, chemical fertilizers, carded wool, and cotton stockings. In fact, the basic food items are all protected by tariffs, and probably would find it difficult to survive without them. Mexico protects, if one wishes to argue that way, its international-exchange position by reducing its imports, but does so at the expense of higher costs, lower industrial efficiency—as in the textile industry—poor products, and a lower standard of living for the mass of its people. To find other activities or increased sources of export that can be substituted for the present inefficient high-cost industries, which can only survive behind a high tariff wall, is a crucial problem.

One Mexican economist, writing after the Second World War, points out that as a result of the devaluation of the

Mexican peso and the increase in tariff duties cotton cloth has a coefficient of protection eighteen times as high as that in 1855. Since 1890 Mexican industry has had a protection of 385 per cent, due to the lower value of the peso.[1] For cotton cloth the tariff provided an added protection of 193 per cent. Similarly cocoa has had an added protection of 85 per cent, rice 400 per cent, woolen stuff 233 per cent, stockings 669 per cent, and carded wool 900 per cent. Production of cocoa is decreasing, and that of the other items is insufficient to meet the national requirements. Further devaluation of the peso in 1948 and 1949 has added an additional barrier against imports.

The most significant changes in Mexican manufacturing are to be found in the metallurgical, chemical, cement, and electrical industries. While not large, these industries suggest that in time Mexico may to some extent achieve independence in semidurable goods. The steel-manufacturing industry has been enlarged by new units in Monterrey, by the development of La Consolidada in Mexico City, using scrap iron, and by a new plant at Piedras Negras, known as Los Altos Hornos. The total steel production in 1941 was about 164,867 metric tons, and expansion now taking place may relieve the country from imports of steel and iron. The industry turns out rails, structural shapes, wire rods, bars, tubes, steel castings, bolts, nuts, springs, cold-rolled sheets, tin plate, and other products.

In the chemical industry considerable progress has been made in the production of sulphur, hydrochloric, nitric, and acetic acids, ammonium sulphate, caustic soda, and a variety of medicines. Cement plants are springing up in various parts of the country, and present capacity is around 1,500,000 tons per year. The electrical industry is represented by the establishment of a plant in Mexico City for the manufacture and assembly of motors, transformers, generators, switchboards, radios, and electrical appliances. The fifteen-million-dollar investment in this undertaking is small for such an ambitious program, but it is a beginning. Partial production was begun

[1] And this before the most recent devaluation of the peso (June 1949).

in 1946. Investment of capital in industrial establishments is continuing, and the production of such items as rayon, foodstuffs, metalware, leather and rubber goods, asbestos, textiles, and glass is increasing.

There is a consistent pressure for the enlargement of the smelting and refining capacity in order to keep within the country the value added in the processing. For the same reasons, henequen, ixtle, and other fibrous plants are increasingly being turned into rope, twine, bags, matting, and hammocks. Finally, efforts are under way to develop a canning industry, especially for tropical fruits.

The total effort, however, is small. In 1940 Mexico's manufacturing plants (not including mines and smelters) produced goods valued at 1,521 million pesos, then approximately 300 million dollars. If the cost of raw materials is deducted, the "value added by manufacture" amounted to only approximately 127 million dollars.

The same is true for the extractive and metallurgical industries, which included oil fields, refineries, mines, and smelters. In 1940 their production was valued at 1,601 million pesos, or approximately 309 million dollars. Here again there must be deducted 72 million pesos for raw materials, half of which were imported.

The annual total of both "manufacturing" and "extractive" industries, other than precious metals, after deducting raw materials, would equal less than half a billion dollars in American money for the entire country. This is the sum available, in addition to the locally produced gold and silver, for internal expansion and for the payment of all external obligations, including imports of both goods and services, profits, amortization, and interest.

2. *Mining*

Historically the mining industry has played the leading role in Mexico's foreign trade and in stimulating internal expansion. But for the lure of the mines, most of what is now northern Mexico would probably have continued to be a haven for wandering Indian tribes, and only the small valleys of Mexico, Puebla, Toluca, Oaxaca, and Michoacán would have been developed. The Spaniards' zest for the precious metals early led them to the mines of Taxco and Pachuca, and during the sixteenth century they staked out such important mineral centers as Zacatecas, Guanajuato, Parral, Mazapil, and Sombrerete. After four centuries these mines are still producing half the silver and a fourth of the gold of the country. The yield from these mines supported the growth of most of the northern cities.

These prosperous mining centers provided the markets for much of Mexican commerce, determined the layout of the roads and trails along which it was carried, and gave occupation to the numerous mule-drivers who traveled the long distances to Mexico City. In addition these mining centers stimulated commerce in coffee, sugar, cloth, vanilla, and a few imported items that could bear the heavy cost of transport. As far as possible, food had to be grown within the neighboring regions. Every mine, therefore, became a center for some agriculture and cattle raising, and the way stations where the mule-drivers rested for the night grew into organized towns.

During the colonial period, and for fifty years afterward, precious metals were Mexico's chief export, amounting to 70 and 80 per cent and in some years, such as 1843, 90 per cent of all the goods shipped in international trade. Toward the close of the eighteenth century and during the early part of the nineteenth Mexico's exports were valued at an average of 21,000,000 pesos, of which about 4,000,000 represented coffee, cotton, vanilla, sugar, dye woods, and so forth, and the rest precious metals. In fact, the mines—chiefly silver—paid for most of Mexico's imports for nearly four centuries, made possible the development of Mexico into a modern nation, justified the building of most of the railroads, and gave Mexico its distinctive place in the outside world.

In addition, the yield from the mines was for a long time the chief source of government income. For many years before the Independence the government received about 30 per cent of its 20,000,000-peso income directly, and perhaps an equal amount indirectly, from the mining industry. When, as a result of the Independence, the mining industry was seriously damaged, the government's income shrank to 9.3 million pesos in 1822, and not until 1877 did it rise above what it had been at the end of the eighteenth century.

In spite of the fact that Mexico began encouraging foreign investment in the mines as far back as 1823, and that both English and German capital entered the field, it was only after 1870 that the industry began its more productive period. American and French capital became interested in Mexican mines during the second half of the nineteenth century.

It was the development of modern mining, smelting, and refining techniques, making possible the working of low-grade ores, that gave Mexico its important contemporary role as a mineral-producing nation. In fact, during the last forty-eight years Mexico has produced as much silver as was taken from the mines in the preceding four centuries.

These changes in the mining industry are reflected in the structure of the industry itself. The estimated billion-peso investment is largely represented by ten mining companies, and the ownership is presumed to be distributed as follows: American, 80 per cent; English, 12 per cent; Mexican, 3.5 per cent; French, 2 per cent; others, 2.5 per cent. This industry now employs about one hundred thousand people in mining and smelting, and apparently contributes about one billion pesos toward the national income. It is a large consumer of local products and such materials as coke, carbide, dynamite, iron, steel, wood products, and cement. It also supplies twenty per cent of the freight on railroads, and twelve per cent of gross railroad income.

In 1940, of Mexico's leading mineral products, gold represented 2.15 per cent of the total world production, silver 30.5 per cent, copper 1.5 per cent, lead 12.5 per cent, zinc 2.8 per cent, and antimony 20 per cent. Mexico occupied second place in molybdenum, and was the world's principal producer of arsenic. In addition, its production of cadmium, bismuth, and mercury was significant in the total world production.

The historically preponderant role of the mining industry in the economy of Mexico is to be explained, in part, by the high cost of transportation. When the cost of sending a ton of freight from Mexico City to Vera Cruz was 108 pesos, or 119 from Guanajuato to Tampico, or 163 from Tehuantepec to Vera Cruz, only those things could move long distances which could absorb the heavy costs. These freight charges continued as late as the middle of the nineteenth century, just before the railroads were constructed, at a time when a ton of corn was worth twenty pesos, a ton of wheat thirty, and a cow ten pesos. It was not until the railroads came to Mexico that other important items could enter the national market.

With the railroads, Mexico began to develop a more complex economy, and the mining industry declined in relative importance, though it continued to occupy first place among exports. It provided 68 per cent of the total in the early years of this century, and as much as 67 per cent in 1940, only to decline, as a result of the war, to 30 per cent in 1944. It ceased, however, to play the important role it once held in the government's income. It contributed only 6.2 per cent of the government's income in 1901, 3.8 per cent in 1925, and 11.3 per cent in 1940. Its contribution to the national income declined from an earlier 30 per cent to an estimated 9.2 per cent in 1940.

Equally striking has been the structural change within the industry itself. Until 1880 gold and silver represented nearly 100 per cent of all mineral production, but these precious metals fell to 85 per cent in 1900, to 40 per cent in 1929. The constant increase in the industrial metals has lessened the relative significance of gold and silver in both the internal and external income of Mexico.

While the production of gold and silver has remained fairly constant since 1925, hovering between 24 and 28 thousand kilograms for gold and between 2 and 3 million kilograms for silver, production of industrial metals has, on the whole, shown marked increase. Zinc, for instance, has increased from 45,770 tons in 1925 to 218,265 in 1944. Mercury, antimony, graphite, arsenic, tin, iron, cadmium, and bismuth have all followed an upward trend. Copper, lead, and rarer metals like molybdenum and vanadium were greatly stimulated by the war, but it remains to be seen how important these changes will prove to be.

As things stand at present, gold and silver, even if they have lost their previous preponderance in the total economy, remain the products of greatest value among the mineral and production exports. If, as seems to be the case, silver and gold have achieved relative stability in production, there is little prospect of an increase of international exchange from that source. For it does not seem likely that the other metals will, for the present, greatly affect the total value of mineral exports from Mexico. The evidence seems to promise no such expansion of the mineral industry as would allow it to offset the growing agricultural difficulties of the country. Even if the mining industry were to expand greatly, the export of minerals still could not be counted fully in the Mexican balance of payments. The foreign ownership of the mines implies that a part of the value of the exports—it has been put as high as fifty per cent—never returns to the country of origin because it is distributed beyond its borders for profits, amortization, administration, insurance, shipping charges, and commissions. What remains in Mexico includes taxes, wages, local transportation charges, and locally bought materials.

What has been said about mining applies in even greater degree to oil. The oil resources of Mexico are estimated by geologists at 1 per cent of the world's total, as against 24 per cent in Venezuela. For a few years, beginning with 10,345 barrels in 1901, Mexico's production was of great importance. It rose to 157,060,678 barrels in 1920, and was as high as 165,514,700 barrels in 1925. It gradually declined to 40,000,000 barrels in 1935, and 33,500,000 in 1943, and the shipments of petroleum and its derivatives fell from 20 per cent of the total exports in 1935 to 3 per cent of the total in 1944. Mexico, which in 1921 produced 25 per cent of the world's oil, produced only 2.4 per cent in 1944.

3. Foreign Trade

A growing population and insufficient domestic food production give Mexico's foreign trade special significance. If it cannot feed its people from domestic sources, it will have to acquire the food abroad, and in the long run it can do that only by increasing its exports. Historically the metals, as we have already seen, occupied the first place in the country's exports, and continued to do so up to 1940, and the international exchange provided by the metals paid for a great part of the imports during most of Mexico's history.

Mexican imports increased between 1935 and 1944 from 406 million to 1,349 million pesos, and to 3,405 million pesos in 1948, excluding imports of gold. Imports of foods increased from 15 million in 1935 to 291 million in 1944, and as compared with the previous five-year period the average for 1935–40 shows a jump of 1,168 per cent in five years. While higher prices had a considerable bearing upon this figure, none of the other items of import—durable consumer goods, production goods, or raw materials—shows any such rise as this, the highest being 260 per cent for raw materials.

Put in a different way, in the five-year period 1935–9, foods represented 5 per cent of all imports. In the period 1940–4 they represented 22 per cent. During these years the import of the following food items increased by more than 200 per cent each: wheat, sugar, hogs, conserved meats, malt, animal fats, butter, cocoa, and cinnamon.

These changes in imports were accompanied by a significant shift in the market from which they were purchased. During the period 1935–44, purchases in the United States rose from 65 to 90 per cent of all imports. Germany, France, and Spain had disappeared from the scene. Britain as a supplier had been reduced to 1 per cent of the total, while Latin America had risen to 5.4 from 0.5 per cent, and all other countries supplied only 3.6 per cent. The immediate effects of the war made the United States almost the sole supplier of Mexican imports, and the American hemisphere provided 96.7 per cent, leaving to the rest of the world 3.3 per cent of the Mexican import trade.

These changes in Mexico's imports during the ten-year period here under consideration are surpassed by those revealed in Mexico's exports. To begin with, the volume of exports declined by about 50 per cent between 1937 and 1944, or from 5,346,000 tons to 2,522,000 tons. If we take the two five-year periods, the last was 55 per cent of the first in volume. The loss was due mainly to the fall in petroleum exports, which in certain years had equaled 3,000,000 tons, or more than half of the volume. But if the volume declined, the value increased, being 750 million pesos in 1935 and 1,133 million pesos in 1944. The loss in petroleum products was made up, it should be noted, not by an increase in minerals, but by forest, animal, and manufactured products.

Minerals, which had from time immemorial occupied first place, and even in 1940 represented 67 per cent of the total exports, fell to 30 per cent in 1944. Among the minerals, exports of the precious metals fell to 1.7 per cent for gold and 3.3 per cent for silver. An equally striking relative decline occurred in petroleum and its derivatives, which fell from 20 per cent of the total in 1935 to 3 per cent in 1944.

The shift in the export position of manufactures is most impressive, for they jumped from 0.4 per cent in 1935 to 22 per cent in 1944. The other important items that changed their relative positions were forest products, from 1 per cent in 1935 to 9 per cent in 1944, and fibers, from 5 to 13 per cent.

The important change, therefore, in recent years is represented by a sharp decline in minerals, and an unprecedented increase in manufacturing, plus a smaller increase in forest, fiber, and animal products and in vegetable foods. As for the future, it remains a question whether this represents a permanent change in the country's foreign trade.

Before considering this point, it will be necessary to note the shift in Mexico's export market. In 1935 the United States took 62 per cent of Mexico's exports; in 1942 it took 91.3 per cent;

the American hemisphere as a whole purchased 99.9 per cent. The market in the rest of the world had practically disappeared, and even in March 1946 the Americas took 97.5 per cent of all Mexican shipments abroad, of which the United States accounted for 80.4 per cent.

We may now look with some greater detail at the abrupt structural change in Mexico's exports. The fall in mineral exports was due to the sharp decline in the export of silver. The flow of capital from abroad, for investment, for payment of goods and services, or in search of safety, made it possible to cover Mexico's needs for foreign exchange without the shipment of silver, which remained in the country as a metallic reserve. The other metals, however, increased their volume and value in the export market, but did not fill the gap created by the loss of silver exports.

The decline of petroleum to 3 per cent of the total export is explained partly by the decline in amount produced, and chiefly perhaps by the increased local consumption, which rose from 4 to 6 million cubic meters between 1941 and 1944, which was almost as great as the total production.

The sudden rise in the export of manufactures from 0.4 per cent of the total in 1935 to 22 per cent in 1944 is represented by approximately seventy different items, most of which had previously not been exported at all and many of which had not previously been manufactured in Mexico. Of these seventy items, six were most important: shoes, sugar, molasses, henequen products, binding twine, and beer; together they accounted for 4.7 per cent of the total exports in 1944. Other items of importance among those that went to make up the 22 per cent represented by the category "manufactures" were: cotton and wool garments, alcoholic beverages, pure alcohol, palm hats, automobile tires, leather bags, manufactured silver objects, sweets, chocolate, chicle, medicines, essence of lemon, books, moving pictures, manufactured steel, iron products, and worked-up zinc.

These manufactured items, which played so important a role as to occupy, next to minerals, the leading place in Mexican shipments abroad, are subject to competitive pressures in normal times, and it cannot be assumed that they will continue in their newly won rank.

Of the other exports little need be said. Vegetable foods, consisting of coffee, garbanzos, bananas, tomatoes, vanilla, and feeds, showed little change in the 1934–44 period, increasing 3 per cent in volume and 2 per cent in value. No marked changes in their relative importance are likely. Fibers, long of some significance, had a doubling of price, but not of volume. In addition to henequen, this group included ixtle, palm, and cotton. But henequen, which represents two thirds of the value and one half or more of the volume in this class, showed a decline by 6,350 tons. It was the sharp increase in price, from 0.17 to 0.90 centavos per kilo, that explains the relative gains of the fibers during the period. There is no likelihood of any great expansion in henequen exports from Yucatán during normal time. The increased competition from many other parts of the world, the high cost of production in Yucatán, and the changing technology of farming have all combined to place henequen at a disadvantage.

What has been said of fibers can be repeated of most products: hardwoods, chicle, guayule, and vegetable wax. The value of these items increased nine times during the war, and their volume doubled. But as with fibers, there is little prospect that they can maintain their increased importance in a normal world market.

Animals and animal products doubled their volume in export, and increased their value six times, between 1935 and 1944. The recent spread of hoof-and-mouth disease in Mexico has stimulated the development of an export industry of canned meats in place of live animals previously shipped abroad.

It can now be seen that Mexico's exports were significantly affected by the war in only three respects:

1. *Minerals.* These greatly declined owing to the flow of foreign capital to Mexico, making possible the retention of the precious metals, especially silver, in the country.

2. *Petroleum.* Export had seriously declined before the war, and it has to a large extent been converted to domestic uses.

3. *Manufactured products.* These showed a phenomenal increase from less than 1 per cent to 22 per cent of the total exports, but the list of articles represented will find serious competition from other better-equipped and more-experienced suppliers.

The end of the war left Mexico in a disadvantageous position. Its European markets are either completely gone or greatly impoverished. It is now, as never before, dependent upon the United States as an outlet for its products. But with petroleum not available for export for the immediate future, and with manufactured articles not likely to find an extensive place in the United States or other markets, Mexico is again forced back upon its traditional commodities, minerals. Of these, the precious metals, perhaps, will once again occupy the leading place, with the other minerals, for all practical purposes, a minor item in the picture. In place of Europe, Mexico has found a market in Latin America, amounting to 14.4 per cent of its total exports in 1945. But here again the things it has to sell to Latin America are chiefly manufactured products, and these will find strong competition, from both the United States and Great Britain and from local industrialization.

4. *Transportation*

If the dream of industrialization, now so insistently preoccupying the country's leaders, is to acquire some real substance, Mexico will have to develop a modern and efficient railway system and greatly expand the production of hydroelectric energy. Without improved railroads the low-cost transport of bulky goods essential to an industrial economy will be unavailable, and without much additional hydroelectric power the energy required by the new factories and growing cities cannot be had.

Between 1925 and 1944, a very considerable amount of

money and energy went into the building of highways. During this period over 14,000 miles of road were surveyed, about 9,000 opened to traffic, and some 4,600 asphalted. This program was largely underwritten by the 750 million pesos derived from the gasoline tax. This income made possible the flotation of public bonds to the amount of 556 million pesos, approximately one third of which have been retired. The total investment in construction and maintenance has run to 1,150 million pesos.

This very remarkable achievement, however, suffers from comparatively low road traffic. In 1946 Mexico had only 205,-494 motor vehicles, of which nearly one third were in the Federal District. Compared with the United States, this gives a motor-vehicle ratio of 1 to 180, when the population ratio was about 1 to 7. Even on the most important and longest highway, that between Laredo and Acapulco, there were on an average only 590 vehicles per day. These yielded a gasoline-tax income per kilometer-year of 4,370 pesos, or barely enough to maintain the road, while on the other roads the traffic was much lower, with a correspondingly smaller income. To place sufficient motor vehicles on this growing highway system, if and when the traffic justifies it, will require an investment of many hundreds of millions of pesos, for most of which foreign exchange will have to be found. It has been estimated that Mexico now spends one hundred million pesos a year on the purchase of motor vehicles.

Roads, useful as they are for trucks, buses, and tourists, are no answer to the problem of heavy freight traffic. For instance, the distance from Manzanillo to Mexico City is about 720 miles by railroad, and the distance from Acapulco is about 270 miles by road. It costs between 15 and 20 pesos to move a ton of freight from Manzanillo to the capital by railroad, and between 60 and 80 pesos by truck from Acapulco, only about a third of the distance. Two thousand tons from Manzanillo can be moved by seven persons; it would take 400 trucks and 800 persons to move such a load from Acapulco. Air transport, which has been greatly developed, even if feasible for heavy traffic, is for the present too expensive. Mexico must therefore look to its railroad system if it is to move the large amounts of heavy low-cost freight required in any industrial economy.

Mexican railroad history makes it doubtful, however, that this essential need can be readily met. The first railroad-construction contract, for the road between Mexico City and Vera Cruz, was signed on August 20, 1837. Between that date and 1898 the theory of nonintervention ruled governmental policy, and the railroad enjoyed complete freedom of action. In 1898, however, the Mexican government changed its policy and bought into the railroads, and in 1937, just a hundred years after the signing of the first railroad contract, it completed the circle by expropriating them. During 1903 the Mexican government acquired a 51 per cent interest in the National Railroad, the Interoceánico, and the Internacional, thus laying the basis for the system now included in the Ferrocarriles Nacionales. At the height of the Revolution, in 1914, Carranza assumed administrative control of all the railroads, which was not surrendered until January 1926.

There were efforts to reorganize the railroads and consolidate the railroad debt in 1922, 1926, and 1930, but nothing of significance was accomplished. The power of railroad labor, the disorganized economy, and the frequent rebellions limited the government's freedom of action. In 1937 Cárdenas expropriated the railroads on the grounds of public utility, promising to pay the owners the real value of the properties, and in 1938 he turned the National Railroads over to a juridical and autonomous organization, with its own patrimony, to be administered by the workers. This administration and, in fact, ownership by the workers came to an end on December 31, 1940, to be replaced by a separate organ of control, directly responsible to the president of the Republic. This, in short, is the history of the Mexican railroads so far as their legal position is concerned.

Of primary importance is the fact that the basic transport system radiating out of Mexico City consists of three roads that run to the United States and two that connect the capital with the Gulf of Mexico. The north is sparsely populated, the country through which the roads pass is largely a desert, and the cities are few and far apart. The railroads to the Gulf are primarily roads connecting with the port of Vera Cruz and serve to carry the imports from, and the exports to, that port. This has left a large part of the country and most of the Mexican rural communities without railroad service.

In 1944 Mexico had 23,299 kilometers (about 14,000 miles) of railroad, divided between twenty-one companies. Six small railroads, with 311 kilometers (less than 200 miles), had gone out of business after 1939. Some additional mileage, however, has since been added by federal construction on the Sureste, which will tie the hitherto isolated peninsula of Yucatán to the rest of the country; on the Sonora-Baja California, which will serve a similar purpose for Lower California, and on the road that will tie Topolobampo in Sonora with the Kansas City, Mexico y Oriente. The only important private railroad in the country is the Southern Pacific on the west coast, between the American border and Guadalajara.

Theoretically at least, the Mexican railroads showed a small profit for the years 1940–2. The total expenditure for the entire system ran up to 96, 98, and 99 per cent of the gross income during this period. The Southern Pacific, however (excepting 1942), the railroads of Yucatán, and the Interoceánico had a higher gross outgo than gross income. In fact, all of the important railroads operated at a loss, and the small profit claimed by the National Railroads is on gross income, without including interest on the railroad debt, amortization, or provision for repair of roadbed or for replacement of wornout equipment. The Mexican railway system was deteriorating, the service became poorer, accidents and wrecks more frequent, and the economic drain upon the country greater in spite of the increased income of the roads during the war.

The war placed a great burden on the Mexican railroads because they had to carry the additional freight previously shipped by sea. In ordinary years before the war the railroads carried an average of 14.5 million tons. This rose to 22.2 million tons in 1944. With this change came an increase in gross intake from 115.5 million pesos in 1935 to 252.8 million pesos in 1944, and the gross income per ton moved rose from 8.5 to 11.3 pesos. But costs of operation rose by 152 per cent. These years, in fact, showed a decline of net revenue of 41.2 per cent. Every item of operational expense had jumped by over 100 per cent, and the cost of equipment rose by over 300 per cent. These financial difficulties were merely a continuing story in Mexican railroad history.

Even before the Revolution the Central Railroad was on the verge of being taken over by its stockholders; the National Railroad, on account of its low income, could not complete its projected trackage; and even the most profitable one, the Mexican Railroad (between Mexico City and Vera Cruz), proved a dubious investment in spite of the low wages to labor and the many favors received from the government. These difficulties were not solved by the consolidation of 1908. The Revolution added to the difficulties, and the assumption of administration by the government, in 1914, merely saved them from formal bankruptcy.

The poor yield has made it impossible to meet the depreciation in shops, machinery, equipment, locomotives, roadbeds, rolling stock, the charges on rented freight cars, and taxes. The presumed net income has been insufficient to meet a third of these obligations, and the roads have literally been consuming their past investments and slowly deteriorating. The payment on the railroad debt, suspended in 1914, has not been renewed (see page 233). Only the increasing traffic caused by a growing population, the greater economic activity stimulated by the war, and the higher passenger and freight rates have kept the railroad system from falling to pieces. The increased gross income per kilometer that saved the railroads is owing to the difference between 73,200 passengers per kilometer carried in 1910, and the 233,200 carried in 1940, and between the 3 and 7 million tons hauled per kilometer, respectively, in these years.

The railroads' survival has been made possible by the great increase in freight and passengers carried without proportionate increase in equipment. The tonnage of freight carried per kilometer between 1926 and 1944 increased 186 per cent, while the traction power improved by only 28 per cent. The number of passengers carried per kilometer rose by 214 per cent, and of coaches by only 46 per cent between these two dates. This more intensive use of the available equipment has added to the rate of deterioration of both the roadbeds and the rolling stock. As a result, freight trains moved more slowly, and the average speed declined in 1944 from 20 to 18.2 kilometers per hour, while for every 100 passenger trains, 78 were late in 1944, 62 in 1943, and 34 in 1940. Accidents in the meantime had greatly increased, and in 1942 there were 225 persons killed and 2,837 injured on the Mexican railroads. In that year, it was estimated, the efficiency of the passenger service on some of the leading railroads was as follows: Sureste, 5.4 per cent; the Querétaro division, 33.7 per cent; the Cárdenas division, 30.2 per cent; and, the Monterrey division, 84.2 per cent. The delay in the trains raised the cost of extra labor time and added to the consumption of fuel. It should further be noted that 35 per cent of the coaches, 50 per cent of the freight cars, and 80 per cent of the locomotives have seen more than twenty-five years of service and need to be replaced. To illustrate what has been happening it needs only to be added that wages and salaries rose from 17.5 million to 168.9 million pesos between 1910 and 1940, and the number of workers from 26,100 to 52,500 within the same period. With the needed addition of at least 33 per cent of equipment at present prices, it would require 800,000,000 pesos to bring the rolling stock and railroad shops into good working order. This would not cover the various hundreds of millions needed to repair the roadbed and to lay new railroad ties and rails.

Such essential new capital represents the deterioration of the physical plant in the years since 1910. In May 1947 the National Railroads reported that they were operating at a loss of 1,300,000 pesos per month, without including servicing charges. If available, the new capital investment is additional to the needs of the Interoceánico, the Noreste, the Southern Pacific, the Kansas City, and the Yucatán. Another 400,000,000 pesos would be required. If a foreign loan is not to be had, the railroads face complete ruin, for an attempt to rehabilitate them out of their own incomes could not stem the rate of deterioration now taking place.

One difficulty among many others is the low ton-kilometer freight traffic available for the Mexican railroads. In 1926–8 the United States railroads carried an average of 1,634,000 ton kilometers of freight, the Mexican railroads 259,000. In 1943 the United States railroads had increased their freight haulage to 3,209,000 ton kilometers, the Mexican to 536,000. The traffic load on Mexican railroads was 15.8 and 16.7 per cent, respectively, of that of the American railroads for these two periods.

The low ratio of traffic per kilometer is merely indicative of the structure of the economy as a whole. A growing industrialism would certainly add to the freight carried by the railroads, but whether it would do so in sufficient amount and with sufficient speed to amortize the new investment in re-establishing the roads is something that only time could reveal. Even if all of the present roads were put into first-class condition, Mexico would still need considerable new railroad construction to open up unused resources, supply the needs of a large section of the country, and make possible the growth of an integrated economy.

Twenty new railroad lines have been proposed, and some of them, such as the road between Mexico City and Tampico, or the road that would connect Mexico City with Acapulco, are of considerable economic significance. All together these roads would add 12,000 kilometers, mostly to be laid in difficult mountain country. A more modest alternate project, for relatively short railroads, of 6,770 kilometers, would, it is estimated, cost 1,537 million pesos for construction alone, and would require about twenty years to complete. In 1947 one estimate put the cost of construction and equipment of these new roads at 200,000 pesos per kilometer. It is clear from the foregoing that Mexico requires one billion pesos for the reorganization of the present roads and at least one billion more for new construction and equipment of needed new trackage.

5. *Power*

Next to the railroads the chief visible obstacle to Mexican industrialization is the insufficiency of easily available power. The coal is located at a great distance from the manufacturing centers of the country and is not economically adaptable to the needs of the manufacturing plants. Most factories, mines, textile mills, and one of the leading railroads depend upon electrical energy for their power.

In 1947 Mexico had electric installations with a potential of 893,449 kilowatts, of which 60 per cent was based upon hydroelectric, and 40 per cent upon thermoelectric plants. Of the available electric power, 70.4 per cent was in public utilities, 21.3 per cent in private industry, and 8.3 per cent in both. Twelve companies, producing two billion kilowatt hours annually, provide most of the electricity used in the country. In addition to what is derived from Mexican companies, about 1.7 per cent is imported from the United States. More than half of the electricity produced is consumed by industrial establishments, and about 40 per cent of the national production is used in the Federal District, including Mexico City.

The relative position of the electrical industry is indicated by the fact that only 1.1 per cent of all Mexican communities have electric service. If we look at this from the point of view of some of the states, the sparsity of electricity is an eloquent testimony of the degree of modernity in the country. Of 780 communities in Aguascalientes, 4 have electric service. Of 3,391 in San Luis Potosí, only 22 have electric service. In fact, this picture is reflected in most of the states, for even in the Federal District, the very heart of Mexico, only 37 of the 260 communities have electrical service. These figures may be given dramatic form by noting that Mexico in 1943 had less than one per cent as much electrical power as the United States, and that it consumed eight per cent as many annual kilowatt hours per person as the United States.

In spite of this poor showing, it has been roughly estimated that Mexico has potential water power for seven million horsepower or more. This prospective hydroelectric development is retarded by the irregular rainfall and by the deforestation of many of the watersheds. This imposes high-cost construction and exposes plants to the danger of rapid silting by the earth carried down during the period when the streams are in flood. In many places, too, the porous soil permits water to seep underground. In addition, the prevalence of earthquakes imposes the need for special care in the construction of dams.

To these natural obstacles have to be added the high cost of initial investment, the slow amortization, the economic and political instability, and the location of many possible sites at long distances from available markets. All of these difficulties have retarded the development of the electrical industry. The insufficiency of the available supply of electric power was indicated by the necessity for a twenty-per-cent reduction of all consumption on the central plateau for a period of three months in 1944.

To meet this situation, a Federal Electrical Commission was created in 1937. It has devoted its energies to the expansion of the available electrical plants and the building of new ones, and to making careful studies of the possibilities of hydroelectric resources scattered over various parts of the country. The commission reports an annual increase of 5.5 per cent in electrical energy produced, as measured by monthly averages between 1940 and 1946. Three plants were started at Ixtapantango, in central Mexico, each of 30,000 kilowatts. The first unit was put in operation in September 1944, and the others were expected to be in operation at an early date. A 25,000-kilowatt thermoelectric plant was put in service by a private concern, the Mexican Light and Power Company, at Nonalco in June 1944, to help relieve the needs of Mexico City. But the demand for electrical energy in the Federal District and Mexico City is growing at about 25,000 kilowatts per year, and even if all the present plans are completed on time, they can barely satisfy the growing demand.

The effects of the federal commission's labors can be seen in states as far apart as Durango, Vera Cruz, Jalisco, and Puebla. In fact, it has sought to group the available plants in the country into five centralized hydroelectric systems and gradually strengthen them by new construction. The commission claims to have increased the total capacity in the units in which it operates by 50,120 kilowatts, and its plans call for early completion of projects that will have a capacity of 218,965 kilowatts.

A fuller appreciation of the magnitude of the undertaking the Federal Electrical Commission looks to is indicated by its report in 1946. It points out that in 1940 there were 1,491 communities with over 1,500 inhabitants each, containing 8.3 million people, most of which had no electric service. Present plans call for an expenditure by 1950 of over 600 million pesos (136 million dollars).

In addition to coal and electricity, petroleum and its by-products are widely used for industrial purposes in internal-combustion engines. In recent years, as was noticed before (see page 207), both production and exports of petroleum have declined, but local use of crude petroleum and its derivatives has greatly increased. Between 1941 and 1946 production fell from 16.4 to 11.2 million barrels. The industry has survived on the comparatively new and highly productive field of Poza Rica, the others being on the decline. Of the 150 perforations made between 1941 and 1946, 31 were dry, 33 came in salt water, and the remaining 95 yield only about 110,234 barrels daily. The refineries at Poza Rica and Atzcapotzalco have been enlarged, and a new refinery for high-test gas has been built at Salamanca. Oil pipelines are in the process of being extended.

The railroads have been unable, on occasion, to deliver petroleum to various parts of the country, and this seriously affects both traffic and industrial establishments. Even in the Federal District the cement industry had to take a serious daily loss for a period, on account of the failure of a sufficient supply of oil.

The oil industry has gone through a series of readjustments

since 1938. While all of the facts are not available, there is reason to believe that the labor force increased from 14,000 to 20,000, and the wage bill, which was about 50 million pesos in 1938, is said to have tripled. The annual losses are estimated at 50 million pesos. It is clear that if Mexican industry is to depend upon oil for extensive development, the oil industry will require very large foreign capital investments.

There is a possible relief available, however, for the pressing need of industrial energy in the supply of natural gas now going to waste at Poza Rica. It is suggested that this gas has a probable life of forty years, and that it could supply a very considerable amount of energy to a growing industrialism if it were piped to Mexico City and other centers. The distance to Mexico City is only 240 kilometers (about 145 miles), though the country is very mountainous. In 1945 it was estimated that to carry 1,250 million cubic meters of gas from Poza Rica to Mexico City would require an investment of 16,635,000 dollars, or, roughly, a hundred million pesos. The gas pipeline from Poza Rica to Mexico City is now under construction.

It must be clear from the foregoing discussion that Mexican industrial growth, now being stimulated both by government policy and by foreign investment, requires, if it is to meet the expectancies of the present-day leaders, a very considerable development in hydroelectric power, petroleum production, and the transport of natural gas. In fact, this essential preliminary investment is of such magnitude that current government and foreign capital going into manufacturing plants is of relative insignificance.

6. *Inflation*

The increased industrial activity of the last decade is partly owing to the impact of the war, to the inflow of foreign capital seeking either safety or opportunities for investment, to the public-works program, to governmental financing of individual industrial undertakings, and to a seemingly deliberate policy of monetary inflation for the very purpose of stimulating industrial activity.

Until 1936 the public-works program was financed out of income derived from taxation. The peso against the dollar was at 3.60,[2] and the government finances were in comparative balance. In 1937 the government began borrowing from the Bank of Mexico in increasing amounts. In that year, the National Bank of Foreign Commerce was established, the Ejido Bank began its operations, and in addition eight million pesos were given to the Bank of Agricultural Credit. Money was allotted for new railroad construction, and port works were financed. The Mexico-Laredo road was inaugurated, irrigation works and schools were constructed, and nine million pesos of public-road bonds were issued, making a total of thirty million pesos outstanding at that time. The government's indebtedness to the Bank of Mexico increased, and in 1939, with an income of 424 million pesos, the government expended over 100 million on public works. The Ejido Bank received 20 million, and the Agricultural Bank 12 million pesos. The National Labor Banks invested 14 million in a new sugar refinery, and more capital was given to the National Bank of Commerce. It is estimated that the borrowings by the government from the Bank of Mexico equaled 123 million pesos and that only small amounts of these borrowings were placed with the public.

In 1938 the peso was devalued from 3.60 to 4.85 to the dollar, thus increasing the price of imported goods, so important to the economy of Mexico. Money in circulation increased by 145 million pesos, or 35.8 per cent over 1935. The government continued borrowing from the National Bank in amounts unknown (it was suggested in 1943 that the government's direct indebtedness to the bank was between 500 and 600 million pesos).

In 1943 the government issued 126.5 million pesos in road bonds, 25 million in railroad bonds, 9 million in bonds for free ports, and announced 200 million in defense bonds, of which only 50 million were actually placed. In 1945 the government issued 60 million for public works, 100 million for roads, and another 8.2 million for ports and roads; in all, 168.2 million. All

[2] In June 1949 it went to 8.65 to the dollar.

of this increased the money in circulation. It was estimated that between 1929 and 1939, while the resources in the credit institutions had increased by 17 per cent, the money in the hands of the public had grown by 222 per cent, and by the end of 1945 the amount of money in circulation (942 million in 1939) had increased to over 2 billion. In 1935–9 the circulating media increased by 6.3 million pesos per month, while in 1940–4 it increased by 36.2 million per month.

This inflationary process was evidenced in both wages and prices. Industrial labor had more than doubled its wages between 1939 and 1943, from 17 to 38.5 pesos per week. By 1945 factory labor received 240 million more in wages than in 1939, petroleum workers 70 million more, miners 180 million, railroad workers 88.5 million, and federal employees 212.6 million more. The wage bill had risen a matter of 600 million pesos in five years, but so had prices.

With 1934 as a base, the cost of living in June 1946 was 412 per cent, and the cost of clothes had risen to 169.6 per cent, while retail prices had risen to 256.5 per cent since 1937. In real wages workers in Mexico City were receiving 83.6 per cent of their 1939 earnings by May 1945. Rural income, as expressed in real wages (with 1929 as a base), had fallen from 119 per cent in 1934 to 62 per cent in 1944.

What is clear is that business activity was increasing, investments in industry were growing, there was more employment, a middle class was developing, and the country was showing evidence of industrial progress. But it was doing so at the expense of those who could least afford it—the industrial and agricultural laboring population. In a country where the standard of living is as low as it is in Mexico, there is a limit to the possible or desirable amount of forced "savings" for industrialization.

CHAPTER 13

The Conditions of Economic Progress: III

1. Labor and Industrialization

LITTLE NEED BE SAID HERE about the place of labor within the Mexican economy beyond what has already been detailed in Chapter viii, except to add that the body of rules, regulations, privileges, and immunities that organized labor has exacted may well be another impediment to the rapid industrialization now being projected. It is not that the wages of labor in Mexico are so high: excepting in the oil industry, the income of Mexican workers is considerably less than that of industrial labor in the United States. Nor are the rules and regulations of trade-unionism and the rights allowed to the workers by law substantially greater than those of industrial workers in many other parts of the world.

It needs to be noted that Mexico is attempting to do two things at the same time: lay the foundation for a rapid capital accumulation, and maintain a high degree of social security and economic equity. This has not been done before, and these two objectives may, in fact, prove incompatible. Industrialism in the United States and Great Britain proceeded with little awareness of the social and human implication of industrial labor. There was little concern about long hours, low wages, or the incidence of unemployment, accident, and death. The needs of social equity were attended to long after these economies had laid the foundations of a basic capital equipment, which made possible the rapid growth of manufacturing and assured an increase in production at a cost low enough to make available a continuous and growing surplus beyond immediate requirements. Short hours, overtime pay, social security in the form of unemployment benefits, sickness and death insurance, vacations with pay, and the hundred other items in contemporary labor policy developed after capital accumulation made the surplus possible. The very expenditures upon public health and education were a by-product of a growing surplus that could be siphoned off through taxation. It remains to be proved that it is possible to develop, with the speed that the Mexican economy seems to require, a rapidly cumulative body of capital equipment and at the same time place upon it in its initial stages the cost of social security and an elaborate body of trade-union rules and regulations. Especially in a country where the resources are inadequate, their exploitation is very costly.

The issues here raised cannot now be evaluated, even by the government. Time alone will determine the answer to the question involved. It is perfectly possible, however, that the Mexicans will defeat their hopes of a higher real income and the greater surplus out of which that income may be derived just *because* they have imposed upon their incipient industry a social security and economic equity that may require the absorption, for the immediate ends of social justice, of the small surplus now produced. This policy may prevent the production of the capital goods upon which a high standard of living for the mass of the population could be developed.

More serious is the growth of a privileged working class behind a high tariff wall. This may, in fact, defeat the very ends of the national market that the present movement for industrialization aims to achieve. As a matter of deliberate policy the government is using the tariff in defense of every new or old industry that undertakes to produce in Mexico things previously imported. The result is a general tariff program that provides an artificial price stimulus to Mexican manufactures and at the same time increases the cost of living for the mass of the people. The artificially high prices serve to protect a few workers and a small amount of Mexican or foreign capital in the production of some special articles, but in the process they also limit the market for these very products.

The essentials for a monopoly situation are, in fact, created for each industry in turn. In effect, a high tariff makes possible a small industry; the resulting high price limits the market for the products of this industry to the small group of industrial and urban workers who because of a high tariff can exact sufficiently high wages to purchase the articles so produced at a high price. But this, in the end, deprives the mass of the people—the rural folk—of access to the benefits of modern science and technique offered as the original justification for the policy. It is clear to Mexican economists that without the rural population no broad market, essential for industrial development, is possible. It is also clear that the combination between the workers, the manufacturers, and the government to raise the tariff as an inducement to industry is preventing the development of the national market, which under the circumstances can be created only upon a basis of low costs, large-scale and efficient production, and a wide distribution at low prices.

A small, industrial-worker upper class, not more than twenty per cent of the total population, is being developed, cut off from the mass of the people, producing a relatively narrow range of products at high cost and of poor quality, to be distributed among its own numbers—leaving the rest of the people no better equipped, perhaps less competent, than they were before to secure an access to the benefits of industrialism.

It may be argued that this is the only condition under which Mexican manufacturing can come into being. This may be true, but it is equally true that this is not going to achieve the purpose broadcast when the movement was initiated. It may, in fact, throw additional doubt upon the validity of the program itself.

In the meantime the urban population is in a position to absorb any additional gain from the newer industrialism, leaving the rural population as poor as they were before in terms of real income, if not poorer. The situation contains the elements of tragedy, and it cannot be that Mexican labor leaders are entirely unaware of what is implicit in the program. If the agricultural workers really become self-conscious and organized, they may well impose upon Mexico a government attentive to their economic as well as to their political needs—and their economic needs are for low-priced industrial goods in great abundance. But the agricultural population is not yet self-conscious in that sense, and their leaders are still city folk with little understanding of the real problem.

Except low-priced industrial goods, clothing, shoes, tools, and services, the things the city has to offer are of little moment to the country folk; but industry is not pointed toward the mass of hungry consumers in the rural areas. There is no important rural market, and the present industry cannot create it, partly because the poor soil and the ancient agricultural tradition impede any rapid change. The Revolution has added to the size of the urban communities, has increased the middle class, and has created for the first time a native bourgeoisie with all of the appetites of a young capitalist class ambitious for gain in a world where gain is not to be had except from governmental favors or from the agricultural population.

Nor has the communalization of the land added to inner unity. The *ejido* and the union may look alike on paper, but they are very different instrumentalities and derive their substance from different relations to the material universe. The *ejido* is a peasant community that with great difficulty can extract a modest living from a semibarren earth. The union, by the magic of a strike for higher wages or the threat of expropriation, can increase its money income, but only at the cost of higher prices and a lower standard of living for the mass of the rural population. *The role of industry in a preponderantly agricultural nation is materially different from what it is in a country where most of the population is industrial, where the resources are large, and where internal plant economies can make up for the higher wages by increased output per worker.*

Even in the United States this issue has been acute, and we have met the problem by many kinds of agricultural subsidies. The ideal of parity, whatever may be said for it, is at least in part an effort to distribute among the nonindustrial population a share of the increased yield from industrial efficiency. But in a country where from seventy to eighty per cent of the population is living upon income from a primitive agriculture, where industry is poorly equipped, where the industrial resources are inadequate, and where there is insufficient capital, there is small prospect for a rapid increase in industrial efficiency or in greater productivity. Higher wages must and, under the circumstances, do lead to higher prices, and the government has not the resources to establish a parity policy.

Economically the rift between the urban and the rural population remains, and is perhaps just as serious as it was before, though it is hidden by the over-all reconstruction effort of the Revolution. The day will come, however, when the Revolution will be over and the internal schism will stand out clearly and remain as largely unremediable as it was before.

In addition to the conditioning features of the trade-union regulations and the tariff, there are a thousand and one government rules prescribing investment and the rights of ownership and determining the kinds of industry that may be developed. These policies are part of the impact of the Revolution, but even more are the result of imbibing theories and ideas neither related to the Mexican milieu nor applicable to its needs. They have proved attractive because of their simplicity and seeming universality. The present-day leaders of Mexico, under the influence of these ideas, have reared a superstructure of governmental regulation that threatens to topple the economy it would order.

The pleasant notions of a planned economy may have their talking-points in a complex industrial society, where the intricacies of the going concern are beyond the ken of the political theorist and are too contradictory for simple political management. An "old" economy, encrusted with tradition, lacking in resiliency, and showing evidence of being incompetent to maintain the older standards of life for a stationary population, may, in despair, turn to "planning" for solution. These extensive controls may be suited to an economy with a stationary or declining population, in which the emphasis is upon security, keeping the wealth that has already been created and seeing that it is properly distributed. It is not, in terms of past industrial experience, a system for the increase of new wealth, especially a speedy increase such as is demanded by a rapidly expanding population.

What Mexico needs is an increase in the rate of capital accumulation, for only thus can it hope to have a growing average annual real income. If it would not remain poor, or become poorer, then the rate of capital accumulation must increase with sufficient rapidity to provide for the increase in consumer goods and services and thus improve the present level of well-being for both the present and the growing population.

It is not sufficient to point to this or that new investment or new industry. It is important to look at the productive picture as a whole and balance the loss in capital goods against the gains in the same goods. Unless the total is accumulating at a *rate* sufficient to keep the growing population at the present level of income *and* leave a margin for annual improvement, the country is, in fact, growing poorer. The emphasis now being put by enthusiastic promoters upon some particular small industrial investments may be misleading. It is entirely possible that over-all depreciation—the continued loss in the fertility of the soil, the deterioration in the railroads, the exhaustion of the mines—is reducing the productive resources at rates more rapid than they are being replenished by new investment, new loans, or new skills and techniques. The country, in spite of its industrial activity, may be growing poorer rather than richer.

The fact that the years 1931–44 probably saw an increase of national income only sufficient to meet the rate of population growth would of itself indicate that the country is not getting richer. This estimate does not include the actual loss by soil erosion, railroad deterioration, depreciation, and exhaustion of mineral deposits. While the Mexicans of the present generation are disputing among themselves over the issue of social justice and economic equality, the thing they are disputing about—the underlying capital accumulation of the country—may be wasted away under their feet. If the argument lasts long enough, the dispute will decide itself, and the Mexican people will go hungry for lack of bare subsistence. These reflections emphasize the significance of the government's attempts to reduce the cost of Mexico's foreign commitments and its effort to increase the local capital resources.

2. *Foreign Investment*

The inner drive since the Revolution has been to reduce the foreign interest in Mexico. This aim has dictated legislative policy and administrative procedure. It has manifested itself in the economic program of every recent government. It has included restrictions upon foreign investments and has limited the place and role of foreigners in industrial management. It has expressed itself in labor legislation, in the elimination of foreign banking and insurance companies, in adjustments of the government's external obligations, and, finally, in the expropriation of such industries as oil and the railroads.

The political aim has been to free Mexico from interference by outsiders in the internal affairs of the country. The economic aim has been to increase the Mexicans' share in the national wealth. Finally, there has been the purpose of reducing the heavy burden of foreign payments that acted as a perennial drain upon the country's foreign exchange.

Mexican economists estimate that foreigners controlled 20

per cent of the national wealth in 1903, and 42 per cent in 1910. This doubling of the foreign interest was represented, in part, by the growth of the oil industry, the expansion of mining, and the increased investments in hydroelectric power. In 1930, according to Mexican economists, foreigners held approximately a 9-per-cent interest in agriculture, 99 per cent in petroleum, 98 per cent in the mines, 99 per cent in electrical development, 42 per cent in commerce and services, and 79 per cent in railroads and streetcars. This does not include the claim upon the national wealth represented by the direct obligations of the government for unpaid loans and defaulted interest, dating from 1914.

Only in agriculture, in commerce, and in the servicing industries did Mexicans own a majority interest. Since 1930 the share of the foreign claim has been greatly reduced. According to Mexican sources, the percentage of the national wealth held by foreigners had fallen to 33 per cent by 1935, and their claims were distributed as follows: United States, 14 per cent; English, 6 per cent; Spanish, 4 per cent; French, 2 per cent; and all others, 7 per cent. This left to Mexicans 67 per cent of the total national wealth.

Many changes adversely affecting foreign investments have occurred since 1935. The oil and railroad industries have been expropriated, the foreign-owned banks and insurance companies have been eliminated, a great deal of land held by nonnationals has been transferred to the peasants, and numerous other steps have been taken to increase the proportion of the national wealth in Mexican hands. In addition the government has attempted to reduce to a fraction of the original commitments foreign claims on account of its foreign bonded debt and the amounts owed on the railroads.

What the situation is at present is hard to define. A very considerable amount of foreign capital has gone into Mexico since 1940, and an appreciable part of it has been invested in Mexican enterprise. As the Bank of Mexico points out, however, all new capital investments by foreigners are now regulated so as to avoid the "undesirable consequences" of the past.

No satisfactory explanation of this profound reversal in national policy toward foreign capital investment can be had without appreciating the continuous drain upon international exchange that this investment imposed. The cost of the capital contributed by outsiders seemed high—higher, in fact, than the country could afford. That, at least, was the judgment of those responsible for Mexican policy. How great the burden was is hard to estimate, for we have no satisfactory accounting of the country's balance of payments, so that we cannot fully detail the various "invisible" items in the total picture, but enough can be pieced together to give an approximate estimate of the country's payments for the benefits it received from outside capital.

Mexico's foreign trade for most of the past four hundred years has shown a "favorable" balance. With few exceptions in all of its history, the figures on the visible trade, including the export of gold and silver, indicated that Mexico was exporting more than it was importing.[1] This balance, mostly based upon the export of precious metals, presumably covered interest, profit, amortization of foreign investments, and the visible imports. Roughly speaking, over the years since 1910 a third of the value of the Mexican exports remained outside of the country as payment on this account. This did not include the services upon the public debt or upon the railroad debt, as these were in suspense after 1914. The last regular service on the foreign debt, made in 1909–10, equaled 26,000,000 pesos, or 23.7 per cent of the income of the government. One Mexican estimate of the country's balance of payments leads to the conclusion that Mexico shipped abroad, for the servicing of the foreign investment and the foreign debt, 149.7 million pesos in 1909, 316.5 million pesos in 1926, and 400.0 million pesos in

[1] Since 1885 Mexico has shown a consistently favorable trade balance, but this was also the period when foreign capital was flowing into the country in presumably great amounts and should have been reflected in the ordinary course of events in a negative rather than a positive trade balance. There is no room here for a full discussion of the question, but it would require full treatment in any economic history of Mexico.

1940, or about fifty per cent of the total value of Mexico's exports for those years.

No accurate record of the total invested by outsiders is available, and even in the seemingly simpler matter of government bonds there has been continuous dispute about the amount for which the government was obligated. One account, in 1921, places the total foreign direct investment at 1,954 million dollars, about one third of which, or 652 million, was said to be American. A later calculation, made in 1931, places American commitments alone as high as one billion dollars.

The figures on the distribution of these investments by industry are estimates, differing as to the amounts assigned to various enterprises. Not to burden the reader, I cite one estimate, which places mining and smelting at 396.3 million dollars, oil 381.5,[2] railroads 196.4, public utilities 226.0, manufactures 48.4, distribution 87.0, and miscellaneous 25.0 million dollars.

Whatever the original investments, their values have now greatly shrunk and in some instances completely disappeared. The United States Department of Commerce in 1936 placed the value of American investments in Mexico at less than half a billion dollars, but since 1936 the peso has been devalued, the oil companies expropriated, and a whole series of other measures developed that have reduced the effective total of foreign holdings. One American statement places United States holdings in 1940 at less than 300 million dollars, and all foreign holdings at less than half a billion. This would be about one fourth of the 1921 estimates.[3]

The Mexican government, by agreement with the United States in 1942, canceled all claims on account of the oil industry for the sum of 24 million dollars. It paid 9 million on

[2] A Mexican official estimate in 1934 gives American investments in the oil industry as 499 million pesos, or 52 per cent of the total in that industry.

[3] This is confirmed by a Mexican economist, writing in 1943, who calculated all foreign investments at 1,881 million pesos, or approximately 380 million dollars.

account, and the rest in regular annual installments over a period of five years, the balance to carry a three-per-cent interest dating from 1938. All other property claims for damage and land expropriations in dispute between the governments were liquidated for 40 million dollars, payments beginning in 1942. Mexico had already paid down 6 million, so that only 34 million dollars were outstanding. During this period, too, the foreign banks and insurance companies were eliminated.

These changes in the position of direct foreign investment still left the government's bonded and railroad debt to be taken care of. In 1929 the government's bonded debt amounted to approximately one billion pesos. There was in addition arrears of interest of some 400 million pesos. This was not the total amount due, for the government had claims laid against it of another 305 million pesos for damages pending before claims commissions for the agrarian debt and other obligations. All together, the seeming indebtedness in 1929 was around two billion pesos.

In 1942 the Mexican Minister of Finance came to an agreement with the International Committee of Bankers for Mexico for the adjustment of the external debt. The debt of 520 million dollars agreed to was converted to a peso debt, and for purposes of final liquidation each dollar was equal to one peso. But as the peso had been devalued to 4.85 to the dollar, the actual reduction of the obligation was from 520 million dollars to 230 million, so that the bondholders would get, at their present value, one peso for one dollar, as if their original claim had been 230 rather than 520 million dollars. Unpaid interest up to 1923 was to be at one per cent upon guaranteed bonds and one tenth of one per cent upon unsecured bonds, the interest to run as against the peso. Between 1923 and 1942 the interest would be approximately one per cent. After 1943 interest would run between one third and one ninth of the contractual rate. The Mexican government was to be able to retire its bonds at this rate up to 1963 or 1968, depending on the type of bond.

The Council of Foreign Bondholders protested, but in 1943

the Mexican government declared the settlement effective because it had been accepted by twenty per cent of the capital interested. In fact, the Mexican obligations had been reduced to ten per cent of their nominal value, and the foreign debt service had been reduced to approximately two per cent of the government's income. One Mexican economic journal, approving of this settlement, made the restrained comment that "the foreign investors, still so necessary, given our small capacity for saving, will have one more incentive, or still better, one obstacle less to adventure upon the undertakings of great promise . . . so necessary to our productivity."

A somewhat similar proposal was made in December 1945 in a law for the settlement of the railroad debt, estimated at 265 million dollars. These changes in Mexico's obligations reduced the pressure on her foreign exchange, and the situation, for the time being, favored Mexico.

The war brought new capital into the country: Mexican laborers who went to the United States during the war sent home remittances estimated at 127 million pesos in 1944, and during that year travelers left more than 101 million pesos in Mexico. For 1945 these two sources of invisible payments are said to have equaled about five million dollars a month, or about 300 million pesos a year.

There was also the continuous investment of foreign funds, averaging perhaps 100 million pesos annually, while the high interest rate and the inflationary prices kept some profits from leaving the country because of the opportunities for reinvestment.

Finally, during this period Mexican exports were drawn to an unusual degree from industries locally owned and controlled: 64.7 per cent of the total in 1942, 74.8 in 1943, 78.2 in 1944, and even higher in 1945. The war had greatly raised the price of such locally owned exports as textiles, fibers, beer, and alcohol, and as a result the profits accrued to Mexico. These various influences, among others, explain the fact that for the first time in many years Mexico's imports were greater than her exports. She showed a negative position for the years

1941–5 inclusive, running over 400 million pesos in 1941 and 1945.

In spite of that, the inflow of outside payments was sufficiently large during these years to make it unnecessary to meet the deficit by the shipment of gold, and the negative commercial balance had no adverse effects upon Mexico's metallic reserve. But this favorable position has been reversed. Since June 1947 imports are greatly exceeding exports. In 1947 Mexico was forced to borrow 50,000,000 dollars from the Export-Import Bank and since then has deliberately cut down imports to protect its foreign-exchange position. In spite of these efforts, Mexico had an unfavorable trade balance amounting to 1,412.9 million pesos in 1947 and 981.7 million pesos in 1948. As a consequence, in June 1949 the peso was devalued to 8.65 to the United States dollar.

3. Public Policy

The government has succeeded in reducing the foreign investment and in laying the basis for controlling foreign investments in the future. In addition, industrial development has been greatly stimulated by high prices and official policy. The objective so long held in view—that of effectuating a policy of intervention and guidance, if not control, of the economy of the nation—is seemingly being realized. It is one of the cardinal beliefs of the present leadership that the government must intervene to protect Mexico against the foreign interest and, even more, to stimulate and direct the industrial and economic development of the country. To this end a long and many-sided series of activities has been fostered, and numerous official and semiofficial institutions have been created. In fact, as stated earlier, the government is involved directly or indirectly, through semiofficial agencies operating with government credit, with governmental personnel, and in conformance with some governmental objective, in almost every economic enterprise in the country.

The central agency in this undertaking is the Nacional

Financiera, S.A., first organized with 20 million pesos in 1934. It has since developed into a complex and many-sided institution, operating with large public and increasing private funds, and assuming a directing, perhaps a dominating, position in the guiding of Mexico's industrial development. Its operations are a combination of activities and powers that might be compared to the United States Reconstruction Finance Corporation, the Securities and Exchange Commission, and an investment trust under governmental auspices. In addition it is the leading instrument for floating government bonds. It also intervenes actively in the market, in support of both public and "private" issues.

On December 31, 1945 the Nacional Financiera had an investment in industrial shares of over 151 million pesos, in stocks of nearly 22 million, approximately 41 million of various bonds, and about 324 million of bonds issued by government units. During the year it had also extended more than 39 million pesos' credit to industrial enterprises. In addition it had operated in the public stock and bond market during 1945 to the amount of 3,469,000,000 pesos, of which 50.6 per cent represented public bonds, 24.4 per cent industrial issues, 22.5 per cent mortgage bonds, 2.4 per cent bank stocks, and 0.1 per cent mining stocks.

Between 1937 and 1945 this public organ floated 259.8 million pesos on its own account, 92 per cent of which was taken up by holders of "participating certificates." Between 1934 and December 1945 it realized a profit on its various operations of over 18 million pesos; for the year 1945 alone its profits amounted to 5 million pesos. In detail, it had taken the initiative in organizing eighteen industrial enterprises with a total capitalization of 256 million pesos, of which it held 49.7 per cent, including common and preferred stocks. In fact, it held 89.4 per cent of the total issues floated by those eighteen firms.

These companies, promoted directly by the government, included a steel industry, a hydroelectric company, a fertilizer firm, an electrical equipment company, and enterprises in coal, glass, meat-packing, cement, rubber, sugar, and copper. This list indicates the range of activities being promoted directly by the government; the investments in the stocks and bonds of thirty-one other enterprises make it clear that there is hardly a field of economic activity in which the government is not participating. These investments are in enterprises that include the manufacture of films, the production of motion pictures, a theater-operating company, a dehydration concern, water distribution, milling, graphic arts, a weekly publication, beer-manufacturing, and a maritime concern. The major investments have been in steel, copper, fertilizers, sugar, cement, electricity, and rayon.

In addition to all of these activities the Nacional Financiera has extended credit and made direct loans to various private and public enterprises. These include the National Railroads, the government-controlled petroleum industry, the town of Laredo, a motion-picture bank, the department of communications, a plastic-manufacturing company, and many others. It also provided credit for the purchase of machinery from the United States to the amount of approximately 170 million pesos. These and many other activities, such as the floating of public issues for federal and state governments, indicate the range of the activities of this institution in the industrialization of Mexico.

The justification for this policy, as seen by the government, has already been indicated. It need only be added that this was, in part, also an effort to develop a local market for public and private issues, which could be tapped only by a device that offered a guaranteed bond at a high price in an easily convertible form. The "certificate of participation" backed by the resources of this institution, having characteristics of shares issued by an investment trust, and supported by the government's bonds, made it possible to float increasing amounts of public issues. Nacional Financiera prides itself upon having floated 40 million pesos of such bonds in 1945 and seeing them oversubscribed in two weeks. There are features of this activity, however, that deserve careful attention, both because of the policy implicit in them and because of the economy represented by them.

All of the issues for industrialization are floated at a high interest rate, usually over seven per cent and sometimes as high as eight per cent. The companies organized are generally expected to pay a guaranteed cumulative profit of between seven and eight per cent; that is even true of mortgage bonds redeemable in ten years. This may indicate that the initial cost of capital is high. It is probably true that this seemingly high interest rate is not excessive for Mexico, even under governmental auspices; but it should be recorded that while the Mexican government was making these investments and establishing these credits, it had received from the Export-Import Bank loans amounting to forty-seven million dollars, at an interest rate of four per cent.

The government-sponsored and stimulated industrial enterprises are therefore setting the pattern of a high initial cost, justified on the ground that it is developing a private market for such industrial issues. We are told that on December 31, 1944 the Nacional Financiera had outstanding more than 204 million pesos in paper, floated mostly during the previous two years. Of this amount, ninety per cent had been taken up by approximately one thousand individuals. This is considered a most flattering result.

It is an interesting question in terms of public policy whether publicly promoted industrialization, paying high interest rates and offering a guaranteed investment of eight per cent, placed in the hands of a thousand individuals, is a flattering affair. It must be remembered that these industries are protected by a high tariff and, if the tariff is not sufficient, by the prohibition of imports of competing products through a system of import controls. It would seem dubious economic policy to raise the cost of living for an entire nation for the benefit of an industrial structure in which the few shareholders are an infinitesimal part of the population, specially protected against loss by the resources of the government itself, and whose holdings, by a decree of February 12, 1946, enjoy the same immunities from taxation, if devoted to the promotion of industrial production, as the bonds issued by the federal government.

That may, in fact, prove to be industrialization at a price greater than the economy of the country can long sustain. In addition, these activities have given justification for the government's direct participation in the minutest industrial affairs of the country, have greatly extended the powers of the bureaucracy, and have raised the issue of the future relations of these industries, governmentally sponsored and controlled, with organized labor in Mexico, which is also governmentally sponsored and largely controlled. Some day the government may have to choose between its guaranteed financial commitments to the holders of the bonds and stocks under its auspices and the demands of the workers. How such an issue can be resolved, except by an increase in prices, remains to be seen. What has happened is that the government has in a short time moved from the political to the economic sphere, to become the arbiter of the Mexican economy. But this change may have complicated rather than eased the industrial development of the nation.

The reduction of the foreign interest, dictated by the nationalist policies of the Revolution, conflicts with the historical role of foreign capital in the development of modern Mexico. In fact, the industrialization Mexican leaders strive for and the economic "progress" they hope for rest upon those past investments which the nationalist policy would reduce or eliminate, and future growth requires additional large-scale foreign commitments. Without them the country cannot hope to carry out a program designed to create an industrial society operating on a national market. It was from capital accumulated outside of Mexico that the railroads were built, the mines developed, the oil industry brought into being, the hydroelectric power plants constructed, the street railways laid out, and the cities lighted. The telephone, the telegraph, the ports, the large commercial establishments, the textile industry, the tobacco industry, the steel works, public sanitation, and even the larger retail trade in tools, machinery, drugs, and department stores were wholly or partly financed by foreign capital, developed by foreign skill, and serviced by foreign technicians. Without this foreign capital and foreign technical aid Mexico would have remained a wholly primitive, agricultural, and disunited nation. The claim that the price for the service rendered was high may be true; but the capital goods represented by the price paid are what Mexico has to look to as a base upon which to build for the future. It remains to be seen whether in the years to come it can secure an equal or greater contribution from the outside at a lower price, or whether it can receive it at all. If foreign capital is not available, then the program of the Mexican government will be indefinitely postponed or be so slowly developed as to be almost imperceptible.

From the point of view of the country's need for foreign exchange to service capital derived from outside sources, it makes little difference whether the servicing is called for by a direct investment or by a loan to the government. Either can be serviced only by the transfer of dollars abroad, and this can be had only from increased exports. The Mexican economy proved incapable of servicing its foreign loans and obligations. It has therefore attempted to reduce the proportion of the foreign interest—even by expropriation—because the burden of payments seemed economically beyond the power of the economy to sustain.

This, of course, raises the whole problem of the impact of foreign investment and government loans. An investment or a loan is, in fact, a payment in advance for goods to be delivered in the future. If the goods cannot be produced, or if they can find no market, the initial capital commitments cannot be liquidated except by default, reduction, confiscation, or agreements such as that proposed by Mexico, which would in fact change each dollar of obligation to about ten cents. The process of adjustment that follows a failure to produce and sell the goods that would satisfy the original obligation raises innumerable political, legal, diplomatic, and social issues. The original purchaser of the bond, his bank, and his government get involved, and the borrower, as in the case of Mexico, is thrown into a series of internal political convulsions and the development of an extreme nationalism in the attempt to extricate himself from an economically impossible and politically difficult situation. Default or expropriation, as for instance in the case of the Mexican railroads, is the child of economic bankruptcy. The failure to service the obligations, including the bonded indebtedness, is a national effort to escape the political and economic consequences of bankruptcy.

What this discussion points to is that, given the Mexican power of repayment, the country was seemingly oversaturated with foreign capital. It could certainly have used a great deal more than it received, but it could not pay even for what it had acquired in both private investment and governmental loans. In the face of this situation the prospect of industrialization in Mexico is confronted with a dilemma from which there is probably no escape. It needs a great deal of foreign capital for primary construction before a sound, large manufacturing development can take place. Various students have estimated Mexico's needs for these primary capital goods as follows:

railroad reconstruction, at least 1 billion pesos;
new railroads and equipment, 1 billion pesos (it has been put as high as 2 billion);
new roads and vehicles, at least 1 billion pesos;
irrigation, 6 billion pesos;
hydroelectric and gas constructions and servicing equipment, 1 billion pesos (as an immediate minimum);
others (airfields, ports, sanitation, etc.), 1 billion pesos;
total, 11 billion pesos.[4]

This seemingly conservative estimate of eleven to twelve billion pesos of new capital equipment is prerequisite for any extensive industrialization. Mexico's record with foreign loans and investments is not conducive to optimism on the part of

[4] All of these estimates were made before June 1948, when official support of the peso at 4.85 to the dollar was abandoned.

prospective lenders. Nor can it be assumed that new devices such as the Export-Import Bank or the new World Bank can profoundly alter this situation. Without the loans the industrialization cannot take place, because Mexico does not have the resources to supply these needs by itself. Nor are Mexican economists unaware of the issues at stake. The *Revista de la Economía* called attention to these contradictions within the Mexican economy when, on August 31, 1946, it said: "We lack the basic investment that would facilitate the development of manufacturing industries for the diversification of our economy. We have no transportation, we have no electricity. We have no irrigation, and we lack the capital that would make it possible for us to make these basic investments by ourselves."

This large investment, a minimum of between ten and eleven billion pesos, is a preliminary condition for the industrialization of Mexico. A competent railway system, sufficient hydroelectric power, a completed program of irrigation, are the prerequisites for the kind of economic program now envisioned. This investment would not in itself contribute materially to the expansion of Mexican exports and would not, therefore, provide the large amounts of international exchange required for the servicing of these new commitments. They could come only from the growth of a wide and complex manufacturing industry. But such new manufacturing plants would in their turn have to draw heavily upon foreign capital, imported raw materials, skills, and machinery, which in turn would have to be paid for by the increasing exports.

Conditions in Mexico are not favorable for a manufacturing program large enough to pay for both the initial basic capital equipment and the factory development. The country's resources are too narrow and badly structured. Even if the initial foreign investment could be had, it is extremely doubtful if it could be converted into manufactures on a scale sufficient to provide the additional exports essential to the program. If the cost of the investment cannot be serviced—that is, if amortization, repair, and replacement cannot be provided for out of the earnings of these investments—the developments will ultimately deteriorate like the railroads. *And this result is independent of any governmental policy.* Expropriation is no answer to the problem. The new investment must amortize and maintain itself by a continuous flow of new investments for repair, replacement, and expansion, or it must deteriorate. Mexican experience is more than eloquent upon this point.

The conclusion is obvious. The proposed program of large-scale investment for capital equipment as a basis for the growth of an industrial society can be achieved only by assuming a burden of cost greater than the country can support. If the Mexican government wishes to meet the basic issue confronting it—that of finding a means of livelihood for its rapidly increasing population—it will have to devise an alternative program, one more consonant with Mexican realities, and one that it can carry out with greater freedom from dependence upon foreign loans and investments.

I recogize that this will seem a policy of despair, but unless some such alternative program is developed, the conditions in Mexico will within a generation or so be well-nigh desperate. Many Mexicans, and some but by no means all of the professional economists, will reject this conclusion. It will be infinitely better for Mexico, however, if it turns its eyes to Switzerland and Denmark rather than to the United States as a model and seeks to find a way out on a local, parochial basis in thousands of little communities, adapting to them all of what modern science and skill can make available for the needs of the little community without making it increasingly dependent upon a national market. There is no virtue in flooding these little towns with poor products from factories at high cost when they can make most of the things they require in their own villages and neighborhoods, with their own hands, by their own arts, and make them beautiful and strong and serviceable. There is no virtue in destroying the Mexican rural community. It is the best thing Mexico has; that is where its strength and resiliency lies. The Revolution proved that certainly.

What Mexico needs is an enrichment of its local communities for increased agricultural production and an increase in the variety and quality of the locally produced handicraft goods sufficient for the local needs and for export as well. *It really needs a philosophy of little things.* The Mexican rural school was that in its beginning, and upon that beginning it ought to build. There ought to be a great emphasis upon little dams, not merely for small-scale irrigation, but also as means for the development of small lakes. With comparatively little effort tens of thousands of small one- or two-hectare ponds and lakes could be built, and built by the villages themselves, without too much overhead, supervision, or direction. Each of these ponds, in addition to all other ends it would serve, could easily become a project for fish-farming, now sufficiently well developed to be taken over by any community that has even the tiniest running brook. Mexico ought to take over and expand the program developed by the state of Missouri. It has been established that an acre pond will supply six hundred pounds of fish annually with a little care and a small expense.

Wherever possible the internal-combustion engine, especially if it is adapted to fuels other than oil (something in the immediate offing), the small electric windmill, or the small hydroelectric plant to serve a given community and its inhabitants ought to be developed.

More important than any of these, perhaps, is the possible adaptability of hydroponics for the growing of potatoes, corn, and other vegetables, which can be easily grown under this system. In Mexico two, three, and for certain items four crops a year could be grown under this method, and it could have almost universal application. In view of the fact that most of the population eat little meat and are not dependent upon wheat, this effort would quickly repay, many times over, the energy put into it. Again, it is something that each village, no matter how small, or even each family, could carry out if the needed chemicals could be procured, and these, from all the evidence, could be produced in Mexico.

The art of making compost ought to be taught in every rural school and in every village. Every effort ought to be made to increase the cultivation of fruit and nut trees of all varieties, not on large plantations, but in every village, in each school ground, and in each man's private yard; and, with it, all of the possible uses of each fruit or nut ought to be developed and taught.

The local crafts and the materials used in their manufacture ought to be studied and improved. Each community ought to be bent in the direction of developing the local resources to make them contribute all they possibly can to the benefit of the local community.

All of this, and a thousand other things, such as seed selection, local sanitation, animal-breeding, and bee-keeping, ought to be developed. To do this would require ten to twenty thousand young men and women trained in the local arts, special skills, and specific sciences adaptable to such a program. They would have to be devoted to their task as the missionaries of old were, and give themselves over completely to redeeming Mexico from the threat of an eroding soil and a growing population.

I must confess to myself with sorrow that both the zeal and the faith have largely departed from Mexico, and a mood of cynicism has taken hold of the country, especially in the cities from which the original impulse for such a program would have to come. The city folk—especially in Mexico City, and particularly the government employees who live there—would have it otherwise. They would make big plans, procure large foreign funds, organize great industries, discover some magic in "industrialization," and have a national economy served by a national market at any cost, even if in their hearts they suspect that it is chiefly a dream, which, because of inadequate resources, cannot be realized. But the ideal of bigness is on them, and they will copy and make plans for the impossible, even if the Mexico they love must be sacrificed to their notion of "progress."

There is nothing in this proposal that would deny both the need and the possibility of industrial development in Mexico.

The extent and the character of such economic expansion, however, can be revealed only by time and experience. An industrial system is a matter of growth and cannot be improvised. Only experience will show what can be done in a country with limited resources, insufficient capital, lack of industrial skill and of the "sixth sense" that comes only with time, not to mention the handicap of a population that by tradition, habit, and attitude is psychologically far away from the "factory hand." It remains to be proved that all of these handicaps can be overcome in a day by government intervention, and it remains yet to be proved that government intervention will in itself not become an impediment to the rapid industrialization of Mexico. It will remain to be proved—for to date Mexico has had past investments in railroads, oil, streetcars, public utilities, telephones and telegraphs, and a thousand other things developed before the recent policies were adopted—that the new policy can do as well as the old or that it can even retain the old services in usable form. I need merely refer to the railroads.

This is not an argument against the present policies. It is merely to point to the fact that these policies are on trial and still have to prove themselves. Even if they do, under the best of conditions they cannot and will not meet the needs of the country if the emphasis is going to be on industrialism for the purpose of a great internal market and a great export industry. If Mexico were wise, Mexican industry would be accepted as a supplement to an agricultural economy, and the emphasis would be upon the marvelous energy and cohesive powers of the rural community. It would use the community to the fullest extent and invigorate it by bringing to it the skills and techniques modern science has made possible for the little place. Mexico, I am convinced, can reach its fullest cultural and economic development only by adopting a policy inherent in its very genius: that of enriching the local community. Any plan that would destroy the vitality of the Mexican rural community is bound to prove tragic in its consequences and repeat the slums of an earlier industrialism without holding out the promise of the increased output that will give employment and sustenance to the fifty or sixty million people who will have to be fed by the end of the century if the present rate of growth continues, as it probably will, during the next two generations.

The Anvil of American Foreign Policy

TIME AND CIRCUMSTANCE have conspired to give Mexico and the United States markedly different configurations. It will always remain an interesting question how two such distinct yet neighboring peoples, with so many difficulties between them, have managed for more than a century to live with each other in peace, even if at times an uneasy peace. For if goodwill, national self-respect, and a reluctant tolerance—but tolerance none the less—can stem from two cultures so variously conditioned, there is some hope that the people of the world may learn to abide in amity.

For those who have read this volume there is little need for a detailing of the issues that gave rise to the bitter controversy between the United States and Mexico from the end of the Díaz regime to the day of our involvement in the Second

World War. The elements of discord are evident in the body of the book. Mexico's latent nationalism, obscured by the fawning upon alien values and the courting of foreign—especially American—capital, turned, with the Revolution, into a violent protest against the outsider and the things he stood for. It aspired to free the native, the uniquely Mexican, spirit, and to strip the strangers, whether Spaniards, Frenchmen, Englishmen, Americans, or Chinese, of any influence over Mexican life.

The very success of foreign enterprise made it a seeming danger. The foreigner was everywhere, seemed to own everything, had the ear of the government, was favored by the courts, flaunted his wealth, and prided himself not merely upon his achievements, but upon not being a Mexican, as if in some way that made him a better man. And the irritation his pride and strutting awakened made him an early object of popular hatred. Because American citizens were most conspicuous and affluent, it was easy for the new movement to become strongly anti-American. Fear of the United States, fear based upon past humiliation, the bitter memory of a lost war, and the despoliation of half its territory, was the stark political reality in Mexico. Just because the Revolution was stirred by a creative impulse toward freedom and popular well-being, the threat implicit in American power turned Mexico to defiance. The leaders of the Revolution were willing to risk the threat of annihilation rather than yield their hopes for a better life for the people and for a nation matured beyond the possibility of outside tutelage.

It is only thus that the long and frequently bitter controversy with the United States can be explained from the Mexican side. The people were fighting not merely for economic justice, but for national dignity. That the argument was often charged with asperity, and at times with a seeming willingness to stir the embers of contention into a flame regardless of the consequence, was owing to a psychological and political insecurity that could not compromise without surrendering all its ambitions and thus being defeated by its own weakness. The Mexican leaders had to risk, and did risk, their own and their nation's destruction to escape spiritual and political thralldom. This choice was not always deliberate. It was rather a stubbornness nurtured in fatalism and pride, an unconscious recognition that if they yielded even a little, the edifice they had reared would tumble and crush them. That is why principle and doctrine seemed so important. When the time came, the "practical" issues could be compromised, but those which symbolized the newly asserted nationalism had to be maintained to the end.

The venturesome challenge to American power succeeded because of events beyond Mexico's borders and beyond its control. In the interval of more than thirty years from 1910 to 1942 the world was torn by two great wars, and United States policy was deeply affected by both the New Freedom and the New Deal. In this troubled and confused period Mexico found it possible not only to defend its social revolution and to reaffirm a doctrine of nationalism that gave the small state a claim upon equal consideration in the world with the large and mighty powers, but also to help pave the way for the acceptance of the idea of the juridical equality of the American nations upon which the Pan-American system was ultimately to be constructed.

If the defense of popular democracy in Mexico contributed in the end to the emergence of a Pan-Americanism based upon the concept of the juridical equality of great and small powers, it did so because for the United States the experience with Mexico during those fateful years proved both a test and a challenge. Its policy toward Mexico could not be divorced from its actions in other parts of Latin America, and its behavior toward Latin America was of necessity but a part of its broader policy in the world at large. The conflict with Mexico had to be resolved in the light of world-wide commitments and responsibilities, not merely political and material, but also spiritual and moral. President Wilson soon lifted the dispute out of its immediate context of Mexico versus the United States and made it heard around the world as an argument of universal implications, one in which the issues were justice, liberty, democracy, national integrity, and the equality of nations. These doctrines were later to be expanded and "humanized" by President Franklin D. Roosevelt.

It is important to remember that of Wilson's doctrines large, perhaps basic segments were first uttered in connection with the difficulties that arose with Mexico; for during his campaign for the presidency and in his first inaugural address there was little reference to international affairs, and by both training and interest he was chiefly committed to internal issues. It was the questions posed by the Mexican Revolution, and especially, perhaps, by the recalcitrance of the Mexican leaders, that brought to the surface as a public utterance a body of ideas that were to become part of the declared international policy of the Wilson administration and later to be reflected in the ideas and ideals of President Roosevelt. The link between the Wilson and Roosevelt administrations is very close and very personal. President Roosevelt was Assistant Secretary of the Navy, Josephus Daniels, his Ambassador to Mexico, served in the Wilson Cabinet, Secretary of State Hull was an influential member of Congress at the same time, and many others held important posts under both Presidents.

More important than the personal link was the ideological one. The heritage of the New Freedom can be seen in the New Deal, and the forces that brought the New Freedom into being were the same that gave the New Deal its strength. Interestingly enough, in their foreign policy both Wilson and Roosevelt fell back upon the support of those same popular elements for whom the New Freedom and the New Deal represent the essentials of domestic policy. In both instances the foreign policy was in a measure the extension of a domestic democratic philosophy and found support among those who accepted the political and philosophical leadership represented by the New Freedom and the New Deal. It was upon the common people, the trade unions, the farmers, and the small middle class that Wilson depended, and it was upon these that Roosevelt rested his policy both at home and abroad. It is no accident that in both administrations the political opponents of the respective domestic policies were often most conspicuous opponents of the foreign, especially the Mexican, policy.

The diplomatic argument with Mexico forced to the surface as an American foreign policy the public formulation of the basic political urge of the American people, and this political urge found in both Wilson and Roosevelt a spokesman who could give it eloquent and dramatic utterance. Underlying this discussion is the assumption that moral ideas are the essence of political controversy. Whatever cynics may say of the matter, it remains true that in the United States the great political debates have always been cast in moral terms, are so cast today, and that first Wilson and later Roosevelt carried these same moral attitudes into the international field and made them the justifying cause for fighting two world wars against German aggression, and for attempting after each of these bloody holocausts to build a world order to make it impossible in the future for arrogant violence to plunge the world into war. What is this but the extension to the outside world of an age-old American commitment to individual freedom and to the equality of the states within the Union?

These ideas and attitudes have been implicit in our foreign policy for a long time, but it was mainly as a result of the painful and disturbing impact of the Mexican Revolution that they were to become an explicit, formal doctrine to be applied abroad. In fact, Americans could not have invoked another. They could speak to the world at large only in the language they talked at home, and the requirement that our foreign policy be justified before the American people every two years at least, at every congressional election, compelled a statement of government policy in terms understandable and explainable within the realm of common experience and belief: liberty, justice, democracy, constitutional government, and the moral integrity of the State. No one had a right to destroy another state, or extinguish it: all of American experience was contrary to that.

In the long run this nation's foreign policy is responsive to public opinion. Individual governments, secretaries of state, and even ambassadors may for a time chart a course of their own, but in the end the people, through the Congress, through the press, through the ten thousand agencies of public expression represented by the churches, the trade unions, women's organizations, and spontaneous public bodies that arise in every crisis, assert themselves and shape a policy that they can approve, one consistent with the special sense of justice and rightness so dominant in American feeling.

That was the case with Mexico. In spite of the many outrages committed against United States citizens, and in spite of the loss of much American property, there was an underlying belief that the Mexican people were struggling for internal justice and order, for freedom from political oppression and economic exploitation, that, in short, they were striving for those very things which have always seemed good and right to the people of this nation, who would not brook the use of force by the United States to fasten upon the Mexicans a system that they did not and could not approve of. Wilson won the battle against the pressure for intervention just because he felt that he was supporting in Mexico those things which the mass of the American people believed in, and that he was opposing abroad the very forces he was battling at home. And we find him saying: "We have seen material interests threaten constitutional freedom in the United States; therefore, we . . . sympathize with those in the rest of America who have to contend with such powers."

This was true later of Roosevelt. He, too, was fighting his gallant battles against reaction both at home and abroad. Neither Wilson's nor Roosevelt's theory of American foreign policy as applied to Mexico can be understood outside of this ideological and moral milieu. The fact that in essence this same policy was projected toward Latin America in general, and later to the world at large, merely gives special meaning to the history of our relations with Mexico. In no small measure the recent public doctrine of American foreign policy was hammered out on the Mexican anvil.

The military *coup d'état of* Victoriano Huerta, nurtured in treason and stained with the blood of the murdered President Francisco I. Madero, precipitated between Mexico and the United States the political crisis that was to run an uneasy course for the greater part of the first Wilson administration. During most of this period the burning issue came to be recognition in Mexico of a government that could meet the test of stability and popular support. The issue was only partially resolved by the recognition of Venustiano Carranza late in 1915.

While this political argument still remained unsettled, another problem crept in to trouble Mexican-American relations, and that was the meaning, reach, and possible effects of the Constitution of 1917. Secretary Lansing raised the question of the retroactive implications of that Constitution even before it was adopted, and from then on to the end of the Cárdenas regime in 1940 its impact upon previously acquired rights of United States citizens was the major if not the sole issue of controversy between our own and the Mexican government.

The Mexican Revolution had begun two years before Wilson's election. The bloody palace rebellion that raised Huerta to power occurred about three weeks before his inauguration on March 4, 1913, and, in spite of much advice, Wilson would not recognize Huerta because he could not.

The role of Henry Lane Wilson, then our Ambassador to Mexico, in this fateful drama has already been noted, but it deserves further detailing because it helps to illumine the contrast in foreign policy before and after the New Freedom. If the United States Ambassador to Mexico laid his major emphasis upon order and the protection of American interests, President Wilson stressed the inherent right of the Mexicans to work out their own destiny, the justice of their effort to reform the social and economic institutions under which they were living, and the moral obligation of the United States to help foster the growth of democratic ways in our neighboring Republic.

The story goes back to the early days of the Mexican Revolution. On March 21, 1911 Henry Lane Wilson informed José Ives Limantour, Díaz's Secretary of the Treasury, that the United States had no intention of intervening unless the government should fall and "not be succeeded by a responsible one," and advised the State Department that the situation could be saved only "by the military pressure of President Taft almost exclusively." Secretary of State Philander C. Knox reminded him that the United States was not concerned in Mexico's internal politics, saying: "You are . . . to observe the strictest impartiality." But impartiality was beyond Henry Lane Wilson, and on February 20, 1912 he reported: "I have . . . endeavored to induce leading members of the Catholic party of the old regime to make some demonstrations of a public character."

The dispatches of Henry Lane Wilson through this period are an interesting study in the psychology of a growing personal aversion. The "apostle" Madero gradually took on in the mind and feeling of the United States Ambassador the eccentricities of a Nero callous to every crime and chargeable with every perfidy. By contrast Madero's opponents appear as disinterested patriots and seeming gentlemen. Wilson searched the English language for its most somber and lurid adjectives to paint the dereliction of the Madero government, and the flood of bitter words poured out of him in a seemingly endless stream.

Two days after the rebellion against Madero had begun, Ambassador Wilson requested instructions of a "menacing character" and "general powers" in the name of the President of the United States. Secretary Knox refused the request because the United States could not assume responsibility for determining the outcome of the conflict. Not content with the rebuff, the Ambassador again asked for power to use the marines and naval vessels in Mexican ports. This was again denied him, but his genius for meddling could not be dampened. He invited the British, French, and German ministers to the Embassy, and on his motion, according to the Mexican Foreign Office, they asked Madero to resign. Madero replied that he would die at his post rather than accept foreign meddling.

Events were moving quickly now. On February 17, 1913 at four p.m. the Ambassador telegraphed that Huerta, Madero's commanding officer, had advised him that Madero would be removed at any moment. "I made no suggestion . . . only that no lives be taken except by due process of law." The next day the President, the Vice-President, and Gustavo Madero, the President's brother, were arrested, and our Ambassador expressed to Huerta the hope that he would "carry out his expression of patriotism." At midnight, "I invited General Huerta and General Felix Díaz . . . to the embassy. I got them to . . . an understanding that Huerta should be provisional president of the republic, and that Díaz should name the cabinet, and that thereafter he should have the support of Huerta for the permanent presidency."

All this took place before Madero had resigned. On February 19 Ambassador Wilson said: "I imagine its ratification [of the agreement] made in the embassy last night will be little more than a matter of form. . . . I have been assuming considerable responsibility without instructions." That same evening he announced: "The President and Vice President have resigned." And General Huerta "explained that Gustavo Madero (the President's brother) had been killed by soldiers without orders." As if that were not sufficient explanation, Huerta informed the Ambassador "that the President and Gustavo Madero had twice tried to murder him." Then Huerta "asked my advice . . . whether . . . to send the ex-President out of the country, or place him in a lunatic asylum. I replied that he ought to do that which was best for the peace of the country"—that just after the murder of Gustavo Madero.

We are told next morning: "A wicked despotism has fallen," and the new government has risen "amid great popular demonstrations of approval. . . . At the request of the wife of the ex-President I visited General Huerta in company with the German minister and unofficially requested that the utmost precaution be taken to prevent the taking of his life or the life of the Vice President, except by due process of law."

This was almost too much for the State Department, and Secretary Knox telegraphed at eleven p.m.: "General Huerta's consulting you as to the treatment of Madero tends to give you a certain responsibility in the matter." On the following day Knox telegraphed again that Gustavo Madero's murder made a most unfavorable impression. "The President [Taft] is gratified to believe that there is no prospect of injury to the deposed President or Vice President, or their families." No comment on Gustavo Madero's death came from the Ambassador, and no evidence is available that he acted upon President Taft's concern for the safety of Madero's life.

With Madero out of the way, the Ambassador busied himself in favor of the Huerta regime. On the day that Taft urged the safety of Madero, the Ambassador assembled the diplomatic corps, and they all agreed that recognition was imperative to enable the new government to impose its authority. "I shall accordingly unite with my colleagues, believing I am interpreting the desires of the Department." Like the unfolding of a Greek tragedy, the events in Mexico moved forward to their bitter end. Madero and Vice-President Pino Suárez were murdered on the night of February 22 while being transferred from the palace to the penitentiary. Huerta explained that they were killed while "trying to escape," and Henry Lane Wilson accepted the story. In addition he said: "I gave a copy of the government version of the killing of the President and the Vice President to the Associated Press, and will ask the Department to accept it as emanating from the Embassy."

Political sensitivity was not Wilson's major virtue, and he remained indifferent to the storm of indignation that swept the United States. He urged the State Department to inform the American public of Huerta's friendly disposition and telegraphed to all American consuls: "In the interest of Mexico, urge general submission . . . to the new government, which will be recognized by all foreign states today." This recognition did not occur; he had had no way of knowing that it would occur.

The callous willfulness of the Mexican tragedy roused a storm in the United States. Knox telegraphed that the American press was horror-stricken and that Huerta could not escape suspicion, and suggested "some modification" of the Ambassador's telegram urging upon American consuls the task of procuring submission to the new government.

Henry Lane Wilson was not to be turned from his purpose, and the American consul at Saltillo, who visited Carranza on instructions from the Ambassador, reported: "Governor Carranza believes the Embassy to be largely at fault for the present condition of affairs." This belief, dragged up by every critic hostile to the United States, colored Mexican-American relations for years to come. Henry Lane Wilson, however, remained imperturbable and wrote to the new Secretary of State, William Jennings Bryan, that Madero was "a man of disordered intellect . . . intrigue shattered his brain . . . his mental qualities, always abnormal, developed . . . that dangerous form of insanity . . . comparable to a Nero in ancient, and to a Castro in modern times." And when his advice for recognition was not heeded, he told the new administration that it was accused of being "secretly in sympathy with the plotters against the integrity of the Republic . . . favoring a repetition . . . of Texas." He was finally recalled in July 1913 and resigned in October. Thus ended a story that has haunted Mexican-American relations to this day.

Woodrow Wilson's first major international crisis was thus upon him before he was firmly seated in the presidential chair. He was profoundly disturbed by the dictatorship risen to power by violence and murder, and sought to promote a policy in the southern Republic more consistent with his own interpretation of American interest and tradition. To this end he sent a personal representative to that country, John Lind, a friend of Bryan's and former Governor of Minnesota, and laid his views before Congress on August 27, 1913.

Lind was to help get Huerta out of the way and to promote peace and democracy. The civil war that had developed between Huerta and his opponents, headed by Carranza, was to be halted, and a free election held. But Huerta refused. President Wilson's repeated assertion that the United States was seeking the extension of "self-government" made no impression upon the new dictator. Huerta replied by saying that Wilson's sincerity would best be evidenced by receiving a Mexican ambassador in Washington.

Huerta's troubles were multiplied by President Wilson's hostility, and his political insecurity provoked him to increasing violence. Private and public enemies dropped from the scene, presumably murdered, and when the Mexican Congress protested the disappearance of a nonconforming senator from Chiapas, Huerta drove the deputies from their seats at bayonet point and cast one hundred and ten of them into the penitentiary. To Wilson this seemed like sheer defiance. He informed the United States Diplomatic officers that, by whatever means, Huerta must now be ousted from power, and on February 3, 1914 he revoked the embargo on arms shipments to permit Carranza, who was heading the rebellion against Huerta, more speedily to drive the usurper from office.

Huerta, badgered and harassed on all sides, soothed his irritation by increasing draughts of good wine, rested upon his stubbornness, and plotted a thousand schemes to keep himself in office. An unexpected event almost turned him into a heroic defender against "Yankee imperialism," but that too failed him. The arrest of some United States sailors in Tampico seemed an incident sufficiently grave, in spite of their release and an apology, to require, in the eyes of the United States admiral in charge of American ships at that port, a formal salute of twenty-one guns. In this the admiral was supported by Wilson, but Huerta refused. In spite of every effort and threat, including an ultimatum, Huerta continued to find one reason after another why the demand from the United States could not be complied with. The United States, he said, wished to humiliate him, and, come what might, he would not accept humiliation. This show of defiance failed to reunite Mexico under his leadership, even against the threat of foreign invasion. The people of Mexico would have nothing to do with him.

Huerta's seeming indifference to American pressure forced Wilson to lay the case before Congress, explaining that force, if necessary, would be used to drive the dictator from power. That same night, April 20, 1914, Admiral Fletcher was ordered to occupy Vera Cruz to prevent a German ship from landing arms and ammunition for Huerta's army. The city was taken the next day, and American troops were on Mexican soil. In spite of President Wilson's pacific intentions, war seemed inevitable, and the rising tension was only relieved by the offer of Argentina, Brazil, and Chile to mediate between the United States and the Mexican leaders. To Woodrow Wilson this was a welcome escape from a painful crisis, and for Huerta it was an opportunity to save face before the world. Carranza demurred, however. He was not quarreling with the United States; in fact, in his own fashion, he thought he was courting its friendship.

Before the mediating board, meeting in Niagra Falls, Wilson laid his program for Mexico: the elimination of Huerta and the fulfillment of those agrarian and constitutional reforms which he believed to be at the root of the Mexican rebellion. The mediators, however, were not interested in the proposed reforms; Huerta's delegates were opposed to turning the government over to Carranza; and Carranza refused to have anything to do with the proposal. Let the mediators mediate between the United States and Huerta; that was a private quarrel. Huerta finally resigned on July 15, 1914 in favor of Luis de Cárbajal, his Secretary of Foreign Relations. The demand for a salute to the American flag was never met.

The resignation of Huerta merely opened the floodgates to chaos. What had been a united force against him was splintered into warring factions under separate leaders, each claiming to speak for the country, each issuing manifestos, sending emissaries to the United States, printing paper money of its own, levying taxes, and imposing forced loans. Mexico City was occupied and abandoned repeatedly by the various military bands, each with a puppet president of its own. The railroads to Mexico City were cut, the mail remained undelivered, and the city was threatened with hunger and riot. The courts were closed. Life hung on the caprice of irresponsible military leaders.

Foreigners and natives in Mexico clamored for relief. Americans protested to President Wilson that their lives were endangered and that their property was being destroyed. On March 20, 1915 the assembled American colony declared: "Mexico is drifting towards destruction from which a mistaken altruism is powerless to save it." To add to the difficulties, the British, French, Spanish, Chinese, and Japanese embassies were pressing the United States to protect their nationals, some of whom, especially Spaniards and Chinese, were being maltreated, robbed, and murdered. To make matters worse, Carranza, who insisted that he alone was the government of Mexico, refused to accept representation from the United States on behalf of foreign nationals other than American citizens.

In the face of a seemingly hopeless situation the State Department threatened to hold Carranza personally responsible for crimes committed against citizens of the United States. Carranza denied all the charges, cast aspersions upon the Brazilian Minister, representing United States interests, and protested that it was beyond diplomatic usage to hold the head of another government personally responsible for a situation he could not control.

On March 11, 1915 President Wilson, as if not to be committed to a policy from which retreat might prove difficult, sent Carranza this remarkable telegram, in effect both an apology and a reassertion of goodwill, and yet something of an implicit threat:

I beg that you will understand that if our messages are occasionally couched in terms of strong emphasis it is only because they concern some matter which touches the very safety of Mexico itself, and the whole possible course of her future safety. We always seek to act as the friends of Mexico, and as their friends it is our duty to speak very plainly.

The chaos was increasing. When no available remedy was apparent because the leaders of the revolution seemed determined to destroy each other and the country as well, President Wilson announced that the United States ". . . must presently do what it has not hitherto done or felt at liberty to do . . . to help Mexico save herself." In August 1915 he turned once again to the Latin-American nations, adding Bolivia, Guatemala, and Uruguay to Argentina, Brazil, and Chile, for the purpose of finding, if possible, by combined wisdom and influence some way out of what had become an intolerable situation.

The only advice that they could give was compromise, conference, mediation, and agreement. Zapata and Villa accepted, and again Carranza refused. His very self-confidence gave him a more impressive character, and his seeming control over his followers held out the promise of stability. On October 19, 1915 the United States, therefore, in co-operation with the conferring Latin-American nations, recognized him as the *de facto* government in Mexico.

If Carranza had the "essentials" of recognition, he did not possess the power to suppress disorder or reduce violence. His infuriated opponents turned to murder and pillage. On January 10, 1916 Pancho Villa's followers took eighteen American mining engineers, returning on the assurance of protection by Carranza, stripped them naked, and murdered seventeen of them in cold blood; one escaped to tell the tale. As if this were not enough, on March 9 Villa, at the head of four hundred followers, raided Columbus, New Mexico, set fire to the city, killed a number of residents, and escaped across the border.

Once again war seemed inevitable. President Wilson met the

storm by ordering American troops to pursue the bandits into Mexico, while Carranza played down the raid and suggested that if Mexican troops were given a similar right of pursuit into American territory, the "forces of the United States may cross into Mexican territory." This eased the tension and gave President Wilson at least mometary relief from the pressure for intervention.

Carranza soon changed his mind, however, and insisted on a formal agreement specifying the number of troops, their armament, the range of their operations, and the time they were to remain on Mexican soil. Wilson hastened to reassure him that pursuit of Villa was "deliberately intended to preclude the possibility of intervention." Moreover, as though the solemn declaration of the President of the United States was not sufficient, a joint congressional resolution, on March 17, asserted that the punitive expedition "shall not be permitted to encroach in any degree upon the sovereignty of Mexico, or to interfere in any manner with the domestic affairs of the Mexican people."

Carranza was in no mood to accept the assurance of the President, even when it was supported by Congress. His susceptibilities, his pride, his own political instability, the fear that once the troops were in Mexico events might conspire to make withdrawal difficult or impossible, and the long story of past grievances and current apprehensions made him eager to get the United States troops out of the country as quickly as possible. Instead of co-operating with the American forces he made their role difficult and their task impossible. He refused them the use of the railroads, and when, on April 12, some American troops were attacked in Parral, he formally suggested their retirement from Mexico.

From the American point of view, withdrawal was out of the question. The bandits remained uncaught and unpunished. Other raids were occurring and threatened, the border was insecure, and the Mexican government was powerless to prevent marauding bands from attacking American towns.

For Carranza, however, the presence of United States troops

on Mexican soil created a major political crisis. He was constrained to insist upon their retirement and to continue feeding the passions of hatred and fear because only by making himself the spokesman of the most extreme nationalism could he retain sufficient influence to ride out the storm. His slogan, therefore, was immediate withdrawal or armed resistance. Our promise to retire the punitive expedition as soon as its objectives were accomplished did not affect his behavior. He recognized that a bending of the knee to the United States would be political suicide.

The perennial Mexican crisis was coming to a head once again, and Carranza, recognizing that American patience was wearing thin, sought to clear himself before the world by casting aspersions upon the United States, charging it with perfidy, and calling for Latin-American sympathy and support by declaring: "It is imperative that the . . . United States . . . define its intentions in order that other Latin American nations might judge . . . the true value of . . . [the offers of] friendship and fraternity made to them for many years past." As if this public attack were not sufficiently provocative, he informed American forces in Mexico that they would be attacked if they moved east, west, or south. Rising passions in Mexico were shown in multiplying acts of hostility against Americans.

The United States government replied to Carranza's bitter attack in a long, detailed, and finely written document. It recounted the long-suffering patience of the American people, their goodwill toward Mexico, the aid extended to Carranza, the failure of his *de facto* government to maintain order and to protect life, and, finally, his refusal and incompetence to cure the evils that had precipitated the immediate difficulty. The note (June 20, 1916) ended by declaring that any attack on the American forces would be resisted. As if to underscore the seriousness of the situation, a copy of the note was given to the Argentine Ambassador with a statement that "Hostilities would be simply a state of war without purpose on the part of the United States other than to end the conditions which menace our national peace and the safety of our citizens."

The line between war and peace had grown thin indeed, and the demand for the immediate release of seventeen American soldiers taken prisoner in a skirmish at Carrizal seemed the final test of American forbearance. Even President Wilson could no longer have resisted the clamor for military intervention. Carranza yielded, apparently at the insistence of Samuel Gompers, president of the American Federation of Labor, and released the men. Once again war was avoided without resolving the conflict, and once again resort was had to a joint commission, doomed to fail because Carranza's pride would brook no compromise. His commissioners would "not even listen" to any proposal other than unconditional withdrawal.

The impasse remained unbroken. Finally, on November 21, after three months of useless negotiations, Secretary of the Interior Franklin K. Lane, chairman of the American commission, informed his Mexican colleagues that President Wilson's "patience is at an end, and that he regards present conditions in Mexico as intolerable." This served no purpose. Carranza would discuss nothing. Wilson was informed that no agreement was possible. The American commissioners, however, recommended the withdrawal of our troops, which was accomplished by February 6, 1917. Carranza had had his way once again, and once again the United States had yielded unconditionally.

In their letter to President Wilson the American commissioners expressed the hope that after the troops had been withdrawn it might prove possible to find a diplomatic approach to the other pending problems. Their optimism, however, was damped by the proceedings of the Constitutional Convention, then meeting in Querétaro, which indicated "a fixed and settled purpose to place in the organic law of the Republic provisions which tend to make the position of foreigners in Mexico intolerable, which open the door to the confiscation of legally acquired property, and which carry with them the germs of serious international friction." This proved a prophetic forecast. One phase of the Mexican diplomatic argument was drawing to a close and another was opening.

If the new Constitution elaborated by the convention meeting in Querétaro endowed the chaos in Mexico with an outline of public policy, it also challenged older concepts of private property and made foreigners apprehensive of their investments. Secretary Lansing evidenced such concern early in January 1917, while the convention was still in session, and later that month informed Carranza that the proposed Constitution was "fraught with possible grave consequences," and that the United States government could not consent to "any direct or indirect confiscation of foreign-owned property."

Carranza, however, promulgated the Constitution and proceeded to enforce it despite the protests of the oil companies that his fiscal and regulatory measures interfered with the use and development of what was theirs under both domestic and international law. But to Carranza the companies' complaints seemed inspired by political hostility, their refusal to abide by the laws and decrees sheer acts of rebellion to be constrained by force.

Protests by the State Department stirred the question of intervention in the internal affairs of another state and provided the occasion for airing in the public press the seeming hypocrisy of President Wilson's repeated concern with social justice and proffered friendliness toward Mexico while the United States government was exerting itself in undue haste to protect American oil companies defying the law of the land.

Similar difficulties arose in connection with the early agrarian legislation. State Department protests had little influence on the course of events, and its repeated arguments merely sharpened the issue at hand. It stood on the "recognized principles . . . of international respect and good neighborhood," and insisted upon the "right of property owners to develop their properties as they may deem appropriate."

The American objections were countered by the assertion that diplomatic protests could not "suspend the effects of the laws," or, as one Mexican official expressed it: "The only road open to the petroleum interests is to amend the constitution, which . . . would destroy the results of the Revolution." That was the crux of the matter from the Mexican point of view.

If the overthrow and murder of Carranza early in 1920 lessened the immediate strain, it did little to change Mexican policy. The bristling self-assertiveness of Carranza had embittered the relations between the two governments, but the suave and politic temper of Obregón proved equally unyielding.

The United States, however, felt that the change of government provided the occasion for reaching a settlement with Mexico by embodying in a treaty, prior to recognition, the essentials of security for previously acquired American property rights. In May 1921, therefore, Secretary of State Hughes submitted the draft of such a document to the Mexican government. This treaty, in Article I, contained the following:

> The United Mexican States declare that neither the Mexican Constitution which went into effect on May 1, 1917, nor the Decree of January 6, 1915, to which the said Constitution refers, is retroactive in its operation; . . . nor any Executive decree or administrative or military order, nor any Federal or state law . . . has or shall have any effect to cancel, destroy or impair any right, title or interest in any property, of whatever nature and wherever situated, which was owned in accordance with the laws of Mexico as then existing, or declared or interpreted; . . . and the United Mexican States recognize that the ownership of all substances which are described in the Code of Mines of the United Mexican States (Codigo de Minas) of 1884 and the subsequent Mexican Mining laws of 1892 and 1909, respectively, on or beneath the surface of lands in that country, are vested in American citizens . . . who acquired title to such lands prior to May 1, 1917. . . .

To appreciate the gravity of the issue here raised, it needs to be recalled that foreigners owned more than 40 per cent of all the national wealth. The treaty stipulated that the Constitution of 1917 should not apply to this vast property, and that the Mexican government should agree that no legislative, administrative, or military decree should "have any effect to cancel, destroy or impair any right, title or interest in any property, of whatever nature or wherever situated. . . ."

In its own view the Mexican government was asked to resign

forever its powers of legislation over nearly one half of its national wealth and to agree to tie its hands as to the rest, because if it could not risk impairing foreign property "of whatever nature," it could not, in effect, legislate for the remaining Mexican property. There was no way of drawing such a line, in either legislation or administration, between foreign and native claims as would not tend to "impair" previously held rights.

Obregón preferred to wait "until the government of the United States becomes convinced of the reality of events." Mexico could not accept a treaty that "would give recognition a conditional character, and would gravely injure the sovereignty of Mexico" and set a "regrettable" precedent for small nations, contrary to the humanitarian doctrines so long supported by the "Government of the White House."

After two years of negotiation an agreement for a joint commission to find a compromise settlement of the differences between the governments was finally arrived at. This commission, composed of John Barton Payne and Charles Beecher Warren for the United States, and Ramón Ross and Fernando González Roa for Mexico, came to be known as the Bucareli Conference, and sat from May 14 to August 15, 1923. The American delegates insisted that the "principles of justice recognized by international law must prevail," while the Mexicans argued that the Constitution of 1917—specifically Article 27—was retroactive neither in character nor in intent. The prolonged legal debate over the nature of private property and the reach of international law, to be so elaborately spun out later, had its real beginning at these meetings. At the moment, both sides seemed determined to reach an agreement. The American commissioners accepted the Mexican principle of "positive acts"—that is, evidence of intent to develop the property—as a basis for a claim to the subsoil. They also accepted the broad definition of "positive acts" given by the Mexican Supreme Court in the Texas Oil Company case in 1921, and they agreed to payment in bonds for *ejidos* of up to 1,775 hectares. The Mexican commissioners promised payment in cash for all other land expropriations. At the final meeting, on August 15, 1923, the American commissioners, in accepting the agreement, reserved, on behalf of both the United States and its citizens, all of their rights under international law, while the Mexican commissioners made a similar reservation of all rights under Mexican law and the law of nations.

The recognition of Obregón on August 31 was followed about ten days later by the signing of the general and special claims conventions covering damages from 1868 to 1910, and from 1910 to 1923, respectively. Two things are to be noted. First, the signing of the claims conventions followed recognition at the request of the government of Mexico; that was the basis of its later claim that recognition had not limited or compromised its sovereignty in any way. Secondly, it fortified Mexico's later insistence that the Bucareli Conference merely represented an exchange of views between the two governments; that, because only views were exchanged, they were personal in character, and that Obregón's promises, even if they were as ample as the United States claimed them to be, did not commit any future government to follow them.

The friendly quiet that had settled down on relations between the two nations after the Bucareli Conference was rudely broken some two years later by an unexpected and violent denunciation of the Mexican government by Secretary of State Kellogg. On June 12, 1925 he declared that conditions in Mexico were not going well, that there were rumors of an impending revolution, and that "this government will continue to support the government in Mexico only as long as it protects American lives and American rights, and complies with its international engagements and obligations," and closed with the challenging remark that "The government of Mexico is on trial before the world."

Two days later President Calles replied in tones equally bitter and violent: Secretary Kellogg's comment on an impending revolution was "a threat to the sovereignty of Mexico"; no country has "the right to interfere in . . . [Mexico's] domestic affairs"; she would not subordinate her foreign relations to the dictates of any nation; no government can create a privileged position for its nationals in Mexico; and Mexico was no more on trial before the world than the United States. These answers from Calles "were matters of surprise and regret to the Department."

Ambassador Sheffield, who was in Washington when the note was issued, lost much of his personal prestige with the Mexican government. He should have known, even if the Secretary of State did not, that threats would only evoke greater recalcitrance. But Sheffield, like Henry Lane Wilson before him, was not particularly sensitive to the Mexican political atmosphere and, like his unhappy predecessor, permitted himself to be influenced in his views by the local American colony. And Sheffield, insulated from Mexican contacts by a lack of knowledge of Spanish, repeatedly told the State Department that a strong stand on our part would bend the Mexicans' pride and force them to yield to the American point of view.

The theme with Carranza was now played over again. The arguments on both sides became increasingly elaborate and obdurate, taking on with each exchange of notes a growing intransigence, impelling both countries once again to that stubborn assertion of foreign rights versus native sovereignty so fraught with the prospects of a cataclysm—a cataclysm acceptable to the genius of Mexico, but so difficult for us to precipitate. The dispute began on the regulatory agrarian and petroleum laws defining the application of Fraction 1 of Article 27 of the Constitution of 1917, submitted to the Mexican Congress late in 1925.

Secretary Kellogg first suggested a personal appeal to remove "the clouds which I perceive on the horizon," but Sheffield urged a formal note to forestall claims that we "did not protest the bill." On November 25, therefore, the State Department presented a note detailing its objections to specific items in the proposed legislation on the grounds that it was retroactive and confiscatory in character and that it impaired, if it did not utterly destroy, previously acquired American rights. Finally, the note added that the United States had no desire to intervene in the internal affairs of Mexico, only reminding the government that the proposed legislation was "in contravention of the understanding arrived at at the Bucareli Conference."

Mexico rose to the argument with the flare of a skilled debater. It seemed incredible that the United States should lay itself open to the charge by "suspicious minds" that it was bringing pressure upon the Mexican Congress by protesting bills tentative in character and not immediately injurious, especially as there was no confiscatory intent in the proposed legislation. Mexico, as a sovereign nation. could freely legislate for all within its jurisdiction, and could not provide a privileged position for foreigners. Finally, the Bucareli Conference, recalled by the State Department, merely evidenced the "mutual respect for the rights of the two sovereign nations" and did not set aside the "provisions of their respective constitutions." The legal debate was now on in full, and would be spun out in all of its possible subtleties.

The theoretical and juridical difference that divided the two countries was clearly stated in the American note of July 30, 1926. The United States government was "unable to acquiesce in the fundamental conception of a vested interest as evidently entertained by the Mexican government. Your Excellency has on several occasions virtually expressed property rights which are commonly regarded as vested in terms of a mere right of user or enjoyment, which might lawfully be interrupted, or wholly taken away by laws or regulations affecting its future duration, or imposing conditions upon future enjoyment. . . . Nor can the American government agree that the Mexican government can, on the pain of forfeiture, constitute itself the sole judge of whether a United States citizen is deprived of vested interests in the violation of the law of nations, by first forcing him to become a Mexican citizen for the property he holds."

On this theory "American owners would thus be forced to

exchange exclusive ownership for concessions of lesser scope and value, into a mere authorization to exercise rights for a limited period of time." The American note rejected the Mexican argument because "It strikes at the very root of the system of property rights which lies at the basis of all civilized society. It deprives the term 'vested' of any real meaning by limiting it to retroactive significance. The very essence of a vested interest is that it is inviolable, and cannot be impaired, or taken away by the State save for a public purpose, and upon rendering just compensation." As if this were not sufficient, the Kellogg note cast doubt upon the validity of the doctrine of "positive acts" that the American commissioners had accepted during the Bucareli Conference, doing this on the ground that it did not apply to an owner of the surface with a vested interest in the subsoil and by recalling the fact that the American commissioners at the Bucareli Conference had reserved all rights acquired under the laws of 1884, 1892, and 1909, which gave an "exclusive property" and not merely an optional right. The American position had now been stated in full.

The issue of retroactivity had become a tangled web of legal definition over which Mexican and American lawyers argued in thousands of pages of fine-spun phrases. The Mexicans said that there was nothing new in their doctrine, that it was the law of Spain for centuries before it was embodied in the mining code issued by Charles VII in 1783, and that it had remained the law until 1884. They said that the laws passed by Díaz in the years 1884, 1892, and 1909 were not true laws and did not mean what Americans said they meant. No government could give away the nation's patrimony. They said that Article 27 was not retroactive in so far as the subsoil was concerned because all property in Mexico from time immemorial was in the nature of a *merced,* a gift revocable at the will of the sovereign. Even a gift had to be accepted by a "positive act," showing some special recognition on the part of the recipient before it became effective. They said that the requirement for registration and the conversion of titles to a concession was not retroactive, but rather confirmatory of the title. They said that no past government could forever bind all future governments, for social life was slowly progressive and not static. This legislation, they said, was universal and applied to all property-holders, that foreigners could claim no exception and had no privileges greater than Mexican citizens, not even that of appealing for diplomatic protection against an injury that was being suffered by all alike, and that foreigners, like all others, had access to the Mexican courts.

The Mexicans argued that the exigencies of social justice and the interests of the commonwealth took precedence over private-property rights, that the demands of public safety and public order could not be surrendered to the demands of a few private corporations or individuals, that a government's just obligation was to the mass of the people, and that need for the survival of the government itself could not be sacrificed or even placed in jeopardy because some foreign or native property-holders were injured in the process. Nor would they admit, even on principle, that the public power could not mold social policy because it affected private interests, and they cited many precedents to that effect.

The purpose of the legislation, they said, was to readjust previous rights to the new Constitution. There could not be two systems of law in the country, one governing the rights acquired by a few people under the laws of 1884, 1889, and 1909, and the general body of law governing all property in Mexico, past, present, and future.

The State Department would not accede to the Mexican view. It insisted that the Conference of 1923 constituted "solemn and binding undertakings," that it saw no reason for modifying its positions and wished "to be understood as maintaining them" with the utmost emphasis, and that "an extremely critical" situation would be created between the two countries if the laws were enacted and enforced so as to violate the principles of international law. The purpose of the correspondence had been fulfilled, and the United States expected that Mexico would take no action that "directly or indirectly" would tend to deprive American citizens of the "full ownership, use, and enjoyment" of their property and property rights.

Answering this warning, Mexico merely reiterated what it had said before, and invited the American government to point out specific instances involving confiscation, "since the Mexican government would be disposed to make indemnity for such violations." In fact, the Mexican government protested against diplomatic objections to a law before it was passed. It objected to complaints after it was passed on grounds that it had not been regulated. It objected to protests against the regulatory laws on grounds that only a specific injury could properly be subject to diplomatic intervention. It objected to specific claims for damage on grounds that the injured individual had open recourse to the Mexican courts. In fact, it repudiated the entire diplomatic argument on the part of the United States while encouraging its continuance.

Thus far the dispute had dealt almost exclusively with the oil and agrarian laws. On December 20, 1926, in a conversation with Mexico's Secretary of Foreign Affairs, Ambassador Sheffield broadened the American case to embrace legislation dealing with colonization, irrigation, forestry, mining, and so on, saying that "these evidenced a uniform tendency to adversely affect" American property in all these other fields as well. In reporting this conversation our Ambassador recorded the hope expressed by the Mexican Foreign Minister that the difficulties would be settled without a "resort to force and violence," and asserted his own belief that Mexico would "yield to the firm position taken by us." But he was mistaken. Calles refused to delay the enforcement of the law. The law, he said, was good, and the "rebellion of some of the companies" was motivated by extraneous issues.

Sheffield, therefore, informed the State Department on April 11, 1927 that drilling permits were being denied to companies refusing to apply for confirmatory concessions, and that the companies might attempt to drill in contravention of the law, with the result that their property would be shut down by *force majeure*. The "concrete" case Mexico has been asking for would thus be at hand. But "such concrete cases, it may be remarked in passing, are already so numerous in other fields as to warrant grave doubts of the 'sincerity' of the Mexican government's alleged disposition to grant reparation, or, indeed, of its capacity to do so. It therefore remains for us to determine how numerous such cases must become before the almost unique career of innovation in international practice thus far pursued by the Mexican government shall be checked." In other words, Sheffield was not only condoning the proposed violation of Mexican law by American companies, but proposing intervention to protect American property rights against "the disposition of the Mexican government to enforce its own legal conceptions stemming from the Constitution of 1917."

One or the other nation would now have either to retreat or to assert its position by force. Mexico seemed determined to exact compliance with its laws. On June 15 Arthur Schoenfield, United States chargé d'affaires in Mexico, reported that there had been an order to employ the army for that purpose, and that "the use of the Federal military to enforce its plainly confiscatory action would seem to constitute further aggravation of a situation which appears to be growing increasingly untenable." Ten days later he reported that he had been informed that the Petroleum Producers Association had passed a resolution on April 27, 1927 to go on drilling in Mexico without any government permits, and that a number of the larger companies were then acting upon this resolution. But on July 14 he noted that the companies had reversed their decision.

Two things had happened in the meantime. One was a statement by the Mexican Secretary of Commerce that, "come what may," the government would enforce the law; the second, that the oil companies were advised by their Mexican lawyer that such action on their part would be considered a "conspiracy against the Mexican government." They hesitated until they were certain of what the United States would do. But they and the Embassy were convinced that "firm resistance by the United States government will force Mexico to find means to change its policy."

President Coolidge, however, was not prepared to pursue this theme to its bitter end. Sheffield was withdrawn, and with him went all the thunder and alarms that had so disturbed the relations between the countries and so nearly brought them face to face with intervention. Dwight W. Morrow went down to Mexico instead.

The appointment of Morrow resolved a crisis that might have led to war. That war did not occur was owing to the essential pacifism of the American people, their opposition to aggression, their belief that the Mexicans were trying to work out a democratic way of life and seeking justice for their common people, and that war on our part would be in defense of a small group of American interests that (especially among the oil corporations) had managed to acquire an unsavory reputation for themselves. The best defense of Mexico, in some measure, was the advocacy of intervention by interests represented by Fall, Doheny, Sinclair, and a host of others who, with the Teapot Dome scandal, had made themselves suspect in the United States, and some of whom were later brought to trial in American courts of justice.

The story is not so simple as this, however. The older Wilsonians, the pacifists, the labor unions, the liberal press, such as the *New York World* and the *Baltimore Sun*, the Protestant church groups, and many others insisted as each crisis arose that the Mexican people must be allowed to work out their own destiny. They won, partly because our participation in the First World War had dramatized the doctrine of the self-determination of nations and the integrity of their peoples. We could not go to war with Mexico over issues of American investment and the rights of American property-holders without denying the moral commitment we had made to the world. For even opposition to the League of Nations was framed to no small degree on grounds that it perpetuated imperialism and the enslavement of unwilling peoples to foreign masters.

It was no accident, therefore, that on January 25, 1927, at the height of the Mexican crisis, the Senate of the United

States unanimously resolved that our differences with Mexico be settled by arbitration. With that resolution American policy was forced back upon an earlier track, the seeking of a peaceful rather than a military solution to our Mexican difficulties.

There is a peculiarly dramatic quality to the reversal in policy here represented. President Coolidge had declared in a public address to the United Press in April 1927 that "The person and property of a citizen are a part of the general domain of the nation even when abroad." But Senator Borah, speaking as chairman of the Senate Foreign Relations Committee, and with the mandate of the Senate's unanimous resolution on Mexico, expressed himself in opposition to the use of force in defense of American property rights.

The appointment of Ambassador Morrow, therefore, proved a turning-point in our policy toward Mexico. His imaginative interest in the country and his genuine affection for its people cleared the atmosphere of the suspicion and fear that hung like a pall over Mexico and impeded every effort at an understanding. The Morrow incumbency is notable not so much for its achievements in solving the basic difficulties between the two countries, for these persisted beyond his day, as for a changed feeling-tone between the two nations.

Morrow went out of his way to popularize Mexico with the American people and to undo the evil effects of years of unfavorable publicity. He invited Will Rogers to Mexico to report from the scene the good that he saw; he arranged a visit by Charles Lindbergh, then the great national hero because of his solo flight to Paris; he broke all formalities and associated with the Mexicans on terms of simple equality, and he built up a personal friendship with Calles through frequent and informal relations.

When Morrow went to Mexico he was advised that he would have to choose between the American colony and the Mexican government. He asked in astonishment: "You mean I cannot be a friend of both?" The answer was that in spite of his great personal prestige it would prove a difficult achievement. He later sent word that he had accomplished the impossible. He had, in fact, perhaps unconsciously made his choice of the Mexican government to which he was accredited, and the members of the older American colony never forgave him. For years afterward they said that they had in fact been betrayed —"sold out," was the phrase—and considered no comment unfitting to describe their chagrin that an American ambassador should treat these "bandits" as if they were his equals, invite them to his home, open the Embassy to them, and try to compromise our outstanding difficulties instead of enforcing the American government's views by the threat of force.

Morrow's great contribution, however, lies just there: in discovering the Mexicans as "people" possessed of a profound and sensitive dignity and in treating them with a courtesy natural among equals. The American Embassy under him ceased to be in the minds of the Mexicans the center of conspiracy, opposition, and threat to them and their aspirations, which it had unfortunately been since the dark days of Henry Lane Wilson. It had taken all these years to wash away the evil memory, and it was done by the simple gesture of open and friendly appreciation of the Mexicans as people struggling under great handicaps toward the achievement of the good life within a design consistent with their own character and tradition.

It proved possible in this changed atmosphere to achieve a compromise of the issues that had so long divided the two nations. We accepted the Mexican doctrine of "positive acts," and the Mexican courts reaffirmed the broad definition of "positive acts" as laid down in the Texas Oil case in 1921 and in the Bucareli Conference of 1923. We also agreed to the contention that fee-simple ownership had to be subjected to a concession before drilling could begin, and Mexico, in its turn, agreed to issue these concessions in perpetuity. The so-called "untagged" lands upon which no "positive acts" were performed were excluded from the agreement, and the oil companies were left free to make their own arrangements with the Mexican government. Both the State Department and the Mexican government accepted this settlement as the conclusion of the long dispute. The companies demurred, but had no other recourse.

A compromise was also attempted in the agrarian problem, and there was talk that land distribution to the villages ought to be terminated. Quiet at last settled down on a scene so long agitated by controversy. The settlement was to prove only a temporary abatement, for when Cárdenas came to the presidency in 1934 the oil and agrarian problems reappeared in an acute form. But the Good Neighbor Policy, the open friendliness of President Roosevelt, and the kindly presence of Ambassador Daniels, who endeared himself to the Mexicans by his simplicity and by his interest in their problems and needs as human beings, greatly eased the solution of the new difficulties.

The appointment of Ambassador Daniels, representing President Roosevelt through all the years when Mexico was finally bringing some order out of the long chaos, seemed natural and fitting. General Cárdenas remarked: "It was my good fortune to have President Roosevelt and Ambassador Daniels representing the American people during my incumbency of the Mexican presidency." While the sudden expropriation of the oil companies on March 18, 1938 revived the older dispute, it did so in a markedly changed atmosphere. Many things had happened in the decade between 1928 and 1938 to deepen the shadows and to bring the threat of a new holocaust to the imagination of men. Bonds of friendship between nations were being loosened, and the fear of war was stalking the earth. Only in the Western Hemisphere, under the inspiration of President Roosevelt and the guiding hand of Under Secretary of State Sumner Welles, was a newer and friendlier basis of co-operation between nations being structured.

The unexpected expropriation of the oil companies by Cárdenas proved a severe shock to the developing pattern and a test of its validity. If the new specter of possible strife between Mexico and the United States was to be laid, it had to be laid within the frame-work of the newly strengthened Inter-American system. Mexico, which justified expropriation on grounds of internal necessity, the rebellion of the companies, and their insult to the national dignity, agreed to pay for the properties within ten years, while the American government conceded Mexico's right of expropriation upon "adequate, effective, and prompt payment."

If President Cárdenas overestimated the available resources of the Mexican people, the oil companies overestimated the readiness of the American people to shatter the developing Inter-American co-operation, essential to our security in an unstable world. Efforts to compromise the differences between the companies and the Mexican government failed, and the final settlement had to come through diplomatic channels.

To work out a basis of a solution for the oil crisis, the United States took up a series of other cases of expropriation in Mexico, cases not so charged with immediate political and emotional overtones. On April 3, 1940 the State Department noted that "during the last 25 years, one American interest after another had suffered at the hands of the Mexican government," and proposed arbitration for the outstanding agrarian claims. Mexico, declining to arbitrate, suggested a joint commission instead. This was accepted, and Mexico made a down payment of one million dollars, with the understanding that a similar amount would be made available annually until the obligation was liquidated, always providing that Mexico's ability to pay was taken into consideration.

Mexico made two important qualifications to this agreement. It denied the requirement for compensation under international law for "general and impersonal" expropriation for the purpose of effectuating social policy, but recognized the justice of recompense under Mexico's own laws. There was, therefore, no conflict between the two governments on that point, even if the reasons for agreement were different. It also made clear that Mexico, in agreeing to pay for the expropriated lands, was setting no precedent for other claims against her.

Later a way was opened for the oil negotiations, which began formally on January 5, 1942 and were terminated on April 17 of the same year. Agreement was facilitated by the private settlement of the Sinclair Oil interests, representing forty per cent of the American claims, and by the overriding exigencies of the war. The Mexican government would consider compensation for only "that part of the companies' justifiable investments which had not yet been recovered." This automatically raised the question of subsoil rights once again, for the companies in all of their public statements based their claims on the older laws of the Díaz regime, the Texas Oil case of 1921, the Bucareli Conference of 1923, and the Morrow Agreement of 1927. They asked payment for the oil still in the ground.

The United States in this instance cut the Gordian knot by merely asking for "repayment of actual sums invested, less depreciation incident to their various operations." The two governments together evaluated the companies' claims at $24,-000,000, and compensation was made by Mexico as explained on page 231. Just as Mexico had made the reservation that no precedent was established when she agreed to compensation on the agrarian claims, so the United States government described this as an exceptional case, providing no precedent whatsoever for future instances of a similar nature.

This settlement of the oil expropriations was made a part of a broader agreement on pending issues between the two countries. This agreement cleared the field by lump-sum payments for the outstanding claims (upon which the general claims commissions had made but little progress), and provided for a reciprocal trade pact, the resumption of silver purchase at pre-expropriation prices, the stabilization of the peso, and the extension of an Export-Import Bank loan for completion of the Pan American Highway.

This was soon followed by a treaty on the long-standing dispute over the distribution of the waters from the Bravo (Rio Grande) and Colorado rivers, by the sending of a railway mission to help Mexico with her railroads, and by many similar co-operative activities on both sides.

The feeling of amity produced by the Good Neighbor Policy made it possible for Mexico to come fully and completely to the support of the United States in the war crisis. At the Pan

American Conference in Lima before we were in the war, and at Rio de Janeiro afterward, Mexico proved one of the staunchest and most eloquent defenders of the United States and one of the most effective advocates of hemispheric solidarity. After the attack on Pearl Harbor she immediately broke off relations with Japan and the Axis powers, and on May 22, 1942 declared war upon the common enemy.

Thus a serious and prolonged difference that more than once had brought the two nations to the brink of war found a peaceful solution, and President Roosevelt could send the following telegram to Ávila Camacho, the President of Mexico:

> Mexico and the United States once again have given a demonstration to the world that the most difficult international problems can be satisfactorily solved when approached with good will and in a spirit of fair play. I welcome this opportunity to express to you and to the people of Mexico the very deep appreciation of my country for the active and constructive collaboration and assistance of Mexico in the cause of freedom and democracy. Our two nations are joined together in unity of purpose, determination and effective co-operation, and the triumph of our cause is certain.

The peaceful settlement of the grave and acrimonious differences between Mexico and the United States is a milestone in our foreign policy, and an important contribution to the developing Inter-American system. It will therefore always be a matter of primary interest how this happy outcome was achieved.

Among the many influences that contributed in the end to the amicable solution was the intransigence of the Mexican leaders. They would not, after 1917, yield their ground, even at the threat of war. On August 14, 1918 Ambassador Fletcher reported that Carranza had told him: "Mexico, in the exercise of its sovereign rights, could not admit interference of foreign governments in the matter [fiscal legislation], and said if this meant war or intervention, he was prepared to confront this alternative, however regrettable."

Carranza, as we have seen, was proud and truculent toward the United States. But beneath his bad temper and seeming ingratitude toward President Wilson, who had so greatly aided his coming to power, there was a theory of international relations. He was not merely a Mexican nationalist; he was also the advocate of a foreign policy that placed the great and small powers on an equal footing, and his dispute with the United States was underlined by the advocacy of a philosophy of universal implications. On September 1, 1918 he laid these views before the Mexican Congress in four basic propositions:

1. All countries are equal; their laws, institutions, and integrity must be mutually respected.
2. No country must intervene in the internal affairs of another in any way, or under any pretext whatsoever. All must accept the principle of nonintervention, without exception.
3. Nationals and foreigners must be equal before the state in which they find themselves; and no foreigner must make his foreign citizenship a basis for claiming special privileges and protection.
4. Legislation must be equal and uniform as far as possible except in cases affecting the sovereignty of the State.

On these principles, Carranza went on to say, diplomacy should not serve to protect private interests or place at their disposal the force and the majesty of nations or put pressure upon weak states. It should watch over the general interests of civilization, and be used for the establishment of universal fraternity. Every Mexican government from that day to this has maintained these principles. In fact, Carranza initiated the foreign policy of the Mexican Revolution, and Obregón, Calles, Cárdenas, Ávila Camacho, and Alemán have merely followed in his footsteps. The original Carranza insistence upon absolute freedom from intervention has remained the Mexican doctrine. He asserted this position from the very beginning, long before he became President of Mexico and when he was merely the head of a revolutionary faction, greatly in need of outside, especially American, support.

It would be difficult to overestimate the theoretical and political implications of Carranza's refusal to accept the offer of mediation by Argentina, Brazil, and Chile in 1914 unless it was strictly confined to the issues pending between Victoriano Huerta and the United States. Carranza would brook no discussion of the internal affairs of Mexico, would listen to no suggestion of a possible presidential candidate and no program of social and agrarian reform urged by President Wilson, and refused to accept from the mediators the very things the Mexicans were fighting for. Carranza's commissioners insisted that no outsider, no matter how powerful or how well-meaning, had any right to interfere in the internal affairs of their country, though it was weak and torn by revolution.

The principle of nonintervention could not have been more clearly asserted, nor could it have been appealed to under more dramatic circumstances. If the Wilson administration was going to deal with Carranza, it had to accept the condition of nonintervention as he defined it, and in accepting that condition, as we did, our government also accepted a precedent that was in time to become one of the cardinal principles of United States foreign policy.

A similar attitude was taken by Carranza in the matter of recognition. He preferred to govern without recognition rather than to compromise his freedom in an effort to obtain it. In 1915, when the United States called Argentina, Brazil, Chile, Bolivia, Uruguay, and Guatemala into consultation on the question of the possible recognition of a Mexican government, Carranza once again would tolerate no intervention and accept no advice. He argued that intervention, even by a group of states, would establish an undesirable precedent for the other nations in this hemisphere. When not invited to join the League of Nations, he declared that Mexico would make no attempt to enter that body until all member nations received equal treatment, for, upon Mexican principles, all states must have the same rights and obligations. He also announced that Mexico had not recognized the Monroe Doctrine as a regional policy because it attacked the sovereignty and independence of Mexico and constituted a forced tutelage over the Latin-American nations.

These same doctrines were asserted by succeeding administrations. As we have seen, Obregón would not accept recognition unless it came completely untrammeled by any previous limitations. Mexico refused to attend the Pan American Conference in Santiago in 1922 because, having no ambassador in Washington, it could not be represented on the governing board of the Pan American Union.

In 1928, at the Havana Conference, Mexico was one of the leading critics of the United States position on intervention. It carried this same battle to Montevideo in 1934. After joining the League of Nations and reasserting its opposition to the Monroe Doctrine, Mexico became a staunch defender of the inviolability of territorial integrity. It supported Ethiopia against Italian aggression and was the only American state that actively aided the Spanish Republic. Mexico also promulgated the Estrada Doctrine in an effort to free governments that came to power through revolution from the need for implicit "approval" that recognition implies. In effect Mexican foreign policy since the Revolution, by emphasizing the juridical equality and the integrity of the small state and by insisting upon the doctrine of nonintervention, became an important influence in the development of the Inter-American system.

If Mexico developed a foreign policy fitting to her needs as a weak neighbor in conflict with a powerful one, it also stimulated the United States government to enunciate a doctrine consistent with American tradition and belief, befitting a great nation devoted to the ideals of individual liberty, representative government, and the equality of states within the nation. These two divergent streams of policy and theory fused to become the foundation upon which the Inter-American system was ultimately to be constructed under the ægis of the Good Neighbor Policy. For in spite of their different inspiration Carranza and Wilson were saying essentially the same thing.

If the Mexican people were prepared to accept self-immolation rather than yield their dignity and national sovereignty, the people of the United States could not and would not accept the sacrificial offer. It went against their grain. *Mexican re-*

calcitrance was taken as a moral rather than as a political challenge. President Wilson first, and President Roosevelt later, met the challenge by enunciating, as Wilson himself said, the applicability of American ideals to the outside world. We would not meet Mexico's defiant attitude either by war or by intervention. A small nation had a right to order its own destiny without the threat of destruction by a powerful one.

President Wilson repeated this doctrine over and over again. In 1914 he said: "We do not want to fight the Mexicans. We want to serve them." A year later he returned to the same theme: "I am proud to belong to a strong nation that says, 'This country, which we could crush, shall have as much freedom in her own affairs as we have. If I am strong, I am ashamed to bully the weak.' "

More than that: "I will not help any man buy a power which he ought not to exercise over his fellow beings. The time has come to call a halt to 'dollar diplomacy.' . . . 'We act in the interest of Mexico alone and not in the interest of any person or body of persons having property claims in Mexico." As a nation among nations Mexico is morally and politically competent to reconstruct its political institutions, "For it is their emancipation they are seeking . . . blindly it may be . . . [but] they are entitled to attempt their liberty." It is an old American principle "that every people has a right to choose its own forms of government, not once, but as often as it pleases. . . . It is none of my business, and it is none of your business how long they take in determining it. It is none of my business and it is none of yours how they go about the business. The country is theirs. The Government is theirs. The liberty, if they can get it, and Godspeed them in getting it, is theirs. And so far as my influence goes while I am President nobody shall interfere with them."

If we have been put to the test in the case of Mexico, it has established that we will not take "advantage of any government in this hemisphere," because our "relationship with the rest of America is . . . [one] of a family of mankind devoted to the development of true constitutional liberty."

What is important in this connection is the extension, first to Mexico and then to Latin America, of a body of doctrine reflecting the commitments of the American people. President Wilson "would like to believe" that in this hemisphere no government can endure that does not rest "upon the consent of the governed. . . . We are only emphasizing the points of our own life" when we detail the elements of "sympathy . . . and interest" that unite us with the people of Latin America. "We should prove ourselves untrue to our own traditions if we proved ourselves untrue friends to them." All that being true, further territorial aggrandizement becomes impossible: "The United States will never again seek one additional foot of territory by conquest."

While this statement, made in 1913, had been anticipated by both Knox and Root, it acquired additional force by being uttered by a president of the United States under circumstances that led many people to expect and even urge the invasion of Mexico. This self-denying pronouncement, bolstered by a theory of equality and nonintervention, led to a doctrine of territorial integrity. We find President Wilson accepting from others the idea of a treaty guaranteeing to the Latin-American states their territorial possessions. He had shown interest in the idea as early as 1914. In 1916 he said: "If America is to come into her own . . . it will be . . . by the States of America uniting in guaranteeing to each other absolute political independence and territorial integrity."

Returning to this theme and recalling his earlier utterance, he expanded the original idea, in a speech to a group of Mexican editors, on June 7, 1918, into a doctrine of universal import:

> The famous Monroe Doctrine was adopted without your consent, without the consent of any Central or Latin American State. . . . There was nothing in it that protected you from aggression from us. . . . Let us have a common guarantee, that all of us will sign, of political independence and territorial integrity. Let us agree that if any one of us, the United States included, violates the political independence or the territorial integrity of any of the others, all the others will jump on her. . . . That was in effect giving bonds

on the part of the United States that we would enter into an arrangement by which you would be protected from us.

Then he went on to say:

> Now, that is the kind of agreement that will have to be the foundation of the future life of the nations of the world. . . . The whole family of nations will have to guarantee to each nation that no nation shall violate its political independence or its territorial integrity . . . and I must admit that I was ambitious to have the states of the two continents of America show the way to the rest of the world as to how to make a basis for peace.

Wilson had projected the American ideals and aspirations, and Carranza the Mexican beliefs and hopes, into a universal doctrine. Strikingly, both were saying essentially the same thing, even if for different reasons.

The roots of Inter-American public law go back to the days of Bolívar and Monroe, to the Congress of Panama, to the beginnings of the Pan American Union, and to the utterances of statesmen and philosophers both north and south for these many generations. As President Roosevelt expressed it in 1939: "A new and powerful ideal—that of a community of nations—sprang up at the same time that the Americas became free and independent." In fact, the history of both continents, in all its complexity, is the essential source of the Inter-American system. But it was the impact of the Mexican Revolution, its truculence, its vehemence, its impassioned and reckless idealism on one hand, and the equally stubborn unwillingness of the United States to deny the essentials of its own commitments to fair play—to the "continued maintenance and improvement of democracy," as President Roosevelt phrased it—on the other, that provided the occasion for fusing the various strands of doctrine into a formal policy. The path was neither easy nor obvious, and the differences seemed beyond reconciliation. But events in the world abroad impressed themselves on the conscience of the people in the Western Hemisphere and illumined their common destiny as well as their interdependence.

While other instances of co-operation between the United States and the countries of Latin America can be pointed to, it was the willingness of the Wilson administration to accept, perhaps even solicit, the help of Argentina, Brazil, and Chile in finding a solution to the difficulties with Mexico that marked the effective beginning of a newer trend. It gave the conflict a continental character, as was recognized by the nations in South America. It was for them the first significant evidence that the United States recognized their right to participate in the solution of problems arising between the American nations. It was more. It was an acknowledgment of the political equality of the countries to the south and an implicit declaration that the Monroe Doctrine was no longer to be considered a unilateral policy.

This impression was strengthened a year later when Uruguay, Bolivia, and Guatemala were added to the original three states for mutual consultation, resulting in the simultaneous recognition of Carranza. Here was additional proof that the tutelary role over the countries of Latin America, hitherto reserved for itself by the United States, was being surrendered. It is from the initial step taken by President Wilson that the Latin Americans are wont to date the beginnings of that change which ultimately led to the Good Neighbor Policy and to the gradual structuring of a system of collective security resting upon the juridical equality of all American states.

Another milestone along the way was Mexico's refusal to participate in the Pan American Conference in Santiago, Chile, in 1922. The long debate precipitated by Mexico's absence resulted in establishing the principle that membership in the Pan American Union was based upon inherent right (*derecho propio*), and was unrelated to recognition by the United States.

The building of the Inter-American system required further implementation. At the center of the problem lay the question of intervention. Carranza had made Mexico's position clear. There must be no intervention on any ground or for any reason. President Wilson had expressed a similar attitude, but the pressure of external events had forced the Wilson administration into the military occupation of Haiti and Santo Domingo, into landing troops in Nicaragua, into financial control of Honduras and San Salvador, while the Platt Amendment still hung like a constant threat over Cuba. These acts denied the avowed intent of the United States policy and laid it open to denunciation for hypocrisy and cynicism.

If the Pan-American system was to develop into something more than a shadowy promise, the right of intervention would have to be eliminated from the public law of the Americas. A serious challenge to the United States was publicly voiced at the Havana Pan American Conference in 1928, and in spite of Secretary Hughes's defense of the right, nay, necessity, of the policy, even if only as "temporary interposition," it proved unacceptable. At best, the question could only be postponed to the next meeting, to be held at Montevideo in 1934. In 1928 President Roosevelt had written: "It is the duty of the United States to associate itself with other American Republics. . . . Single-handed intervention by us in the internal affairs of other nations must end."

The situation, however, had improved. President Hoover had withdrawn the marines from Nicaragua. Later President Roosevelt not only had proclaimed the Good Neighbor Policy, but had called together the Latin-American representatives in Washington during the crisis in Cuba in 1933 and had told them that there would be no intervention by the United States alone. But Secretary Hull, who headed the American delegation to Montevideo in 1934, could not go the whole way. He accepted the doctrine of nonintervention, but reserved United States rights under international law.

An important step, however, had been taken, and at the next meeting, in Buenos Aires in 1936, which President Roosevelt visited in person, the United States signed an agreement that "No state had a right to intervene in the internal or external affairs of another for any reason whatsoever." This was later confirmed once again in the Declaration of Lima in 1938. Roosevelt, speaking before the Pan American Union on April 14, 1937, recalled his conference with the Latin-American ministers in 1933 over the Cuban affair and remarked: "Out of that first meeting have come the very remarkable, the amazing results that culminated last autumn in Buenos Aires."

Thus at last the position taken by both Carranza and Wilson became the formal doctrine. The essential commitment had now been made upon which the Inter-American system could be built. When the war came, the nations like Mexico, which had most opposed the United States in previous years, were its most eloquent supporters. A sense of common identity and interest had at last been created.

The acrimonious controversy with Mexico had, it is evident, precipitated a body of ideas that have influenced American world policy. These ideas include the doctrine that in "some measure" we are the guardians of "constitutional liberties" the world over; that governments must rest upon the consent of the governed; that peoples have a right to work out their own destinies that spiritual and moral interests take preference over material ones; that the United States will not go to war in defense of American investments; that foreigners have no rights other than those of native citizens; that small states have a right to the same treatment as powerful ones; that in the American system all states are juridically equal; that no state has a right to intervene in the internal or external affairs of another; that the Monroe Doctrine is a multilateral rather than a unilateral doctrine; that the recognition of new governments in this hemisphere is to be arrived at by consultation; that the territorial integrity of the American states is to be secured by collective agreement. Finally, there was the proposal of a Confederation of American States. It was against a background of attitude and policy saturated with these ideas that it was possible, when the world crisis was upon us, to build the system of collective security against external aggression at Havana in 1940, later to implement it by treaty at Chapultepec in 1945, at Rio de Janeiro in 1947, and at Bogotá in 1948, and to include the doctrine of territorial integrity and collective security against internal aggression as well.

We may now draw together the threads of the argument by indicating that the refusal to recognize the Huerta dictatorship was consistent with a similar refusal to protect American investments against the interests of the Mexican people. One emphasized the American belief that governments must rest upon the consent of the governed, the other that social justice takes precedence over property rights. These two ideas have governed relations between Mexico and the United States since 1910. The fact that the issue is often obscured, that the Department of State and individual ambassadors give the argument, upon occasion, another turn, is merely evidence that the period is formative and the policy in a state of development. But when the crisis was upon us and a policy had to be framed, it was always framed to satisfy the inner urge of the American people. That was true not only of Wilson and Roosevelt, but of Coolidge as well.

The insistence by the United States government upon the right of Mexico to self-determination, upon its political integrity, upon its equality and independence, upon the fact that if we are powerful we must also be just, that the great nation has no rights in international affairs greater than those possessed by the small nation, and that force must be used only against injustice and tyranny, made it possible to carry on a world-wide campaign against German aggression in two world wars. Belgium, Poland, Czechoslovakia, Manchuria, and China could be defended with complete conviction by Wilson and Roosevelt because we had also defended Mexico against ourselves.

Finally, intervention in Mexico by force of arms, leading to conquest and annexation or even only to the imposition of a government dictated by the United States, would have made it impossible to develop the Pan-American system. More than that, had we followed the traditional and expected policy of the great nations in regard to little ones, then our present role in the world as champion of the small state against direct or indirect subversion could not have had the force of public approval it now carries, and perhaps the role itself could not have developed.

If the Good Neighbor Policy has solidified the Inter-American system, it has done so by implementing and expanding ideas and ideals long cherished by the American people. The modern doctrines, seemingly so new, have roots deeply embedded in the American conscience. In 1843 the New York State Senate adopted the following resolution:

> Resolved, that the acquisition of foreign territory, by conquest, is at war with the principles of our government; fosters a spirit adverse to the permanency of our institutions, and should receive the disapprobation of all who regard the stability of our government more than the extension of our boundaries, and the splendor of our arms.

If this seems to some a case of mere special pleading during the controversy over the extension of slavery, the following from Senator Charles Sumner, on December 1, 1870, during the debate over the annexation of Santo Domingo may prove more convincing:

> Santo Domingo is the earliest of that independent group destined to occupy the Caribbean Sea, toward which our duty is plain as the Ten Commandments. Kindness, beneficence, assistance, aid, help, protection, all that is implied in good neighborhood,—these we must give, freely, bountifully; but their independence is as precious to them as is ours to us, and it is placed under the safeguard of natural laws which we cannot violate with impunity.

The doctrine of the good neighbor is congenial to the American spirit, and with it the hope that it can be spread to the world at large. President Wilson expressed it in the following terms:

> I am proposing, as it were, that the nations should with one accord adopt the doctrine of President Monroe as the doctrine of the world: that no nation should seek to extend its polity over any other nation or people, but that every people should be left free to deter-

mine its own polity, its own way of development, unhindered, unthreatened, unafraid, the little along with the great and powerful.

President Roosevelt said:

The twenty-one American Republics present proudly to the rest of the world a demonstration that the rule of justice and law can be substituted for the rule of force.

Secretary Hull said:

I hoped, if my health permitted me to remain in office, to persuade Russia to adopt the policy of co-operation and nonintervention that prevailed in the Western Hemisphere and to make this a solid world policy to which all nations subscribed. Under this Pan-American policy transplanted to Europe, Russia could have the friendliest political relations and the liveliest economic exchanges with her neighbors while refraining from interfering in their internal affairs.

President Truman has declared:

We are following a foreign policy which is the outward expression of the democratic faith we profess.

The Good Neighbor Policy, to which our experience with Mexico had so greatly contributed, was moral and spiritual, and not merely political and economic. It stood for the old American ideal of the dignity of man and the equality of the state. It sought to resolve the persistent conflict between the large and the small powers by accepting a multiple universe, the members of which were of equal juridical status, possessed of equal privileges and similar responsibilities. As Sumner Welles has expressed it: "It lightens the darkness of our anarchic world. It should constitute a cornerstone in the world structure of the future."

Significantly, also, Latin-American statesmen agree. Oswaldo Aranha, former Brazilian Secretary of Foreign Affairs, wrote recently: "The Americas have anticipated the international organization of the future."

Index

A NOTE ON THE TYPE

The text of this book is set in Caledonia, a Linotype face designed by W. A. Dwiggins, the man responsible for so much that is good in contemporary book design and typography. Caledonia belongs to the family of printing types called "modern face" by printers—a term used to mark the change in style of type-letters that occurred about 1800. It has all the hard-working feet-on-the-ground qualities of the Scotch Modern face plus the liveliness and grace that is integral in every Dwiggins "product" whether it be a simple catalogue cover or an almost human puppet.

The book was composed, printed, and bound by Kingsport Press, Inc., Kingsport, Tennessee.

Progreso
Mérida
YUCATÁN
QUINTANA ROO
of
eche
Campeche
Ciudad del Carmen
L. de Términos
CAMPECHE
B A S C O
lahermosa
Usumacinta
Tuxtla Gutiérrez
I A P A S
Grijalva
GUATEMALA
Ciudad Chetumal
(Payo Obispo)
BRITISH HONDURAS
Beliz
Gulf of Honduras
Puerto Barrios
HONDURAS
Huehuetenango
Quezaltenango
Guatemala
EL SALVADOR
San Salvador
90°

Date Due